# The Hundred Percent Challenge

# The Hundred Percent Challenge

## Building a National Institute of Peace

### A PLATFORM FOR PLANNING AND PROGRAMS

**Edited by Charles Duryea Smith**

Conflict Analysis Center

**Seven Locks Press**

*Publishers*

Cabin John, Md./Washington, D.C.

Copyright © 1985 by the Conflict Analysis Center

**Library of Congress Cataloging in Publications Data**

The Hundred percent challenge.

   Includes bibliographies and index.
    1. Peace—Study and teaching—United States.
2. National Academy of Peace and Conflict Resolution.
I. Smith, Charles Duryea, 1941-   . II. Title: 100% challenge.
JX1908.U6H86 1985     327.1'72     85-2205
ISBN 0-932020-30-5
ISBN 0-932020-31-3 (pbk.)


Manufactured in the United States of America
Designed by Lynn Springer—Concept by Chuck Myers
Printed by the Maple Press Company, York, Pennsylvania
*First edition, April 1985*

### Seven Locks Press
7425 MacArthur Boulevard
P.O. Box 72
Cabin John, Maryland 20818
301-320-2130

*We dedicate this book to our friend and colleague, the late Milton C. Mapes, Jr. A man of optimism, conviction, and great humor, Mike was a true and gifted leader of the drive to establish a national peace institute. He often said* "si vis pacem, para pacem" — *if you want peace, prepare for peace. He did.*

# Acknowledgments

Work on *The Hundred Percent Challenge* began over two years ago. Along the way new friendships were made and old ones strengthened. From the time this book was only an idea, John R. Dellenback, James Laue, Richard C. Sullivan, Jr., and my wife Ruth Gutama Smith gave wise and caring guidance.

Review is important to complex, scholarly writing, and our generous reviewers for the chapter in Part One were John Norton Moore on just-war theory; Lieutenant Colonel Augustus Richard Norton, Colonel Jesse Harris, Charles C. Moskos, and Charles Cotton on peacekeeping; and John Scanlan, Jerry Tinker, Roger Winter, Norman L. Zucker, and Naomi Flink Zucker on forced migration.

Among those who provided much-needed financial support were the Dynamic Strategies Research Foundation, the George Gund Foundation, the National Peace Academy Foundation (now the National Peace Institute Foundation), the Parten Foundation, the National Education Association, John P. Dunfey, Roger and Jennifer Fajman, Neil and Wendy Kotler, Roger Landrum, and Lois Murdough Smith. When funds were slight and there were better uses than rent, we found hospitality in the Georgetown Visitation Preparatory School. We are deeply grateful to all.

*The Hundred Percent Challenge* is produced by the Conflict Analysis Center, a Washington-based nonpartisan, nonsectarian, and nonprofit corporation established in 1982. The authors are responsible for the content of their contributions. Editorial responsibility rests with the editor. The Center is concerned about the management of conflict and the preservation of human rights, and its special interest is the implications of citizenship for international violence and peace, forced migration, and democratic governance. Its directors are John Norton Moore, president; Paul A. Kerschner, secretary; Leon F. Bouvier, treasurer; William J. Byron, S.J.; Paul M. Kalill; and Elizabeth Midgley. Its members are Raymond G. Helmick, S.J., John A. Herzig, Aiko Herzig Yoshinaga, Charles Duryea Smith, and Ruth Gutama Smith.

Charles Duryea Smith
February 1985
Washington, D.C.

# Contents

# Foreword

MARK O. HATFIELD
*United States Senator*

Peace is not "mad," mutually assured destruction, or war and the threat of war. It is not desperate, frightened, and oppressed people. Nor, because it is a basic human need and human beings are bounded by time and space, is it guaranteed. In that sense, peace is like bread. It nourishes life, yet it must constantly be replenished; if left to sit, it becomes stale and unfit for use.

When the 98th Congress amended the Defense Authorization Act to create the United States Institute of Peace and appropriated funds to launch it, we acted on the understanding that peace is more than the absence of war: it is justice, and it is an ongoing process. In biblical terms, it is *shalom*—"wholeness." Never out of our thoughts were the children, those growing up under the shadow of nuclear annihilation and those we hope will come into and create a better world than ours. We also understood that every 45 minutes, the world spends enough money just arming itself to operate the national institute of peace for two years.

The immense investment in war machinery made us question the noble idea of a Department of Peace, which Benjamin Rush and Benjamin Banneker initiated in 1792 and Senator Matthew Neely proposed in 1935. The view that peace is secured by preparing for war, *si vis pacem, para bellum,* could too easily consume any federal peace institution that was not insulated from the bureaucratic momentum of the central government. George Orwell, in *1984,* warned against corruption of language, when peace would simply be a different name for war. So we guarded against diversions, especially from political forces: the national institute of peace will not participate in policymaking, and it will not intervene in disputes. Through research, education and training, and an information service, the institute will focus on the elements and practical methods of peace among nations.

We also wanted the institute to belong to all Americans, whether or not questions of international peace are a direct part of their daily responsibilities, and we designed it carefully. We directed it to consider both government experience and that of the American people, particularly as we resolve local, regional, and national problems fairly and without violence. Most of its directors will be drawn from private life. A substantial amount of its federal funding will be used for grants and contracts. And it will develop a significant program of outreach and information flow to the general public. The institute's heritage is American, and because of that, its doors will be open to people from other nations. I hope that others will see our institute as worth emulating, in their own cultural, social, and political manner.

The institute's public mandate is based on democratic principles of citizen participation. We guide education, local welfare and safety, and state and national policy decisions through parent-teacher associations, school boards, city councils, and the activities of state legislators and United States Representatives and Senators. In international affairs, however, our democratic ways are much less practiced. Americans are not isolationists, and there is deep public interest in relations between the United States and other countries. Yet once we move past our borders into the more distant spheres of international relations and diplomacy, we seem to enter the territory of the specialist where there are signs that say "off-limits."

Secrecy and management by the chosen few may appear easiest and most in keeping with a world that largely is not democratic, is not peaceful, and is often heavy-handed in using power. But leaving life-and-death decisions up to experts is risky and not to be tolerated in democracies. It may be that the national institute of peace will see fit to examine the importance of public opinion in a democracy's foreign policy. It is an important subject. But more important is that the institute itself serve the American thirst for information on international peace. Peace is more certain when the public achieves a voice in the nation's international activities like the voice it enjoys in domestic matters. An informed and self-confident public will moderate unsettling swings in foreign affairs that at times accompany electoral change and shifts in the policymaking elite. A nation so equipped is better able to apply its talents to peace.

*The Hundred Percent Challenge: Building a National Institute of Peace* is the first book on the United States Institute of Peace. It gives a full picture of the background and prospects of the institute. It makes an excellent text, too. The original and seminal essays on just-war theory, peacekeeping, and forced migration are in the finest research tradition of the field. The stories of the Camp David mediation and of the negotiation and conciliation surrounding American hostages in Iran and Colombia are rich in training value. *The Hundred Percent Challenge* also sets a high standard for the institute's information services component. It is well written, timely, and attractive; it is responsible and imaginative about questions of war and peace; it extends the discipline of conflict resolution; and it starts a tradition of on-going examination of the institute's purposes and methods.

Stop for a moment and consider bedrock causes of instability, violence, war, and revolution. They lie behind more headlines than we often realize. In my judgment, the greatest destabilizing force in the world, more ominous than the arms race, is famine and hunger. It accompanied genocide in Cambodia, and today there is starvation in a number of heavily armed and unstable countries in Africa. I am glad that *The Hundred Percent Challenge* places refugees in the peace lexicon along with the theology of war and the peaceful uses of the military. Such integration of issues represents the insights promised by the institute itself.

I am confident that, from the vantage point of the twenty-first century, the seemingly small step we took to establish the United States Institute of Peace will be seen as one of the most important post-World War II acts of the United States government to bring peace to the world. The record of good fortune in developing a national peace institute is in the pages of *The Hundred Percent Challenge*. That the book is produced now, just when we are ready for it, is a good sign for this exciting and hopeful new aspect of American life. May we meet the challenge.

# Contributors

KENNETH E. BOULDING. Distinguished professor of economics, emeritus, University of Colorado. Research associate and project director, Program of Research on Political and Economic Change, Institute of Behavioral Science, University of Colorado. Oxford University, B.A. and M.A. Founder and former director, Center for Research on Conflict Resolution, University of Michigan. Former president and chairman of the board, American Association for the Advancement of Science. Editor of ten books and author of 24 books, including *A Preface to Grants Economics: The Economy of Love and Fear* (Praeger, 1981); *Stable Peace* (University of Texas Press, 1978); *Beyond Economics: Essays on Society, Religion, and Ethics* (University of Michigan Press, 1968, Ann Arbor Paperback, 1970); *Conflict and Defense: A General Theory* (Harper, 1962, Harper Torchbook, 1963).

KATHARINE SWIFT GRAVINO. Graduate School, Department of Sociology, University of Maryland. University of Maryland, B.A. Former research assistant, Military Manpower Policy Project, Twentieth Century Fund; academic investigator, Department of Military Psychiatry, Walter Reed Army Institute of Research. Author, with David Segal, "The Empire Strikes Back: Professionalism and Technology in the South Atlantic War," in Brown and Snyder, eds. *The Regionalization of Warfare* (New Brunswick: Transaction Books, forthcoming).

MARK O. HATFIELD. United States Senator (R-Oregon) since 1966. Chairman, Senate Committee on Appropriations, and Subcommittee on Energy and Water Development; member, Committees on Energy and Natural Resources, and Rules and Administration; member, Joint Committees on Printing and on Library. Willamette University, B.A.; Stanford University, M.A. (political science). Former member, Oregon State legislature; governor of Oregon, two terms; U.S. Naval officer; professor of political science. Author of *Between a Rock and a Hard Place* (Waco, Tex.: Word Books, 1976); *Conflict and Conscience* (Waco, Tex.: Word Books, 1971); *Not Quite So Simple* (Harper, 1967).

FRANK K. KELLY. President, University Religious Center, University of California at Santa Barbara; senior vice president, Nuclear Age Peace Foundation. University of Missouri-Kansas City, A.B. Former vice president and senior fellow, Center for the Study of Democratic Institutions; staff director, U.S. Senate Majority Policy Committee; speech writer for President Harry Truman. Nieman Fellow, Harvard University; Wilton Park Fellow (British Foreign Office). Author, *Court of Reason: Robert Hutchins and the Fund for the Republic* (New York: Macmillan, 1981); *Your Freedoms: The Bill of Rights* (Putnam, 1964).

DAVID LITTLE. Professor of religious studies, University of Virginia. College of Wooster, B.A.; Union Theological Seminary, B.D.; Harvard University, Th.D. Former professor of Christian ethics, Yale Divinity School. Author of articles principally on history, religion, and ethics, and four books: *Religion, Order and Law: A Study in Pre-Revolutionary England* (Harper & Row, 1969; University of Chicago Press, 1984); with R. S. Khare, *Leadership* (The University Press of America, 1984); with S. B. Twiss, *Comparative Religious Ethics* (Harper & Row, 1978); and *American Foreign Policy and Moral Rhetoric: The Example of Vietnam* (Council on Religious and International Affairs, 1969).

MILTON C. MAPES, JR. Former executive director, National Peace Academy Campaign. Mr. Mapes died in 1984, only a short time before the United States Institute of Peace Act became law. U.S. Naval Academy, B.S.; Yale Law School, J.D.; American University, M.A. (Russian area studies); University of Maryland, M.A. (political science). Former official, Departments of Commerce and State (Agency for International Development), for export expansion, small business development, international trade, and third world economic development. Special Counsel, U.S. Senate Committee on Interior and Insular Affairs. U.S. Navy service, World War II and Korean War. Private law practice, The Dalles, Oregon.

JENNINGS RANDOLPH. Associate editor, *West Virginia Review,* lecturer, visiting professor, business consultant. Salem College, A.B. Former United States Senator (D-West Virginia, 1958-1984), with most recent committee membership in Senate Committees on Environment and Public Works, Labor and Human Resources, and Veterans' Affairs; United States Representative (D-West Virginia, 1933-1947); airline executive, journalist, professor of public speaking and journalism, and athletic director. Author, *Speaking That Wins.*

RONALD S. SCHEINMAN. Senior associate, McManis Associates, Inc., an international management consulting and research firm, Washington, D.C. Brandeis University, B.A., University of California, Santa Barbara, M.A. and Ph.D. (political science). Former director of refugee policy research, U.S. Select Commission on Immigration and Refugee Policy; program officer (Geneva, Kinshasa, Dakar), United Nations, Office of the High Commissioner for Refugees; professor of political science. Author, "Refugees: Goodbye to the Good Old Days," in John Scanlan and Gilbert Loescher, eds., *The Global Refugee Problem: U.S. and World Response*, The Annals of the American Academy of Political and Social Science 467 (1983); with Norman Zucker, "Refugee Policy," *The New York Times, News of the Week in Review*, May 24, 1981.

DAVID R. SEGAL. Professor of sociology and of government and politics, University of Maryland. Guest scientist, Walter Reed Army Institute of Research. Editor of the journal *Armed Forces & Society*. Harpur College, B.A.; University of Chicago, M.A. and Ph.D. Former chief, Social Processes Technical Area, U.S. Army Research Institute for the Behavioral and Social Sciences. Author of articles principally on military studies and two books: with Jerald G. Bachman and John D. Blair, *The All-Volunteer Force: A Study of Ideology in the Military* (University of Michigan Press, 1977); and *Society and Politics* (Scott, Foresman, 1974); also with Nancy Goldman, eds., *The Social Psychology of Military Service* (Beverly Hills: Sage Publications, 1976).

CHARLES DURYEA SMITH. Senior associate and founding member, Conflict Analysis Center. Associate editor, *Interpreter Releases*, the weekly immigration and nationality law reporter of the American Council for Nationalities Service. Phillips Academy; Oberlin College, A.B.; Washington University, M.A. (English literature); Boston University Law School, J.D.; Harvard Law School, graduate study. As former special assistant to the chairman, organized and wrote the final report of the Matsunaga Commission on the National Academy of Peace, *To Establish the United States Academy of Peace*. Research director, U.S. Commission on Wartime Relocation and Internment of Civilians; legal staff, U.S. Select Commission on Immigration and Refugee Policy. Coauthor of *Right to Counsel in Criminal Cases: The Mandate of Argersinger v. Hamlin* (Cambridge: Ballinger Publishing Co., 1976). U.S. Peace Corps volunteer, Ethiopia.

# The Matsunaga Commission on the National Peace Academy

SPARK M. MATSUNAGA. Chairman, U.S. Commission on Proposals for the National Academy of Peace and Conflict Resolution. United States Senator (D-Hawaii) since 1976. United States Representative (D-Hawaii) from 1962-1976. Member, Senate Committees on Energy and Natural Resources; Finance, Labor, and the Human Resources; and Veterans' Affairs, and the Select Committee to Study the Committee System. Chief Deputy Minority Whip. Principal sponsor of legislation to establish U.S. peace academy, while in House and in Senate, 1963-1984. University of Hawaii, Ed.B.; Harvard Law School, J.D. Officer in the all-Nisei 100th Battalion/442nd Infantry Regiment, World War II, retired as Lieutenant Colonel from Army Reserve. Author, *Rulemakers of the House* (with Ping Chen; University of Illinois Press, 1976).

JAMES H. LAUE. Vice chairman. President and executive director, The Conflict Clinic, Inc., working in close collaboration with the Program on Negotiation at Harvard Law School. Professor of sociology, University of Missouri-St.Louis. Harvard University, Ph.D. Authority and practicing mediator and trainer in the field of conflict resolution. Former director of program development for the Community Relations Service, United States Department of Justice.

JOHN M. ASHBROOK. United States Representative (R-Ohio) from 1960-1982. Died in 1982 while running for the Senate seat from Ohio. In the House, member of Committees on Education and Labor, Judiciary, and Select Intelligence. Harvard College, B.S.; Ohio State School of Law, J.D. Candidate for 1972 Republican nomination for President. Only commissioner to dissent from commission's recommendations, asserting that peace studies is not an accepted discipline and that mainstream American thinking had not accepted a national "peace office."

ARTHUR H. BARNES. President, The New York Urban Coalition, since 1975. Former vice president, Institute for Mediation and Conflict Resolution. Previously associated with Consolidated Insurance Companies for twenty-one years.

ELISE BOULDING. Chair, sociology department, Dartmouth College. Member, United Nations University Council; UNESCO Peace Prize jury; several international commissions to study peace strategies. Editor, International Peace Research Association newsletter. From 1967-1978, the Department of Sociology and the Institute of Behavioral Science at the University of Colorado, Boulder. Author of eight books and more than seventy articles, pamphlets, and chapters on sociology, including transnational and comparative cross-national studies on conflict and peace, development, family life, and women in society.

JOHN R. DELLENBACK. President, Christian College Coalition, Washington, D.C. Yale University, B.S.; University of Michigan Law School, J.D. Former United States Representative (R-Oregon) 1966-1974; director of the United States Peace Corps from 1975-1977; college professor; practicing lawyer; Navy officer.

JOHN P. DUNFEY. Founder and president, Dunfey Hotels Corporation (Omni-Dunfey Hotels); industrial developer, Maine and New Hampshire. Former representative, African Trade Mission, Department of State, September 1979; member of national committee, "Americans for SALT II"; member of national committee to raise funds and encourage citizen support for Senate approval of Panama Canal Treaty.

DAN GLICKMAN. United States Representative (D-Kansas) since 1976. Member, House Committees on Agriculture, Judiciary, and Science and Technology. Chairman, Science and Technology Subcommittee on Transportation, Aviation and Materials. Co-chair, Congressional U.S.-USSR Study Group. Principal sponsor of peace institute legislation in 97th and 98th Congresses. George Washington University, J.D.

WILLIAM F. LINCOLN. Director, National Center for Collaborative Planning and Community Service, Inc. Professional arbitrator and mediator on the environment, education, prisons, discrimination, and Native American affairs. Wilton Park Fellow (British Foreign Office). Lecturer, Harvard University, Kennedy School of Government and Graduate School of Design; academic conference leader, Harvard Law School and Willamette Law School. Former New England Regional Director, Department of Community Dispute Services, American Arbitration Association.

# Introduction

CHARLES DURYEA SMITH

In October 1984, the drive for a national peace academy led Congress and the president to establish the United States Institute of Peace. The institute is modeled closely on the recommendations of the Matsunaga Commission on the National Academy of Peace. The commission, in turn, was part of a two-hundred-year movement for a national institution devoted to peace. *The Hundred Percent Challenge* grew out of the work of that commission, and its parts are unified by the vision of what a national peace institute can be.

Peace is the absence of war, it is the effective application of peacemaking techniques, and it is the presence of social justice. As Senator Mark Hatfield makes plain in his foreword, viewed singly the definitions are incomplete; together, they give a whole picture. The three chapters in Part One represent these three perspectives.

Approaching peace as the absence of war, David Little brings just-war theory into the nuclear age. Mankind for centuries has taken up the sword and justified its slaughter on both sound and specious grounds. Argued over in varied historical contexts, just-war theory is about God, death, and individual responsibility. The classical just-war writings are by Aristotle, Cicero, St. Augustine, and Thomas Aquinas, while the father of early modern just-war thought is Hugo Grotius. When the Catholic bishops wrote their *Pastoral Letter on War and Peace,* they entered the just-war fray. So, whether we know it or not, just-war theory is an important part of today's ongoing debates over arms control and disarmament, retaliatory strikes, the protection of noncombatants in wars of liberation, and conscientious objection.

One way to enable a just peace to develop in a troubled area is to introduce a peacekeeping force. David Segal and Katharine Gravino write about this most difficult military mission, which relies on techniques aimed at separating disputants and keeping civilian fears at bay. It buys time for other peacemaking methods, such as elections, mediation, and negotiation. Whether they act as police or buffers, peacekeeping soldiers become vigilant strangers for whom boredom goes with the territory. Peacekeeping needs special leadership, particularly as peacekeepers depend on sophisticated intelligence, and it cannot endure without solid political support. Despite difficulties, dramatized by terrorist attacks, peacekeeping may be the most important contribution that the military can make for policymakers who seek options beyond nuclear-based peace through strength. It is also one way to make home safe for people who otherwise would enter the stream of forced migrants.

The forced migration of millions of men, women, and children across national borders is one of the identifying marks of the second half of the twentieth century. Sometimes people move because efforts at peace have failed, and sometimes their presence itself threatens peace. Ronald Scheinman considers forced migration as a question of social justice and peace. Forces that drive people against their will into urban centers or new countries, where they often are unwelcome sojourners, include persecution, economic instability, unmanageable population growth, environmental devastation from deforestation and drought, and war and revolution. His picture of migration forces in the world of tomorrow is sobering; the headlines today tell us no less. People on the move in massive numbers demand—from the United Nations, governments, voluntary agencies, and religious organizations— protection, redress of injustice, and peace. As they make history with their feet, forced migrants challenge the nation-state system, traditional legal constraints, and long-held concepts of citizenship.

The authors of Part One are versed in philosophy, religion, sociology, psychology, political science, and history. They demonstrate that the investigation of peace, war, and conflict requires a variety of intellectual disciplines, and they make it clear that the social sciences and the humanities are as important as science and technology in learning about and managing peace.

What should we expect from a national peace institute? In Part Two, three people devoted to the national peace academy movement answer that question. They consider the institute's research purposes, its training and education impact, and its information role. A national peace institute, they say, simultaneously will reflect special American qualities and be a model for other countries setting up their own peace institutions.

Senator Jennings Randolph describes how the Senate shaped the Matsunaga Commission's national peace academy legislation. He stresses the careful selection of the national peace institute's first directors, and he poses eight questions for the first congressional oversight hearing. Senator Randolph's career in Congress began in 1932 and ended with his retirement in January 1985. He was a principal sponsor of the legislation that created the United States Institute of Peace. In his honor, the institute will establish the Jennings Randolph Program for International Peace, providing a sabbatical base to scholars and leaders from around the world.

Kenneth Boulding, economist and author of classic books on conflict, looks at progress in conflict management. This skill, he argues, is a discipline that can be taught and examined, and it is based on the scholarly and scientific ethic that truth should be sought through evidence, not bribery or threat. Thomas Kuhn spoke of a ''paradigm shift,'' which like the theory of relativity changes the ways we structure and organize our images of reality. Conflict management is a paradigm shift, especially in the international arena, that confounds the usual array of nay-sayers and cynics. The institute, he suggests, is a major advance for this practical field, which itself may preserve our future and make a safer world.

Milton C. Mapes, Jr., was the executive director of the National Peace Academy Campaign and Foundation. He completed his essay just before his death in 1984. He found the world at an historical crossroads, where nuclear destruction lifts all bets but one: Unless we concentrate our resources to make fundamental changes in the way society deals with conflict, we have cancelled the future. The establishment of a national peace institution in the United States, he saw, will be a firm promise to future generations and a message to other nations that through their own national academies of peace they, too, should join in exploring affirmative ways to resolve conflicts without violence and to create the necessary conditions for stable world peace.

The landmark work of the Matsunaga Commission on the National Acadamy of Peace was the catalyst for the United States Institute of Peace. In Part Three, Frank Kelly, former speech writer for President Harry Truman and vice president under Robert Hutchins of the Center for the Study of Democratic Institutions, introduces this report. He traces the history behind the national peace institute from the Founders' early struggle over federalism and the Constitution, through Tennyson's ''Locksley Hall'' and the Civil War, into twentieth-century efforts to establish a prominent national institution devoted to international peace. Selections follow from the commission's study, including its introduction to peace research, United States Ambassador Diego Ascencio's recollection of negotiating his freedom while a captive of M-19 guerrillas in Colombia, Professor Roger Fisher's account of the Camp David mediation strategy, and the Reverend John Adams's story of conciliation in Washington and Teheran during the Iran hostage crisis.

There is one appendix: the legislation that established the national institute of peace. The United States Institute of Peace Act stands as the institute's charter, and it embodies the recommendations of the Matsunaga Commission and the congressional deliberations. This law sets the institute's purposes, design, limits, and power. It, too, should be read.

# PART ONE

# The Just-War Tradition
# And the Pursuit of Peace

DAVID LITTLE

> As it is most true that magistracy in general is of God for the
> preservation of mankind in civil order and peace—the world
> otherwise would be like the sea wherein men, like fishes, would
> hunt and devour each other, and the greater devour the less—so
> also it is true that magistracy [in its particular forms] is of man....
> All lawful magistrates in the world...are but derivatives and
> agents, immediately derived and employed as eyes and hands,
> serving the good of the whole. Hence they have and can have no
> more power than fundamentally lies in the [political] bodies...
> themselves, which power, might or authority is not religious,
> Christian, etc., but natural, human, and civil.
>
> Roger Williams,
> *The Bloody Tenent of Persecution* (1644)

The just-war tradition offers a set of moral standards to regulate
force in political conflicts. It is a product of the Christian West, but it
achieved its modern form only after the lesson proclaimed here by Roger
Williams was learned: that established political ''power, might, or
authority is not religious...but natural, human, and civil.'' The lesson
did not come easily. Just-war teaching is the result of several centuries of
cultural struggle, and the relevance it has to the forms and use of force in
the conflicts of today is best appreciated in light of that troubled story.

The principal intention of the just-war tradition is the pursuit of
peace, and that pursuit, in turn, is grounded in the belief that a necessary
condition of peace is the *just administration of force*. There is nothing in
the tradition that rules out consideration of nonviolent and preventive
alternatives to the use of force. In fact, it encourages them. But there is
also the conviction, for better or worse, that whatever else is involved,
peace within and between societies depends on the measured use of
coercion. In that sense, the comments by Dr. Joseph Short of Oxfam in

his testimony before the Matsunaga Commission on the National Academy of Peace reflect the spirit of the just-war tradition: "There is a symbiotic relationship between peace and justice and...injustice is the most important source of conflict."[1]

There is a second sense in which the just-war tradition pursues peace by restraining force. It establishes *standards of public accountability*, according to which a government's resort to force should be subjected to stringent scrutiny by the citizenry, as well as by the international community. The idea is to put obstacles in the path of any government contemplating the use of force so as to reduce the risk that force will be employed mindlessly and arbitrarily, and thus work to undermine a just peace. This condition, as we shall see, has some important implications for the "sovereignty" of each citizen's conscience regarding the use of force and the pursuit of peace.

That a just and virtuous peace is the primary objective of this age-old set of teachings about war is already made plain by Aristotle, who apparently was the first to use the term "just war." "We wage war in order to have peace," he wrote, and he meant a peace governed by the moral and intellectual virtues of the upright person, including restraint in the exercise of coercion. "No one," he stated, perhaps a bit naively, "chooses to wage war or foments war for the sake of war; he would have to be utterly bloodthirsty if he were to make enemies of his friends simply to have battle and slaughter."[2]

Cicero, the Roman philosopher, adopted a similar view, except that in keeping with Roman legal thinking of his time, he began to elaborate and refine some of the standards of moral restraint that were to distinguish a just war from an arbitrary exercise of violence. These moral standards were rooted in natural law, as Cicero and his Stoic colleagues referred to it. "We are born for Justice, and that right is based, not upon men's opinions, but upon Nature."[3] Conforming to the dictates of natural justice alone assures lasting "fellowship and union" among all human beings. This Stoic belief in natural law strongly influenced early Christian thinking, as, for example, in St. Paul's famous remark in the Letter to the Romans: The gentiles "do by nature what the law requires" and therefore "show that what the law requires is written on their hearts" (2: 14-15). This conviction would help to shape centuries of subsequent Christian reflection on war and peace.

The first instinct of the early Christian church was to detach its primary religious and moral ideals from the activity of the state. It created, thereby, a sphere of independent judgment constituted by a strong disposition toward the use of peaceful means, particularly in matters of religious faith and practice, and by some pointed skepticism about resort to force in general. These attitudes set the early Christian movement apart from its Graeco-Roman context, which included the classical doctrines of just war. If Aristotle, Cicero, and many sympathizers advocated restraint in war, they nevertheless regarded civil coercion and armed conflict as a natural activity. In fact, for Cicero and his Roman compatriots, wars if they were just had positive religious significance.[4]

After the establishment of Christianity in the fourth century A.D., Christians attempted to combine Biblical teachings with Graeco-Roman just-war notions and relate them to the realities of international politics. But this attempt created difficulties. The message of Jesus and the early church emphatically set a vision of peace and nonviolent practice in direct contrast to the use of armed force. The early churches were purely voluntary communities of believers consciously independent of ''Caesar.'' They preached their message and practiced their beliefs by peaceful means, by persuasion, and by an appeal to personal responsibility, without any direct reliance on physical coercion, civil or otherwise. This was a movement whose preference for the ''sword of the spirit'' caused believers to devalue, if not to repudiate altogether, the ''sword of steel.'' Jesus' well-known reference to what we may call the ''pathology of force'' took firm hold on the early Christian conscience. ''For all who take the sword will perish by the sword'' (Mt. 26:52) expressed the conviction that force always stands ready to consume its users.

But both Old and New Testaments were accepted as sacred scriptures by Christians, so there remained a need to reconcile such nonviolent passages in the New Testament with contrary passages such as Paul's defense of the legitimacy of the state and its use of ''the sword,'' in the thirteenth chapter of the Letter to the Romans. Moverover, there was the entire Old Testament tradition of explicit ''holy wars'': wars initiated and directed by Yahweh himself and conducted without restraint. Passages from Deuteronomy reflect these brutal directives: ''You shall destroy all the peoples that the Lord your God will give over to you, your eye shall not pity them....'' (7:16). ''In the cities...that the Lord your God gives you for an inheritance, you shall save alive nothing that breathes, but you shall utterly destroy them...as the Lord your God has commanded; that they may not teach you to do according to all their abominable practices....'' (20:16-18).

Christians, then, had the unenviable task of trying to cope with three strongly divergent positions on the use of armed force: the emphasis on peace and nonviolent methods so central to the teachings and to the life and death of Jesus; the just-war doctrine generated by the classical Graeco-Roman tradition; and the holy-war doctrine so important in the Old Testament. Western Christianity represents a shifting series of efforts to respond to these conflicting positions, and in some cases to combine two or more of them. Generally speaking, pacifism, characteristic of the Christian sects, adopted the first and simply rejected the other two. But the rest of the church—the Roman Catholic and the mainline Protestant—took a more inclusive approach toward the options before them. It is this part of western Christianity that, endeavoring to harmonize the three positions, elaborated and refined just-war teaching and eventually, following a painful process, presented that teaching to the modern world.

Simplifying shamelessly, we may organize just-war thinking under three general rubrics: the medieval perspective, the post-medieval reaction, and modern developments and dilemmas.

## The Medieval Perspective

The way that Augustine, the first great theologian of established Christianity, attempted to harmonize the three approaches to force structured the framework for medieval reflection. In the first place, he domesticated the nonviolent prescriptions of the New Testament by turning them inward . For Christians to take up arms was not illicit in itself, so long as they did it in the right spirit. Turning the other cheek was not primarily a matter of behavior, but rather of inward attitude and disposition. If charity and the desire to achieve peace motivated a soldier or policeman, then the use of force to restrain violence or to punish wrongdoing was, according to Augustine, fully in accord with Jesus' teaching. With the right attitude, a resort to armed force became an exercise in "benevolent severity."

The way thus opened for just-war thinking. Augustine agreed with Aristotle, Cicero, and other classical authors that the exercise of government entailed the administration or regulation of force, and he borrowed liberally from them in elaborating the standards for the proper use of force. According to the tradition, the standards for determining whether a given use of force is "just" or not are worked out in response to four basic questions:

1. Who is it that has the authority to order a resort to force?
2. What are the reasons (causes) necessary and sufficient for such an order?
3. What special, additional considerations ought to govern the decision to employ force?
4. What is acceptable conduct, under conditions of armed conflict, in respect both to armed antagonists and to unarmed bystanders?[5]

Augustine accepted Cicero's view that the emperor or other duly authorized civil magistrate was qualified to give the order to fight. But in addition to the "secular" authorities, Augustine, in an assertion of the gravest consequence for later just-war teaching, held that the church, at least indirectly, might properly engage the coercive services of the state in the protection and advancement of Christian orthodoxy. The relation was "indirect," so as to maintain the appropriate distinction between sword and spirit, but it was nevertheless to be a potent connection.

On the reasons or causes for employing force, Augustine again supplemented standard Roman thought. Just wars avenge injuries: in defense against aggressive attack, in recovery of wrongfully seized assets, or in punishment of wrongs done in the past. Augustine's crucial innovation was to specify, in addition to these secular or temporal causes, certain "religious" causes, such as offenses of various kinds against Christian orthodoxy. In particular, he authorized imperial persecution of heretics and those guilty of sacrilegious acts. By including "injuries" of this sort alongside the more conventional forms of belligerent acts, Augustine provided a foundation for considering the crusades against the Muslims, and other heretics and infidels after the eleventh century, as a "just" use of force.

As one would expect from his preoccupation with the inward side of human action, Augustine gave great weight to correct intentions on the part of those undertaking and participating in armed conflict. War ought to be initiated only in the interests of achieving peace, which Augustine defined as "the tranquility of order" and as the just arrangement of "things equal and unequal, each to its own place." As with the Stoics, force for Augustine must always serve justice. Moreover, there ought never be thirst for revenge nor delight in the use of arms as an end in itself.

In fact, in response no doubt to the early church's attitude, Augustine was highly sensitive to the pathology of force. War was at best a lamentable activity. No thoughtful individual could contemplate it except "with pain on these great evils, so horrible, so ruthless."[6] What is more, Augustine seemed to suggest that one of the special infirmities of armed conflict is its tendency to generate passion and rage and thereby to distort, prejudice, and oversimplify the matter of rights and wrongs in going to war.[7] The case for using force may not be as one-sided or as open-and-shut as each party is ready to think.

That fact, coupled with Augustine's unrelenting reminders concerning the subtle corruption of all human endeavor and especially endeavor involving power, enjoins a spirit of restraint and of scrupulous self-examination on the part of those considering a resort to arms. Incidentally, Augustine's conviction that monks and clergy should be exempt from combat further underscored his deep reservations about the use of force.

Still, there is a darker side to Augustine's advice about the dispositions and other considerations that ought to govern a decision to employ force. When it came to religious persecutions, what Augustine took to be proper orthodox motives served to relax the spirit of restraint and anguish with which he otherwise approached the subject of force. An aggressive policy of punishing heresy and unbelief was, for Augustine, an act of benevolent instruction, carried out for the eternal good of the unorthodox.

When he came to define acceptable conduct toward armed antagonists and unarmed bystanders under conditions of armed conflict, Augustine generally believed in moderating the conventional brutalities of warfare. He ruled out wanton violence, profanation of temples, looting, massacre, vengeance, atrocities, and reprisals.[8] He thereby intended to suggest, though he certainly never developed or elaborated, what later became known as the "principle of noncombatant immunity" or the "principle of discrimination." Augustine thereby assumed a moral distinction that was to take on the greatest significance in the just-war tradition. However difficult it might be to draw a totally satisfactory line in the real world, there is a primitive and unmistakable difference between an armed soldier intent upon killing an enemy attacker, and a defenseless infant gurgling in its crib. Soldiers locked in combat might with good cause attempt deliberately to inflict severe injury upon each other, but there could be no justification for such action in respect to the infant.

This fundamental moral distinction is embedded in the classical and especially in the Stoic tradition of "natural justice." Natural justice referred, among other things, to certain incontestable and indefeasible ways of treating or not treating people. The tradition holds that there are certain forms of behavior, such as forbearing the deliberate infliction of serious injury upon innocent persons as an end in itself, that are always and everywhere—"by nature"—indubitably wrong. For Augustine, such a view began to define, from a Christian perspective, what constituted loving and unloving conduct. There is, though, the predictable qualification in respect to Augustine's application of this inchoate principle of noncombatant immunity. For Augustine, it turns out that "any violation of God's laws, and by easy extension, any violation of Christian doctrine, could be seen as an injustice warranting unlimited violent punishment. Further, the...guilt of the enemy merited punishment of the enemy population *without regard to the distinction between soldiers and civilians*. Motivated by a righteous [religiously motivated] wrath, the just warriors could kill with impunity *even those who were morally innocent*."[9]

In his reflections on force, Augustine concocted an unstable mixture of the three positions available to him. Without much apparent perplexity, he tried to force together the pacific impulses of the New Testament, the moderating spirit of the just-war tradition, and the no-holds-barred attitude of the Old Testament holy war. During Augustine's time, the Christian church itself came to embody the conflict. On the one hand, the church was the depository of quintessentially noncoercive, voluntary belief and action. On the other hand, the church might regulate and propagate its message both at home and abroad by forceful means, and it might do that with righteous ferocity, after the fashion of the wars recorded in the Books of Judges and Joshua.

The instability and tension inherent in the Augustinian synthesis determined the debate over the use of force throughout the Middle Ages. In the first place, while the pacific tradition was hardly a dominant influence on medieval thought, there are, occasionally, eloquent expressions of it by some Franciscans and Hussites, for example.[10] In the thirteenth century, Roger Bacon, an English Franciscan, concluded a critique of the crusades with the following comment: "The faith did not enter into this world by force of arms but through the simplicity of preaching, as is clear."[11] The lesson to be learned, Bacon argued, was that war does not avail against the unbelievers for they are not converted that way, but instead are "angered more and more against the Christian faith because of those wars... and are inflamed to do Christians all possible evils."[12]

## The Crusaders

In sharp contrast to these sentiments, the crusading strand of medieval thought embraced the holy-war themes reactivated by Augustine, and pushed them to the limit. The standard just-war questions about the authority, cause, intention, and execution of a resort to force continued to be discussed. But the responses were governed by "an extreme theory of papal world-monarchy."[13]

However firm the disjunction between church and the use of force in early Christianity, those limits were greatly relaxed by the apologists of the crusades. Increasingly, the church itself, without waiting for civil authorities, assumed the right to initiate and supervise armed action against unbelievers. Moreover, the church came to regard itself as the final court of appeal in the disputes among Christian civil rulers as well as the supreme authority on the legitimacy of all uses of force.[14]

As to the just causes for resorting to arms, this crusading point of view became preoccupied with the mortal threat to Christianity posed by "blasphemy" and unbelief. In inaugurating the crusades against the Holy Land in 1095, Pope Urban II reminded his audience that the "Holy Sepulchre of our Lord is polluted by the filthiness of an unclean nation....Therefore go forward in happiness and confidence and attack the enemies of God."[15] Christian soldiers fighting the enemies of God performed not homicide but "malicide," and those who died in battle earned eternal salvation.

Some supporters of the crusades held that unbelievers were enemies simply by dint of unbelief, or by refusal to pay a special tribute to the Christian authorities, and were therefore the fit subjects of armed attack every bit as much as were common aggressors. Because of their unbelief or their recalcitrance, they forfeited their rights to life, property, and self-determination. Others argued that unbelievers might be attacked only in response to invasion, acts of violence, and other "temporal" reasons for just retaliation. Otherwise, they ought to be left in peace . But despite the difference, there was no ambiguity over what was taken as the special and particularly sinister threat to the church represented by unbelievers, or over the need for the church to deal with that threat by force if necessary.

Since, to this way of thinking, the key to civil peace and justice—both within and between states—was a dominant and encompassing church, the intentions of those participating in the crusades to extend and secure the church's spiritual, political, and geographical control were taken as inspired by the worthy objective of a just peace. So complementary were Christian vocation and military activity that the tradition of exempting clergy and monastics from combat was frequently waived. There were monastic military orders such as the Templars and the Knights of St. John. One first-hand report from an early crusade describes a priest who ''at one and the same time...communicates the body and blood of God and becomes a man of blood, for this barbarian is no less devoted to sacred things than to war.''[16]

The crusaders and their defenders did not express much reluctance or revulsion over the effects of the wars against unbelievers. Various forms of restraint on the use of force that were being developed during the Middle Ages outside of the crusades had very little impact upon the behavior of the crusaders.

> Crucifixion, ripping open those who had swallowed coins, mutilation—Bohemond of Antioch sent to the Greek Emperor a whole cargo of noses and thumbs sliced from the Saracens—such exploits the chroniclers of the crusades recount without qualm. A favorite text was a verse in Jeremiah, ''cursed be he that keepeth back his hand from blood.'' There was no residue here of Augustinian mournfulness in combat. The mood was strangely compounded of barbarian lust for combat and Christian zeal for the faith.[17]

There was virtually no attention to Augustine's prohibitions against atrocities, wanton violence, profanation of temples, and so on, nor much interest in observing the principle of noncombatant immunity.

> [In the capture of Jerusalem] some of our men (and this was more merciful) cut off the heads of their enemies;...others tortured them longer by casting them into the flames....But these were small matters compared to what happened at the temple of Solomon, a place where religious services are ordinarily chanted....[I]n the temple and portico of Solomon, men rode in blood up to their knees and the bridle reins. Indeed, it was a just and splendid judgement of God, that this place should be filled with the blood of the unbelievers, when it had suffered so long from their blasphemies.[18]

By extending and redefining the just-war tradition so as to accommodate holy-war themes, the crusaders came to consider heretics as ''outside the law'' and therefore to be proper subjects of a ''war of extermination.''[19] The imperatives of restraint, either from the New Testament or from the just-war tradition, were all but consumed in the heat of crusading passion.

## The Moderates

But there is another side to the medieval perspective. In comparison with the crusading spirit, and no doubt partly in reaction to it, other thinkers like Thomas Aquinas emphasized, up to a point at least, precisely the imperatives of restraint which were ambiguously present in Augustine and were minimized, if not altogether disregarded, by the crusaders. It is this other side that advanced just-war thinking, even if the ghost of the holy war was by no means completely exorcised. That would happen only after a revolutionary restructuring of the relations between the church and the state, something that lay well in the future.

Whereas the crusaders had greatly relaxed the tensions between church and state that were characteristic of the primitive church, Thomas went part way toward restoring them. While he did believe that princely authority is subordinate to the Pope who "holds the apex of both powers, namely, spiritual and secular," Thomas also asserted and elaborated the difference of function between church and state, especially in regard to the use of the sword. He affirmed that "the Church of God, which is never bound by worldly laws, has no sword except the spiritual sword...."[20] That meant, among other things, that the church had no authority on its own recognizance to initiate a resort to force. It might, it is true, induce others to wage war, but that was only by indirection.

This differentiation between church and state pointed to a more general distinction between supernatural and natural things so central to Thomas's thought and to the thought of other medieval moderates, and so indispensable for the development of just-war thinking. While the supernatural or spiritual realm had final priority, the natural order, including the natural political and legal order, had relatively autonomous authority. There was no disparaging a prince's right to run his own affairs for the temporal welfare and security of his subjects. What is more important, Thomas stood firmly with those who regarded infidel princes as being thoroughly legitimate on natural law grounds, despite their unbelief.

In discussing the question of the legitimate causes for resorting to force, Thomas did not ignore religious causes altogether, but he qualified them, at least in comparison with the crusaders, and he thereby reinforced the importance of the secular or temporal causes for war. These were the standard causes relevant to the life of the natural political order: "defending the commonwealth from external enemies"; recovering assets that were "unjustly carried away"; and punishing wrongdoing as defined as severe offenses against the natural-moral law rather that against religious laws. In Thomas's words, "wars are lawful and just...insofar as they defend the poor and the whole commonwealth from injustices of the enemy."[21]

The key question highlighted by the crusades was whether unbelief in and of itself constituted an intolerable and unjustified threat to orthodoxy, and whether, therefore, it might be cause for armed action against unbelievers. Thomas is unwilling to deny flatly that it is, but he is more restrained than the crusaders. For one thing, he emphasizes, up to a point, the early Christian predilection for extensive freedom of belief and conscience. In the words of one of his commentators, "the only valid act of faith is that which proceeds from a free, interior choice." "Unwilling belief is an impossibility."[22] Therefore, Thomas will not justify compelling unbelievers to accept the Christian faith or punishing them coercively for their belief. In fact, Thomas holds rather radically that, although belief in Christ is necessary for salvation, it is wrong to affirm such belief for any reasons other than those one has freely embraced of one's own accord.

There is a basis here for what Thomas and others called a doctrine of "invincible ignorance," which was to become of great importance in later just-war thinking. The idea is that certain forms of deep and considered belief are so profoundly a matter between a person and one's own conscience that they are not susceptible to any form of coercive alteration. Trying to "conquer" those beliefs by taking arms against them is simply senseless, however disagreeable or unacceptable the beliefs may be to others. The doctrine of invincible ignorance was important in inspiring an attitude of respect and toleration for the religious and other heartfelt convictions of unorthodox and dissenting groups.

There is, incidentally, further evidence that Thomas deepened and extended the idea of the sovereignty of conscience in regard to the use of force. He suggests that all the citizens within a regime are bound to scrutinize for themselves a prince's policies, including decisions to use force. "Man is bound to obey secular rulers to the extent that the order of justice requires. For this reason if such rulers have no just title to power, but have usurped it, or if they command things to be done which are unjust, their subjects are not obliged to obey them; except, perhaps, in certain cases when it is a matter of avoiding scandal or some particular danger."[23] Should a citizen conscientiously conclude that the policy is unjust, because for example the prince lacks authority to determine the policy or invokes an unjust cause, the citizen is conscience-bound to disobey the policy. This is a radical doctrine, but its full force would not be felt until much later. Thomas grew increasingly conservative politically, and more and more he was inclined to bear down hard upon the prudential provisos about "avoiding scandal or some particular danger." Still, by enunciating and dwelling upon the idea of free conscience, Thomas had, whether he liked it or not, advanced that idea's cause.

Despite the surprising degree of support in his thought for the idea of independent judgment and civil disobedience, Thomas's commitment, even theoretically, to these ideas was highly qualified. He makes a great deal of a distinction between simple unbelievers and those who wilfully turn their back on the true religion. Heretics and apostates, writes Thomas, "at one time professed the faith and accepted it; they must be compelled even by physical force, to carry out what they promised and to hold what they once accepted."[24] In other words, heretics and apostates are unfaithful to their solemn promises and, as with contractual default in all weighty dealings, deserve civil punishment. Accordingly, punishing what might be called "treason" against the faith becomes in Thomas's mind a central religious cause for war.

As to the special, additional considerations Thomas believed should govern a decision to resort to force, he predictably gives priority to intending "the prosperity of [true] peace," which is, following Augustine, a just peace.

> It can happen that even if the authority declaring the war is legitimate, and even if the cause is just, nevertheless the war is rendered unlawful on account of a perverse intention. For Augustine says in the book *Against Faustus*: "The desire to inflict harm, the cruelty of taking vengeance, an unreconciled and implacable spirit, the fever of rebelling, and the lust to dominate, and things like these— these are the things which are justly condemned in wars."[25]

*****

> Even those who have a just war can sin in taking booty through cupidity from a perverse intention, namely, if they fight chiefly on account of booty and not on account of justice.[26]

Finally, while Thomas, like other medieval moderates, does not devote extensive attention to restraints on the conduct of war, he makes some important comments. He preserves and elaborates on the principle of noncombatant immunity implicit in Augustine's writings and thereby advances the discussion.[27] In fact, in dealing with this question, Thomas

imposes more stringent conditions on the treatment of innocent bystanders than later just-war thinkers were to accept. Not only is the direct and
intentional killing of innocent persons prohibited, but their indirect and
unintentional killing is prohibited as well. "Therefore the Lord teaches
that the wicked should be permitted to live and vengeance reserved until
the last judgment rather than that the good be killed together with the
wicked."[28] Thomas's opinions concerning noncombatant immunity,
together with other authoritative teaching, were gradually interwoven
with and influenced by the essentially secular prescriptions of the
chivalric code, which respected innocent life as a matter of knightly
virtue and etiquette.[29] Still following Aristotle, Thomas permits the
enslavement of enemy prisoners in favor of killing them. He allows the
seizure of booty and the use of ambushes, but only in the prosecution of a
war deemed just on grounds of authority, cause, and intention. And he
requires strict adherence to agreements arranged with enemies.

## The Post-Medieval Reaction

The fragmentation of medieval society into a variety of independent nation-states and the collapse of the geographical and political
dominance of the Roman Catholic Church had the profoundest effect
upon the just-war tradition. On the one hand, the common spiritual and
institutional foundations which had secured the unity and harmony of
medieval civilization, including the arrangements for limiting force and
the agreements regarding humane treatment, were undermined. The
church had served as a supranational court of appeal and source of
compromise in political disputes and conflicts, and, consequently,
just-war standards were, up to a point, authoritative and effective.[30] But
by the fifteenth and sixteenth centuries, the demise of a respected central
authority left nations "in the state of nature" where standards regarding
the use of force were self-applied and thus susceptible to extensive
partiality and bias.

On the other hand, and equally important, a countervailing process
was set in motion that favored the impulses of moderation, impulses that
were firmly if ambiguously embedded in the western Christian tradition.
So long as the church remained established and ascendant, so long as it
was capable of controlling the sword directly or indirectly while advancing its purposes, holy-war imagery continued to exert enormous influence in contradiction to the pacific dispositions of the early church and
the restraining sentiments of classical just-war thinking.

What is more, the medieval establishment encouraged the church, in face of some reluctance, to consider force a legitimate means for manipulating the conscience and for punishing and dispossessing the unorthodox. In short, by embracing religious causes and religious legitimation for resorting to war, the medieval perspective—whether understood in reference to the fulminations of the crusaders or the more temperate reflections of Thomas Aquinas—served, in crucial respects, as an inspiration for extending and decontrolling the use of force.

It is true that the potency of the holy-war tradition did not expire with the collapse of medieval society. After the Reformation, it continued to fire the imaginations of some reformers and their followers, as well as some militant sectarians like Thomas Müntzer, one of the leaders of the German Peasants' Revolt in 1525. The Reformed tradition reveals a particularly acute ambivalence over the use of force, but there can be no question that the Genevan reformer John Calvin and many of his followers shared the medieval enthusiasm for an established, uniform church. That very enthusiasm for bringing church and sword into close alliance, when replicated among conflicting religious groups and territories, helped to generate the bloody and protracted wars of religion, as well as the wars of imperial expansion and colonization so characteristic of the near post-medieval period.

But as we would expect, given the diversity of contending attitudes toward war and peace within the tradition, the crusading spirit did not go unchallenged. The sixteenth and seventeenth centuries were a particularly creative period for the advocates of restraint. In an outspoken protest against Spanish colonial policy toward the beginning of the sixteenth century, a Dominican friar illustrates a growing revulsion to the brutal military practices of the time:

> Tell me, by what right or justice do you keep these Indians in such a
> cruel and horrible servitude? On what authority have you waged a
> detestable war against these people who dwelt quietly and peace-
> fully on their own land?...Are these not men? Have they not
> rational souls? Are you not bound to love them as yourselves?[31]

The influential writings of early modern just-war thinkers—both Catholic and Protestant, such as Francisco de Vitoria, Francisco Suarez, Alberico Gentili, and Hugo Grotius—are in many ways but elaborate glosses on this statement.

## Early Modern Just-War Thought

These early modern writers saw all about them grim evidence of the pathology of force, and in response they articulated something of Augustine's earlier anguish over armed combat. They became consumed with the cause of international peace, and they identified that peace with achieving a just administration of force.

> Throughout the Christian world I observed [writes Hugo Grotius] a lack of restraint in relation to war, such as even barbarous races should be ashamed of; I observed that men rush to arms for slight causes, or no cause at all, and that when arms have once been taken up there is no longer any respect for law, divine or human; it is as if, in accordance with a general decree, frenzy had openly been let loose for the committing of all crimes.[32]

And Grotius continues:

> Least of all should that be admitted which some people imagine, that in war all laws are in abeyance. On the contrary war ought not to be undertaken except for the enforcement of rights; when once undertaken, it should be carried on only within the bounds of law and good faith.[33]

They all also reasserted and elevated the idea of natural law as the basic standard for the just administration of force, a standard conceived as independent of and prior to religious revelation. Correspondingly, they all, though with different degrees of stringency, restricted and reduced the place of religious causes in legitimating force. The strong surge during this period respecting the "natural" rights of conscience, possession, and self-government of all peoples is, therefore, linked directly to the declining appeal of the holy war.

For example, Grotius, the Dutch lawyer and Protestant theologian, makes the momentous claim that it is possible to grasp and apply a "body of law" "concerned with the mutual relations among states" that "would have a degree of validity even if we should concede...that there is no God."[34] Because a law of right relations among human beings is taken to exist, and to exist independently of any belief in God, that law is incumbent upon and knowable by all human beings without regard to religion. No one is entitled by special religious privilege to override forcibly fundamental requirements of freedom and fair treatment.

The result of such views is that the sphere and sovereignty of each individual's conscience in relation to the use of force dramatically expands. Coercion in regard to matters of religious belief and practice is sharply curtailed, so that individuals have more room for stretching their consciences unmolested. Just as significantly, the degree of each person's responsibility for evaluating and supervising the use of armed force is increased. The concern of these early modern writers with individual responsibility and conscientious objection in face of a summons to war greatly outstrips anything found earlier, though it was, of course, anticipated by Thomas Aquinas and others.

Grotius had particularly liberal views. He rejected medieval notions of collective guilt and punishment according to which whole groups could properly be sanctioned for their leaders' derelictions. For Grotius, citizens were responsible to take charge of their own actions and suffer the consequences accordingly. That meant that they were bound to expand the reach of their consciences and to scrutinize and assess unrelentingly the words and deeds of their leaders, particularly those involving the resort to force.

Grotius urges all potential combatants to assess the "lawfulness" of a given war (in respect to just-war criteria), and "they should altogether refrain from [serving], if it is clear to them that the cause of the war is unjust."[35] He even suggests that if a strong doubt exists about the justifiability of a war policy, a citizen should disobey, since "disobedience in things of this kind, by its very nature, is a lesser evil than manslaughter, especially than the slaughter of many innocent men."[36] In response to a defense of "executive privilege," whereby a leader might think it acceptable to keep the reasons for war secret, Grotius retorts that all attempts at justification "ought to be clear and open."[37] He implies that if a leader is unable to provide a coherent and compelling public defense for the use of force, then any reluctance on the part of soldiers and citizens serves the leader right.[38]

In the interest, then, of moderating what Grotius saw as the "frenzy" of violence that had seized post-medieval Europe, he and the others set to work to elaborate and refine, in a relatively systematic way, the four general categories of just-war concerns that had been struggling for life for a long time.

In regard to *legitimate authority,* there is a new and stronger emphasis upon the responsibility of secular rulers in matters of war and peace along with a substantial reduction of the temporal role of the church. Catholics like Suarez and Vitoria still ascribed some authority to the Pope in resolving international disputes and in recommending the use of force where the church was threatened. Even Grotius, the Protestant, recommended the use of an ecumenical confederation of church leaders to arbitrate interstate disputes. But in all these proposals, the role of church authority was vestigial in comparison with the medieval perspective.

It it important to refer in passing to the emergence during this period of new conceptions of consent and popular sovereignty as the basis of political authority. These ideas were in many ways simply an extension of the new emphasis on the sovereignty of each citizen's conscience in respect to the conduct and organization of political life, including the administration of force. These ideas implied that citizens in concert held the upper hand over their rulers, and if they judged the rulers unworthy, they might, at least in extreme circumstances, resist them and even "delegitimate" them.

All this posed for just-war theorists the tender subject of revolution. Thinkers like Vitoria and Grotius had uncorked notions which had a logical implication, in many cases, of stark revolution. Yet, did not such a prospect foreshadow more rather than less strife and bloodshed? Especially Gentili and Grotius, as they grew older, thought it did, and consequently they became less and less enthusiastic about revolutionary stirrings. The problem of revolution would continue to be a sore point for just-war thinking ever after.

As to the question of *just cause,* there is, as expected, a strong emphasis upon "natural" or "moral" offenses as a warrant for using force, and again only a vestigial reference to religious causes. The writers reiterate the standard temporal just-war causes—self-defense, recovery of assets, and punishment of wrongdoing—but they also make something of the distinction between self-defense as a "defensive" war, and punishment as an "offensive" one (with recovery of assets somewhere in between). Defensive wars are direct responses to an imminent or existing unjust armed attack or seizure of property; the notion also was broadened to include operations intended to "defend" foreign citizens against unjust rulers—what we might call "humanitarian intervention"—and defense of allies.[39]

There is no unanimity among the writers concerning the question of certifying or verifying the existence of a just cause. Indeed, for obvious reasons, this was to become one of the most vexing problems for just-war theory, since belligerents are called upon, in effect, to try their own cases. Opinions varied sharply. Gentili's view was that, so long as both sides "aim at justice," they may legitimately fight, despite any doubts. Grotius took a harder line. If there is any doubt at all about the causes of war, then force must be foresworn. This difference produced the equally controversial doctrine of *simultaneous justice,* according to which both sides in a war might well be justified. While Grotius, for one, rejected the idea that from a moral point of view both sides could be equally right, he readily conceded that one or both of the belligerents might understandably, if mistakenly, *believe* themselves to be in the right. It was his sensitivity to "invincibly" biased interpretations concerning the authorizing reasons for war that led Grotius and others to counsel self-restraint and a modest and tolerant attitude in pleading the case for war. The pathology of force was always at hand.

The special, additional considerations, as loosely and somewhat informally discussed in the Middle Ages, were taken by the early-modern theorists and classified, clarified, and, in some cases, modified. The requirement of having a *peaceful intention,* so important to Augustine and Thomas, is reduced somewhat in significance, no doubt because of the preference of these writers for evaluating deeds rather than motives.[40]

Next, all of them singled out and emphasized that force be used only as a *last resort*, which means that all other reasonable means for solving a conflict peacefully must be exhausted.[41] They also laid down the rule that any resort to force must conform to *general proportionality*. The cause, even if just, must be "grave" or "weighty" enough to warrant risking life and national treasure. In addition, the costs of using force must be proportional to the foreseeable consequences, again however just the cause. A related test requires that there be a *reasonable hope of success*. This is, of course, a counsel of prudence: It is generally irrational to undertake a costly and risky venture faced with a high probability of failure. Finally, some attention is given to requiring a *formal declaration of war*, including a statement of charges, presumably to assure full accountability.

These seven considerations—legitimate authority, just cause, peaceful intention, last resort, general proportionality, reasonable hope of success, and formal declaration—comprise a set of criteria that came to be grouped under the title, *jus ad bellum*, meaning those conditions which must be met before a decision to go to war is considered justified. Three additional conditions, present in the tradition but also somewhat revised and systematized by the early-modern theorists, make up a second category, called *jus in bello*, meaning the conditions for the permissible conduct of war.

The first of these additional criteria is the principle of *discrimination* or *noncombatant immunity*. The writers, distinct from Thomas, permit the unintentional killing of innocent civilians and thereby introduce the so-called *principle of double-effect*. It works as follows: If there are two effects of an action, one good and one bad, such as attacking a military installation, but in the act unavoidably killing several innocent civilians lodged therein, then the action is permissible so long as the destruction of the installation is the only effect intended and directly and deliberately sought. The killing of civilians in that case is regarded as an unintended and indirect or "collateral" side-effect. The principle of double-effect would rule out such terroristic acts as taking hostages or directly threatening the lives of innocent civilians in order to extort compliance from the enemy.

Incidentally, all the thinkers wrestled with the problem of defining "innocent civilians." They included such groups as young children, old people, "all unable to bear arms," clerics, monastics, farmers, and so on. Moreover, the thinkers worried in various ways over "indiscriminate" weapons, and they offered strictures against the use of such weapons as wild animals and poison, because their effects were so hard to control.[42]

There is some indication that, although the condition of discrimination was regarded as very important, it was not absolute for these writers, as it has become in some later just-war positions. They hold that under certain dire circumstances "military necessity" might permissibly override the prohibition against directly threatening or killing civilians.[43] In that case, what we may call the condition of *military proportionality*—the efficiency relationship between weapons or tactics and specific military objectives—would take precedence. Such permission, incidentally, constitutes a direct violation of the principle of double-effect, though the authors do not appear to worry much about that. The whole point of the principle of double-effect was to prohibit deliberate and direct attack upon innocent civilians under any circumstances, and the temptation to tamper with the principle would not end with these early modern theorists. In any event, as proportionality begins to assume increasing importance during this period, the writers expend considerable effort elaborating, as Grotius did, both qualitative and quantitative measures that ought to be applied to a prudent calculation of the costs and benefits of military actions. Nevertheless, they did not carry very far the attempt to apply this condition in practice.[44]

The last condition concerns the *treatment of prisoners*. While the thinkers favor some measure of restraint in dealing with prisoners, their opinions vary over the degree. Grotius recommends that only those prisoners guilty of grave offenses or serious excesses in the line of duty ought to be punished.[45] Beyond the matter of ascribing guilt and punishment, there does not appear to be much discussion of prison conditions, post-war treatment, and the host of conditions that have in more recent years been developed. Still, the beginnings of a concern to protect prisoners are found in the writings of these theorists.

## Modern Developments and Dilemmas

After the disintegration of the Middle Ages, something of a puzzle confronted those concerned about creating conditions of international peace and justice. On the one hand, it appeared that only by eliminating established religion of the medieval and reformation variety was there any chance of loosening the grip of holy-war thinking and of liberating the spirit of restraint associated with the conjunction of early Christianity and classical just-war thought. "Secularizing" political life and the terms for using force, as Grotius and others advocated, seemed to be one of the necessary requirements for developing standards to moderate violence and promote humane treatment.

On the other hand, once the church and the cultural unity it represented was removed, there was no longer a respected supranational authority to help define and enforce a semblance, at least, of effective international order. The emergence in the post-medieval period of a myriad of independent, self-determining, and often antagonistic nation-states seemed by its very nature to defy the establishment of any effective set of international regulations for governing the use of force, for the elementary reason that each nation, in effect, constituted its own judge and jury.

Extensive discretion in interpreting and applying the rather abstract just-war standards worked out by the end of the early modern period did little to increase their credibility. Moreover, the state of affairs was particularly dangerous with the invention of new and more devastating armaments and techniques of warfare. In short, the dilemma was this: What was to become of the cause of peace when the chances for restraining violence were at once improved and retarded by post-medieval circumstances?

After the seventeenth century, two general responses to this dilemma presented themselves, the *positivist* and the *legalist* [46] positions. These positions continue to exert influence up to the present. While different in some of their assumptions, both responses conclude that, under modern conditions, we have dispensed with the need for just-war thinking as conceived in the traditional terms of a moral theory independent of and superior to the law.

The proponents of a positivist theory of international law gained ascendancy in the eighteenth and especially in the nineteenth centuries. They simply despaired of ever discovering a natural law—an objective moral foundation—on which to build determinate and operative prescriptions for regulating the relations of states in war and peace. The only hope for working out a viable international law was, so to speak, to catalogue and codify *after the fact* the actual agreements, determinations, and behavior patterns of existing states. Not how states "ought" to relate to each other in matters of war and peace, but how they in fact "do" relate to each other, tells the tale. Rulers might learn some lessons regarding international behavior by observing customary or conventional practice, and they clearly might better estimate the costs of violating custom by knowing what it is. But the sovereign positivist principle in all matters is "the reason of state"—the protection and enrichment of the state by all means necessary and expedient.

Agreements and pacts for mutual benefit might well serve to regulate the use of force and the treatment of combatants and noncombatants during wartime. However, as soon as the benefits for one side expire, that side is bound by the terms of positivism to disregard the agreement, if it can do so with impunity. For the positivist, behavior in war is dictated by two rules: "circumstances alone determine proper means," and "war gives a nation an unlimited right of exercising violence against the enemy."[47]

Proponents of a legalist theory sympathize with the formulations and background of the just-war tradition. They agree that standards of the sort developed and elaborated by just-war thinkers regarding *jus ad bellum* and *jus in bello* are required for a secure international order, and that a positivist approach, in its preoccupation with "naked national self-interest," ultimately destabilizes international order.

Thanks to a series of international covenants in the twentieth century, such as the Covenant of the League of Nations, the United Nations Charter, and treaties governing the law of war, legalists claim that just-war standards by now are "legalized," and therefore that the "classical doctrine of *bellum justum* may be seen to be comparable in policy with contemporary prescriptions."[48] At long last, the dreams of Grotius and other just-war thinkers that their standards might become part of international legal thought and practice are beginning to materialize.

For this reason, a just-war theory independent of and superior to the law is no longer much use. In fact, without authoritative and effective instruments for defining and applying just-war standards, an independent just-war theory self-applied by contending parties is impotent. For the legalist, just-war theory moves from abstraction into the real world through effective legislation. This, in turn, changes the character of the theory. Once the legal instruments are in place and working, the theory becomes part and parcel of the existing body of law.

The legalist makes a case worth considering, though it is deficient in two respects. The strength of the position lies in the fact that, when it comes to justifying and assessing a resort to force between states, just-war standards, like those now embedded in much of the existing international law of war, are precisely the reference points according to which the justifications and assessments are discussed.

For example, however difficult it may be to define "international aggression," there is a widespread assumption that, under some circumstances, we can know it when we see it, and that "flagrant cases of aggression" constitute, unmistakably and unexceptionably, a just cause to respond with force. Hitler's invasion of Poland in 1939 would appear to be a paradigm case. Such judgments, insofar as they are made, rest on a set of venerable just-war beliefs: that the international community is composed of independent states with rights of territorial integrity and political sovereignty, and moreover that unprovoked threats or use of force by one state against another constitutes an act of aggression, an impermissible "injury," and may be legitimately counteracted by force in self-defense.[49]

Furthermore, even though international covenants such as the Convention on the Prevention and Punishment of the Crime of Genocide have not been ratified by all states (inexplicably, the United States, as of this writing, is still delinquent), "acts committed with intent to destroy, in whole or in part, a national, ethnical, racial or religious group as such" are regarded throughout the international community "as a crime under international law." Whatever their actual behavior, nations would not be indifferent to accusations of genocide.

The same is true of the so-called International Humanitarian Laws, such as the Hague Conventions of 1899 and 1907, "Respecting the Laws and Customs of War on Land," and the Geneva Conventions of 1949 governing treatment of the wounded and sick in the field and at sea, prisoners of war, and protection of civilians in war. Although nations no doubt violate these provisions from time to time, even violators endeavor invariably to disprove charges against them. That is the tribute vice pays to virtue, and as the legalist rightly argues, it is not an insignificant tribute. It means that at the level of international expectation certain norms are widely shared and are vigorously "operational" in the judgments made about the behavior of states. In that respect, the just-war tradition has vindicated itself against positivist theory.

The legalist, however, is not right in trying to put just-war thinking in its traditional form out of business. Just-war thinking took root in the West as the result of conjoining classical Graeco-Roman themes with the predilections of the early Christian church for erecting a sphere of conscientious judgment independent of and superior to the use of force. However ready the church might be in medieval and reformation times to surrender its birth-right to the lure of the legal establishment and the glittering images of the holy war, the idea of a "right of conscientious objection" was always nourished by the tradition, even in the most bellicose of times. It is this part of the tradition that, in societies like ours, eventually produced provisions for conscientious objector status.[50]

The implication is that each citizen is personally responsible, in face of public decisions to employ force, to "try the government" in the internal forum of conscience according to the standards suggested and elaborated by the just-war tradition. In that sense, just-war thinking inspires a grand campaign of public education. It calls for informed, open, and thorough discussion on the part of government and citizens of the issues involved in using force, so that each citizen may conduct a "fair trial" and arrive at a thoughtful verdict.

Naturally, existing international law should play an important role in these deliberations. Making that law known is part of the educational task. But according to the just-war tradition, individual conscience is never reducible to established law, however enlightened. To affirm the "sovereignty of conscience" is to preserve a realm of irreducible moral independence. For the just-war tradition, war is too important simply to be left to the policymakers or the lawyers.

In addition, while the international legalization of just-war standards is by no means to be disparaged, the full complement of legal mechanisms for authoritatively interpreting, applying, and enforcing the law hardly exists under present conditions. This is the grain of insight in the positivist position. Though things have improved since the sixteenth and seventeenth centuries, nation-states to an important degree still live in the state of nature. In respect to using force, nations still try their own cases, and the bigger the nation, the greater the degree of discretion.

Discretion breeds controversy. Precisely because of the lack of binding and authoritative procedures, the range of divergent opinion within and among nations as to what the law means in given instances is unavoidably broad. This indicates that there remains considerable room for "just-war theorizing," among other things, in the spirit, if not always in the terms, of Augustine, Aquinas, and Grotius. There is continuing need for critical reflection on and proposals concerning the restraint of force in the modern world. Existing international law surely will condition such reflection, but the unfinished nature of the law itself demands creative and independent reflection.

## Contemporary Dilemmas for Just-War Thinking

Particularly since the eighteenth century and the advent of the positivist theory of international law, just-war thinking has been under serious attack. If anything, in more modern times criticism intensified.

There is a point to much of the criticism. It touches on many of the perplexities and dilemmas that confront any person who tries to put just-war standards to work. For one thing, there is not, as should be evident from our historical review, anything even approximating a settled just-war "theory," if we mean by that a coherent, authoritative, and elaborate set of practicable standards for evaluating force. The number of standards, their definition, their order of importance, the terms of their application and verification, even their moral foundations, are subject either to conflicting interpretations, or are left very much in the air. Futhermore, there are legitimate questions whether, in the modern world of revolutionary and insurgency wars and of high-technological conventional warfare and nuclear weapons, standards formulated during an age of relatively primitive and discriminate weapons and tactics make any sense.

In response, it may be suggested that, if it is hard to live with just-war standards under modern conditions, it is equally hard to live without them. That means that should just-war standards prove hard to apply to contemporary kinds of war, those standards nevertheless appear, much as in the legal discussion, to constitute unavoidable reference points in guiding conscientious judgment in regard to using force. Two poignant examples help to substantiate this.

The intense and extended debates over U.S. military involvement in Vietnam during the '60s and early '70s dramatically illustrate both the difficulty and unavoidability of employing just-war standards in discussions of armed conflict. The difficulty in applying the standards to that confused and confusing war is fairly obvious, and it is revealing that two authors, William V. O'Brien [51] and Michael Walzer, [52] come to conflicting conclusions regarding the "justice" of U.S. policy in light of the same just-war standards.

Sharp disagreement attends the application of nearly all the criteria. Was the government of Vietnam (GVN—South Vietnam) a *legitimate government* in the first place? Indeed, how is a legitimate government to be defined and determined under revolutionary conditions? Did an "aggressive assault" in fact take place against the GVN by another independent government, the Democratic Republic of Vietnam (DRV—North Vietnam)? Did the GVN therefore have a *just cause* to fight in its own defense and to invite members of the international community to join in that fight? Was the U.S. decision to use force in defense of the GVN itself legitimate, given the ambiguities surrounding the Gulf of Tonkin Resolution? In fact, should there have been a *declaration of war* at some point?

Was force administered with a *peaceful and just intention*, or was the U.S. really serving some surreptitious and illicit economic, military, or symbolic interest? Did the U.S. involve itself militarily only as a *last resort*? Had it in fact exhausted all means of international mediation, including the UN? Was there indeed a *reasonable hope of success*, given the often-advertised liabilities of fighting a land war in Asia in an altogether unfavorable environment? Could the GVN survive on its own accord, once the U.S. departed? Was it worth trying to help it do so? Was there a measure of *general proportion* between the overall objectives of victory and the costs of the war in terms of the destruction of Indochina, loss of life, and the impact on U.S. domestic and fiscal life?

With respect to the conduct of war, was sufficient care taken to respect *noncombatant immunity*, or was the Mylai massacre symbolic of a generally "indiscriminate" war the U.S. was fighting? Were weapons such as napalm, and the tactics such as "search and destroy" missions, extensive bombing, and population relocation humane? Was there *military proportion* between arms and tactics and the purposes for which the arms and tactics were used, or was the famous utterance by the U.S. officer, "We had to destroy the village in order to save it," illustrative of the general irrationality of the use of force in Indochina? What about the *treatment of prisoners* on both sides? Did the DRV honor its obligations? Did the U.S. and the GVN? What about the "tiger cages?"

O'Brien, for one, has serious problems with some of the *jus in bello* standards, especially compliance with noncombatant immunity and military proportionality, but on balance he believes that the overall justice of the cause produced a passing grade for U.S. policy. Walzer, on the other hand, leaves no doubt that for him U.S. policy failed the just-war tests. The differences between O'Brien and Walzer as they look back and evaluate U.S. military policy are hauntingly reminiscent of the differences in the U.S. population at large during the "Vietnam years."

But if it was hard to apply just-war standards to the Vietnam war, it should at the same time be obvious, from stating the questions as we did, that traditional just-war standards constituted precisely the terms of discourse over U.S. policy in Vietnam. People came to their conscientious judgments about that case within the framework of considerations long established by just-war reflection. They emphasized certain just-war standards over others and had to say why; they had to provide definitions for the standards and to indicate how the standards should be applied. They had to reveal how they went about verifying and certifying their judgments, and so on. Ironically, it was partly because of the difficulty in applying the standards to that war that interest in just-war standards intensified.[53]

Skepticism about the relevance of just-war standards to military and deterrence strategy involving nuclear weapons appears to run deep. Right off the bat, three of the tests would seem to be nonstarters when applied to nuclear weapons. What sense does it make to speak of a *reasonable hope of success* in a nuclear exchange? In a nuclear war, who wins? And precisely what is won? The same goes for the tests of *general proportionality* and *military proportionality*. In either case, how can a nuclear exchange be proportional to anything? What are the conceivable benefits that outweigh the costs, once the war is over? As for the test of *noncombatant immunity* or *discrimination*, nuclear weapons appear clearly to flunk. The only realistic distinction that could be made in reference to the victims of a nuclear attack would be the grotesquely living and the grotesquely dead.

Nuclear deterrence strategy does not fare much better. Despite some inconsistency among early modern theorists in applying it, the principle of noncombatant immunity stands squarely against the intentional and direct infliction of severe injury upon innocent people, as well as against the *threat* of doing that, as in hostage-taking. It is hard to see how present-day deterrence policy is anything more than a massive hostage-holding operation.

A number of contemporary just-war advocates have tried ingeniously to avoid the force of this claim, but without much success. Paul Ramsey, for one, has tried to vindicate the principle of noncombatant immunity in an age of nuclear deterrence by proposing that nuclear weapons be aimed so as to threaten only counterforce, rather than countercity, targets.[54] Accordingly, the principle of double-effect would then be respected, because there would be no intention directly and deliberately to assault innocent people. However great the civilian casualties from such an attack, they would be the result of indirect "collateral damage."

Incidentally, the Reagan administration has seized upon this same idea without, perhaps, recognizing its roots. They insist that their policy of targeting directly only installations of military and industrial significance is morally superior to a counterpeople targeting policy. The problem, of course, is that there are sixty-odd such installations in Moscow itself and some forty thousand across the Soviet Union. Noncombatants will be hard to avoid. Leon Wieseltier argues:

> The counterforce strategy of the present Pentagon is what counter-force strategy [in a nuclear age] has always been — sheer sophistry. The concern of counterforce for innocent lives is purely cosmetic. Innocent lives [in huge numbers] will surely be lost [in a nuclear exchange]; and the lie that they will not, which flourishes in the strategic formulas of the Soviet Union and the US, only makes the loss of these lives more likely....Counterforce was conceived as a consequence of improvements in the accuracy of intercontinental ballistic missiles, which made it possible to hit small targets very far away, but the accuracy of missiles does not limit the damage they cause.[55]

Other just-war advocates have attempted to protect the relevance of the tradition to nuclear policy by arguing that even deterrence strategy premised on the threat of civilian destruction is justifiable so long as no actual use of weapons is ever intended. The policy is mere bluff, and therefore the intentions remain morally pure, though, of course, that fact is necessarily concealed from the enemy.

But this argument is not very powerful either. Whatever the hidden intentions of U.S. policymakers might be, U.S. military preparations must be as they are: sufficiently convincing to lead an adversary to believe that nuclear weapons are intended for use. Such action is obviously sufficient to constitute a coercive threat against innocent people.

That fact also undermines Michael Novak's apparent suggestion that so long as the "fundamental" intention behind a deterrence policy is to prevent nuclear war, any "secondary" intention to be ready to use the weapons is morally neutralized.[56] Whatever merits there are to such a distinction, his suggestion clearly contradicts rather than refines the tradition. Direct threats on the lives of innocent people, whatever one's "fundamental" intention may be, is an unmistakable violation of the principle of double-effect.

Finally, the Catholic Bishops, in their *Pastoral Letter on War and Peace*, "acknowledge the need for [a nuclear] deterrent," and concur with Pope John Paul II that a deterrence policy "based on balance" and "as a step on the way toward progressive disarmament" is "morally acceptable." But, they do not demonstrate how their judgment can be squared with the principle of double-effect.[57] This is particularly peculiar in light of their explicit unwillingness to take refuge, like Ramsey, in counterforce deterrence doctrines. Until this issue is faced and resolved, the Bishops' attempt to harmonize just-war standards with deterrence theory must, like the other attempts, be adjudged unsuccessful.

Given the character of nuclear weapons and the massive damage even a small number of them would undoubtedly produce, there is no escaping the irrelevance of attempts to maintain purity of intention in making ready and threatening to use such weapons. It would appear, then, from a scrupulous reading of the just-war tradition, that on a number of counts—reasonable hope of success, proportionality, noncombatant immunity—both the use and the threat to use nuclear weapons are morally objectionable. But if that is the verdict of the tradition, must we conclude with the skeptics that just-war theory is obsolete?

Might we not better conclude, in keeping with the just-war tradition, that instead it is nuclear weapons and policies premised upon them that are obsolete? It seems clear that the widespread revulsion toward nuclear weapons is in fact inspired to an important extent by the conviction that such weapons are *morally irrational*. Their use could not conceivably serve a good or just end, and their effects would obliterate any meaning to the distinction between combatants and noncombatants or proportion and disproportion. In other words, by the very terms of the just-war tradition itself, it seems reasonable to conclude that nuclear weapons are the very symbol and embodiment of violence—of unjustifiable and illegitimate infliction of severe suffering on human beings—which just-war thinking has always been in business to try to prevent.

If this is true, then far from being excluded by the circumstances of a nuclear age, just-war standards make an appearance at the back door after having been thrown out at the front. The criteria are partially vindicated by the judgments many people find themselves inclined to make about using or threatening to use nuclear weapons.

Anyone who seeks, within the just-war framework, to decide what is to be done about deterrence policy, seems to have two fundamental options. One may consistently conclude with the ''just-war absolutists'' or ''nuclear pacifists'' that the acquisition and deployment of nuclear weapons as a deterrent is morally illicit, and that any country engaging in such an activity ought on moral grounds to stop forthwith. Some form of unilateral disarmament would appear to follow.

The other option is to take up the so-called ''necessity excuse,'' which was unsuccessfully toyed with by the early modern theorists, and to interpret and apply it more rigorously and self-consciously than has been done in tradition. To be clear, an ''excuse,'' in the relevant sense, is very different from a justification. It is offered to reduce a person's responsibility for doing something that is admitted to be wrong. An excuse of ''necessity'' would be offered in a situation where, whatever one does or does not do, the effects are morally abhorrent. Threatening the life of a terrorist's infant, where that remains the only means to prevent the explosion of a nuclear device planted in the midst of a city, is a familiar example. The crucial ingredient is the presence of a profoundly divided will: One wills, and has the capacity to prevent, untold human misery; at the same time, however, one wills to achieve that end by means of threatening, and presumably intending (if need be), the death of an innocent infant. This is sometimes described as an example of ''right against right,'' but it is probably better understood as ''wrong against wrong.'' In any event, it is a case of necessity because it is a case where the moral machinery jams. In such a situation one is excused from full responsibility for the evil effects that are intended or that result.

The situation we find ourselves in regarding deterrence strategy and the Soviet Union appears to have the features of a case of necessity. As Walzer puts it, ''Against the threat of an immoral attack, [both sides] have put the threat of an immoral response.''[58]

Now if we accept this as a proper description of our moral situation, we may draw some conclusions. First, we must admit outright the force of the negative just-war appraisal of nuclear weapons. They *are* immoral weapons for all the reasons mentioned. And deterrence strategy is morally wrong for the same reasons. It *is* a policy of reciprocal international terrorism. Both sides *are* holding each other's innocent citizens hostage. There is no prettying up these unpleasant facts. The best we can hope for is to provide an excuse for persisting in so morally dubious a policy, an excuse grounded in a fervent concern to prevent untold human misery or abject capitulation, and a firm belief that deterrence is the only remaining, if deeply regrettable, means to achieve that end.

Second, we must prove our excuse. We must be able to demonstrate that deterrence is indeed a "last resort," and that it is in fact an efficient and reliable means to prevent the sort of evils we seek to prevent.

Third, we should, on this view, be morally prompted to eliminate the conditions of necessity as quickly as we can. Just because we, along with the Soviets, are "in the wrong," even if our responsibility is diminished, we are bound, if we can, to find ways to remove our colossal moral burden.

On this reading, any moral appraisal of the firing of nuclear weapons or their role in deterrence must acknowledge the irreducible antinomy in which we are caught: Since firing them would be evil, the only conceivable excuse for threatening to fire them is to prevent the first evil from occurring. The "ethics of deterrence" have to do with extricating ourselves from this predicament, in a reasonable and balanced way, as fast as we can.

Accordingly, the pertinent questions to such considerations as "first-use," mutually assured destruction, and nuclear freeze are whether they contribute or not to maintaining a credible and reliable deterrent and thus to reducing the likelihood of nuclear war, so that we gain breathing space to set about negotiating the end or at least the serious modification of our predicament. In this sense, calculations of utility do play a special role in respect to deterrence, but only so long as we remember that such calculations are forever tainted by their context.

In any case, the appeal to the necessity excuse, like the nuclear pacifist position, asserts the moral irrationality of nuclear weapons as adjudged by just-war criteria. Thus it pays tribute also to the salience of the just-war tradition.

However just-war standards are finally applied to specific contemporary dilemmas, it is useful to remember that the just-war tradition has deep European roots that extend not only to the new world of America, but to Russia and the Soviet bloc as well. The language is not unknown there, and it often unwittingly informs the public statements of Soviet leaders no less than it does the statements of U.S. leaders. It is part of our inherited and common way of evaluating the use of force. Furthermore, since the just-war tradition gradually has become part of international legal and moral consciousness, any nation that openly rejects or disregards the basic provisions of the tradition is not likely to be regarded with indifference.

The tradition still is very much in the process of being shaped and interpreted. There is considerable room for debate and discussion over the precise meaning and application of the various categories, if only because they are so general and formal. While developments in the international law of war have helped to specify and make practicable some of the just-war standards, the law itself is, as I have suggested, quite unfinished. The law and the tradition urgently need help from broader, ongoing public consideration of the problem of the just administration of force, both within and among nations. An important first step toward informed and sophisticated public discussion is an understanding of the origins and history of the just-war tradition.

# Peacekeeping
# As a Military Mission

DAVID R. SEGAL
KATHARINE SWIFT GRAVINO

In February 1984, the United States Department of Defense authorized awarding the Purple Heart to military personnel wounded in the course of peacekeeping operations or as a result of terrorist attacks. The Purple Heart is a combat medal for soldiers exposed to physical danger in the interest of national security. This new usage marks peacekeeping as a legitimate part of the American military mission.

It is our thesis that, in an age of nuclear technology, the role of military forces in maintaining peace is unlikely to be limited to the "peace through strength" doctrine of deterrence. Increasingly, military forces will be called on to participate actively in conflict resolution. Work as peacekeeping troops is a relatively new role for American forces, and analysts concerned with conflict resolution have largely ignored the role of the military in this process. Military analysts, for their part, have focused on high-intensity conflict and ignored the role of the military in peacekeeping except in the sense that they regard military victory as conflict resolution.

We see peacekeeping operations as a form of low-intensity conflict. This conclusion is reflected in a number of studies showing that American military personnel feel that peacekeeping is the kind of mission they are most likely to perform during the next decade.[1] But little is known about the peacekeeping process in general or about the most appropriate forms for American participation in peacekeeping. Our review of changes in the nature of the military function, the history of peacekeeping operations, and the issues that remain to be resolved demonstrate that those concerned with the means and techniques of international peace as a process of conflict resolution must count the military into that process.

Warfare is an ever-present characteristic of human life. Quincy Wright, in his classic study of war,[2] asserted that war has existed at every historic epoch. Similarly, Stanislav Andreski assumes war to be "the constant feature of the life of humanity."[3] These scholars and others suggest that warfare is a social process predating the emergence of social institutions solely dedicated to the waging of war: military organizations. The constancy of war as an element of the social process continues today. At any point in time, there are scores of wars being waged in the world. They tend to involve smaller nations rather than larger and low levels of intensity rather than high. Frequently, however, they do involve major nations and almost always the use of modern military technology. And whether small nation or large, low-intensity war or high, this armed conflict kills, maims, and displaces people, and destroys property and economic capacity.

Organized armies appeared with the development of political systems.[4] Even in primitive societies, the growth of a warrior class coincided with increasing cultural complexity. Early civilizations produced armies to the extent that (a) economic surpluses permitted the support of soldiers not directly involved in economic production, or (b) soldiers could be released from the domestic productive economy by season, for example between sowing and harvesting in agricultural societies, or (c) armies provided their own economic support through imperial conquest. Under any of these conditions, the function of the army was to wage war, offensively or defensively. When wars were not being waged, armies were demobilized and soldiers set to work in the domestic productive economy. The development of organized armies, in contrast to less organized groups of opposing forces, produced clear differentiation between combatant and noncombatant which became formulated into an ethic of war. Combatants were identified through uniforms, could commit acts of violence on behalf of the state, and were legitimate targets for opposing soldiers. Engaging in combat when not identified as a combatant, for instance by wearing civilian clothing, came to be regarded as a crime of war, as did the unnecessary killing of noncombatants.

Keeping large standing armies in peacetime was a luxury most societies could not afford. Thus, once political complexity allowed the growth of armies and experience dictated distinctions between combatants and noncombatants, it continued to be the case that soldiers returned periodically to civilian pursuits: combatants became noncombatants.

More importantly, war became a temporally bounded event. When soldiers were mobilized and engaged in battle, it was wartime. When they were demobilized and engaged in civilian economic pursuits, it was peacetime.

## Mass Armies and Mobilization

Recognizing that large standing armies during peacetime were an inefficient use of resources and that such armies were a potential threat to the democratic political process, the industrial nations of the West, at least from the time of American and French Revolutions through the first part of the twentieth century, used a mobilization model of military manpower. They maintained relatively small nuclei of military organizations during peacetime, and in times of conflict, they expanded the force by taking large numbers of people out of civilian pursuits and making soldiers of them. This was the task of conscription.

Economic mobilization accompanied the mobilization of such "mass armies," and the productive resources of society were expanded and converted from consumer-oriented production to the production of war materials.[5] The mass army reached the peak of its importance in the western world during the first half of the twentieth century. The armies of that era were mass in terms of their great size, numbering in the millions when engaged in war. They were mass in terms of having low levels of organizational differentiation and division of labor, with the infantry serving as the prototypical model of the soldier. And they were mass in terms of the mobilization of people and resources drawn from the civilian sector.[6]

Mobilization assumed that, in the event of war, the states involved would have time to raise, train, and field their fighting forces, and that the peacetime nucleus could fill the organizational and training functions until the newly mobilized force was ready to take the field. Technological changes in the mid-twentieth century, however, deprived nations of the luxuries of time and distance from the battlefield that the mobilization model required.

## The Advent of the Garrison State

Shortly before the middle of the twentieth century, political scientist Harold D. Lasswell noted changes in military technology that he proposed would change the relationship between military forces and their host civilian societies.[7] In a world where modern military technology (then conceived of as airpower) would make civilians as vulnerable to attack as military personnel, Lasswell projected that military elites, which he termed "specialists in violence," would become a major force in the governance of societies and that economic production would become regularized and geared primarily toward military rather than consumer goods. Note that Lasswell did not intend to apply this "garrison state" model to the United States and indeed, evaluating the model a quarter of a century after its formulation, he found it most applicable to the Warsaw Pact nations.[8] Still, his model has been extremely influential in setting the conceptual agenda for the analysis of the structure of civil-military relations in America. Analyses of the American power elite and of the military-industrial complex[9]—perspectives which assert increasing military influence in American political and economic life and militaristic values driving the decision-making process—can be seen as elements of the garrison state concept. Central to this concept is the notion that airpower puts civilians at risk as targets of military activity although they may be far removed from the battlefield. This "socialization of danger" through increased vulnerability of noncombatants changed the ethic of war.

World War II added nuclear weapons to the airpower that had concerned Lasswell, and these two technologies undermined the mobilization model's assumptions of time and distance from the battlefield. And World War II ended with the major nations of the world divided into ideologically opposed camps, one centering on the United States and her allies in Western Europe, and the other on the Soviet Union and Eastern Europe. Each felt a need to respond rapidly to external threats expected from the other and began to maintain larger peacetime forces in the post-World War II period than previously. With no demobilization, the old distinction between peacetime and wartime lost relevance. A spatial dimension replaced the temporal dimension of war.[10] At any point in time, there are places in the world where war is being waged and other places where it is not: war places and peace places.

## Deterrence as a "Peacekeeping Strategy"

In the nuclear age, the major nations of the world recognize that a confrontation between them which used advanced military technologies would be at best a Pyrrhic victory. At worst, nuclear winter would destroy life as we know it. Not just combatants, but whole societies would be devastated. And no known technology provides security against nuclear attack. In this context, purely military strategies such as preventive war, preemptive attack, or massive retaliation—attractive, effective, and arguable strategies at lower levels of military lethality— lose their appeal. In their place has grown the "strategy of deterrence."[11]

Deterrence asserts that even if a major power is attacked and a large proportion of its military power and indeed its society are destroyed, it has sufficient nuclear capability to retaliate and impose a level of destruction on the attacking nation that the attacker would find unacceptable. A society does not have to have weapon superiority to assume a deterrent posture. It merely needs sufficient retaliatory strength to impose unacceptable destruction on an enemy after suffering a massive attack. The irony of this doctrine of "peace through strength" is that it requires the major powers to seek assurances that a significant nuclear arsenal will survive an attack, and thus to constantly upgrade and expand their weaponry— a process that can at least as logically contribute to war as to peace. And the consequence of deterrence, to the extent that it succeeds, is not the achievement of peace, but rather the spatial displacement of war. The nuclear powers may avoid going to war against each other, but deterrence does not by the same logic preclude a major power from going to war against a non-nuclear power: the United States in Grenada or the Soviet Union in Afghanistan. Nor does it preclude nations that are not members of the nuclear club from going to war against each other, even if they are allied with a nuclear power.

## The Constabulary Concept as an Alternative to Deterrence

Recognizing the limitation of deterrence strategy to the upper end of the intensity spectrum, sociologist Morris Janowitz in 1960 proposed the constabulary concept of military force:

> The use of force in international relations has been so altered that it seems appropriate to speak of constabulary forces, rather than of military forces....The military establishment becomes a constabulary force when it is continuously prepared to act, *committed to the minimum use of force, and seeks viable international relations, rather than victory*....The constabulary force concept encompasses the entire range of military power and organization.[12]

Janowitz suggested that military men would look upon such police-type operations as less prestigious than traditional military operations, in part because involvement in domestic police activities is seen as detracting from the national security mission. He emphasized that the constabulary concept did not refer to domestic police operations, and indeed that "extensive involvement of the military as an internal police force...would hinder the development of the constabulary concept in international relations."[13] Because the dividing line between war and peace is space rather than time, "no longer is it feasible...to operate on a double standard of 'peacetime' and 'wartime' premises. Since the constabulary force concept eliminates the distinction between the peacetime and wartime military establishment, it draws on the police concept."[14]

The term "constabulary" was an unfortunate choice, we believe. It carries the image of the unarmed British constable, keeping peace through civility, morality, and his whistle. The bobby stands behind the popular conception of a constabulary military force. Janowitz assumed the military shared this popular conception because peacekeeping is viewed as being restricted to the low end of the combat-intensity spectrum:

> The military technologists tend to thwart the constabulary concept because of their essential preoccupation with the upper end of the destructive continuum and their pressure to perfect weapons without regard to international politics. The heroic leaders, in turn, tend to thwart the constabulary concept because of their desire to maintain conventional military doctrine and their resistance to assessing the political consequences of limited military actions which do not produce "victory."[15]

Although Janowitz rejected as not feasible the development of specialists in peace, in the abstract one can posit a "peace force" parallel to the armed force, the former being peacekeepers maintaining viable international relations, while the latter would take the field if peacekeeping fails. However, because of the interrelatedness of war and peace and of the international system itself, attempts to move beyond deterrence in the quest for a stabilized international system must involve a "transformation...[which] must take place within existing operational units. For the military profession, the overriding consideration is whether a force effectively committed to a deterrent philosophy and to peacekeeping and the concept of military presence can maintain its essential combat readiness."[16] As we shall see below, this issue assumed more than academic interest when elite American combat troops became involved in multinational peacekeeping operations in the early 1980s.

The need to merge the peace and war functions, as Janowitz's constabulary concept dictates, itself emanates from the disappearance of the temporal periodicity of war and peace. Prior to World War II, during the era of mobilization and the mass armed force, there were periods of peaceful international relations; persuasion and economic coercion were replaced by force when peaceful means did not achieve desired objectives.[17] In the deterrence era, by contrast, persuasion and the threat of force are used concurrently rather than serially in the quest for stabilization. Thus the deterrent force, or peace force, must be constantly prepared to wage war.

It is difficult to keep combat readiness in a large military force during what in days past would have been regarded as peacetime. According to Janowitz, the problem is least severe in the Air Force, where "the routines of flying aircraft create military units in being," in Navy units, which "have traditionally represented a force in being and maintained a group solidarity derived from the vitality of seamanship," and in missile and radar crews, which "because of the deadly character of the weapons they handle, feel a sense of urgency which helps them to overcome boredom."[18] The problem is most severe in ground combat units, which are the most likely elements of military organization to be called on to participate in actual constabulary operations, as distinct from deterrence posturing. Interestingly, for ground forces Janowitz sees the problem of combat readiness as least severe among elite combat units, because of the risk and danger of their training. These of course are the very units that have been assigned as the American contingents in recent multinational peacekeeping operations: a point to be discussed later.

To produce a military prepared for both constabulary and combat operations, Janowitz prescribes a program of civic/professional education for military personnel at all levels, to help them understand the political context and implications of the range of military operations they may be required to perform in pursuit of stabilization of the international system. Historically, the American military has not had such training, and more than two decades after introducing the constabulary concept into the vocabulary of military analysis, Janowitz reported that, "military personnel have rejected, or at least resist, the concept of a constabulary because to them it sounds too much like police work." While there were some indications "over the years [that] substantive elements of the constabulary force concept have increasingly entered into the civic consciousness of the military establishment," the trend seemed weak.[19]

## Students of Peacekeeping

Neither the League of Nations nor the United Nations established the international armed force that their charters allowed. Both, however, mobilized national armed forces under joint command for specific peacekeeping duties. The League of Nations fielded the Saar International Force (1934-1935) before the advent of social science analysis of the peacekeeping phenomenon; therefore, most analyses have addressed later peacekeeping efforts under UN auspices.

Between 1945 and 1970, there were twelve UN peacekeeping missions.[20] Writing in 1971, a decade after Morris Janowitz promulgated his concept of constabulary forces, Larry Fabian sought to systematize the lessons learned in international peacekeeping in order to improve the ability of the UN to undertake future peacekeeping missions.[21]

Fabian saw these twelve operations as spanning three generations of UN peacekeeping preparedness. The first generation, 1945-55, was characterized by overt hostility between the Soviet Union and the United Nations, rooted in part in the domination of the UN by the West and in part by Stalin's leadership style. There was no clear international constituency for UN peacekeeping preparedness, and the level of such preparedness was low. The year 1953 set the stage for the advent of the second generation; Josef Stalin died and Dag Hammarskjold was elected UN Secretary-General. The second generation, 1956-65, was the only one to begin with any promise for peacekeeping preparedness. The new Soviet leadership was more flexible, the cold war was less intense, and Hammarskjold built a middle-power constituency for peacekeeping preparedness from the expanding membership of the United Nations. In addition, he enjoyed the active support of the United States, and initially, the passive acquiescence of the Soviet Union, a resource his predecessor, Trygve Lie, lacked. However, Soviet opposition to the UN peacekeeping effort in the Congo, the largest and costliest of the international body's peacekeeping operations, shattered consensus. By 1966, Soviet opposition to a Canadian peacekeeping proposal immobilized the Secretary-General and his middle-power constituency. The third generation was distinguished by the recognition of the importance of super-power approval for any plan to build a true international peacekeeping force. In part a reversion to the first generation, this stage was characterized by unilateralism, a lack of formal structure, diffusion, and experimentation.

These experiences led Fabian to propose a ten-point program for the establishment of a United Nations peacekeeping capability:

1. The United States and the Soviet Union must begin a dialogue and reach consensus on issues involving the exercise of broad political responsibility for peacekeeping preparedness.

2. Political responsibility must be shared with the Soviet Union, rather than dominated by the United States.

3. Superpower involvement in peacekeeping activities should be reduced and the role of the medium-sized and small powers increased. Fabian was concerned here not only with the source of peacekeeping troops, but also with the political proprietorship of international peacekeeping, and presumably too with the financing of such missions.

4. Preparedness activities should be selective rather than collective. That is, security will depend on those states willing to contribute to it, with perhaps two dozen states bearing the burden of maintaining international security. These states should represent a political, racial, and geographic cross-section of UN members, including Third World and Eastern European states.

5. Greater centralization of peacekeeping activities is required, as is a recognition that this goal must be worked toward slowly.

6. Since preparedness will continue to rely on national military forces, more needs to be known about how such forces are to be shaped if international peacekeeping preparedness is to be achieved.

7. Institutional arrangements among the General Assembly, the Security Council, and the nations providing the peacekeeping forces that will protect the preparedness system from excessive disruption by the major powers are necessary.

8. Resources must be provided for the United Nations to establish centralized planning based on technical and political factors, and to disseminate information to member governments.

9. Political understandings regarding a commitment to peacekeeping will have to precede the establishment of a stable system of preparedness.

10. Peacekeeping will continue to be performed by states acting as agents of the United Nations, rather than by a permanent United Nations force.

The conditions specified by Fabian in the 1970s have not been met in the 1980s, and the peacekeeping operations of the 1980s have continued to be:

• unilateral, representing the political interests of individual nations and alliances and not necessarily those of the world system;
• decentralized and not coordinated by an international body or even necessarily by a joint military command;
• informal, rather than necessarily governed by treaty or formal arrangement; and
• under auspices other than those of the United Nations.

A second major research effort of the 1970s also contributed to contemporary thinking about UN peacekeeping efforts. Using a very different methodology from the historical approach adopted by Fabian, sociologist Charles Moskos spent about six months in the field with personnel from seven nations assigned to the United Nations Force in Cyprus (UNFICYP). Moskos's findings intersect in two important ways with Fabian's analysis.

Fabian had recognized that a permanent UN peacekeeping force was unlikely to evolve, at least in the short run, and that peacekeeping missions were going to have to be performed by national military forces. This raised the problem of whether traditional soldiers, whose allegiance was to national political entities to be defended by force of arms if necessary, would develop a commitment to the supra-national goal of maintaining viable international relations and would accept the doctrinal importance of minimizing their use of force in pursuit of that goal.

Moskos's research suggested that this was not a problem. Soldiers assigned to UNFICYP became increasingly committed to constabulary norms; as more and more time was spent in the field, these soldiers believed that peacekeeping required special skills and that it could be performed without using force. Interestingly, they did not become more "internationalist" at the same time. Their commitment to peacekeeping was rooted in military professionalism and in a recognition that their mission was a reflection of national policy, rather than in a belief in transnational political institutions.[22]

Reflecting Fabian's position that once consensus on basic peacekeeping principles is reached the superpowers should maintain "distance and detachment" from the peacekeeping system, Moskos hypothesized, "Soldiers from neutral middle powers are more likely to subscribe to the constabulary ethic than are soldiers from major powers."[23] Moskos's findings led him to soften this position. He found no difference in constabulary orientation between British soldiers assigned to UNFICYP and soldiers from neutral middle powers. Viewing military training and professionalism as the best predictors of peacekeeping effectiveness, one could infer from Moskos's analysis that the best soldiers would be the best peacekeepers. Nonetheless, he concluded that the realities of international politics were critical elements, too, making the neutral middle powers the primary and appropriate source for international peacekeeping forces. We shall consider below the implications of deviation from this principle by the Sinai and Beirut peacekeeping operations of the 1980s.

## Peacekeeping Activities: An Overview

The complexities of international peacekeeping operations can be illuminated by considering the historical experience of the League of Nations, the United Nations, and other international bodies that have organized such missions.

With relatively little success, the League of Nations used the peacekeeping concept in attempts to couple the use of multinational military forces with League mediation in the settlement of international disputes. The first proposed League multinational peacekeeping force was to assist in the settlement of an argument between Poland and Lithuania over the status of Vilna, the former capital of Lithuania. The conflict was exacerbated by Russia's concern with her nearby western border. In September 1920, Poland requested League assistance in settling the dispute and preventing warfare.

League mediation led to a diplomatic resolution of the dispute: a neutral zone between the forces of Poland and Lithuania would be maintained by a military force to be provided by the League, and a league civilian force would oversee a plebescite to decide the status of Vilna. The proposed force would include troops provided by Sweden, Norway, Britain, France, Italy, Spain, Belgium, and Greece. In March 1921, however, primarily in response to Russian protests that League forces in Lithuania threatened Russian security and to a Lithuanian request to postpone the plebescite, the League suspended plans for the plebescite and for the international force.[24]

The first real use of a League force in conjunction with mediation of an international dispute occurred in 1933. Leticia Trapeze was a large area east of the Andes that had been ceded by Peru to Colombia in a treaty ratified in 1928. In 1932, the Peruvian province of Loreto, adjacent to Leticia, invaded and reclaimed Leticia, apparently without the prior consent of the government of Peru. Peruvian military forces blocked attempts by Colombian forces to retake the province. Initial mediation attempts by Brazil to break the impasse were unsuccessful.

Peru requested League intervention and, in early 1933, the League proposed that a commission be appointed to administer Leticia for one year while negotiations took place. The province was to be returned to Colombia at the conclusion of the negotiations unless another settlement was agreed upon. These terms were initially unacceptable to Peru. However, in April, following the assassination of the Peruvian president and in the face of growing militancy in both Peru and Colombia, Peru accepted the proposal. A League commission, with members from Spain, the United States, and Brazil, administered Leticia for one year while negotiations took place, and then it returned the province to Colombia as agreed. The Commission was supported by a seventy-five-man military force designated a League international force. Although the soldiers wore League force insignia on their uniforms, they were all Colombian.[25]

Under League auspices, a true international military force assembled the following year to maintain order and oversee a long-awaited plebescite in the Saar Basin of Western Europe. By international agreement at the end of World War I, the Saar had been governed by a League commission since 1919, with the anticipation that in 1935 a plebescite would determine whether the region would join France or Germany or would remain a League protectorate. The withdrawal of French troops from the Saar in 1927, the growing strength of National Socialism in Germany, and the withdrawal of Germany from the League of Nations in 1933 (accompanied by a call from Germany for the immediate return of the Saar to Germany without a plebescite) raised concerns within the Saar and internationally. To insure order in the Saar at the time of the January 1935 plebescite, the League approved the creation of a multinational force.

Expenses of the force were borne by the Plebescite Commission of the League of Nations. Within a period of a few months in late 1934, the force was approved, raised, supplied, and deployed to the Saar by contributing nations. The Saar International Forces arrived in the region in mid-December 1934, and they were popularly received by the Saarlanders. Commanded by British Major General Brind, and centrally staffed by British officers with English speaking officers from the other national contingents serving as liaison to the command staff, it totalled

3,300 soldiers. National contingents were selected by the contributing nations and included elements of the Essex and East Lancashire Regiments from Britain, Italian Grenadiers, Dutch marines, and Swedish soldiers. During the weeks preceding and following the plebescite they maintained high visibility, engaging in parades through the city and in band concerts and sports events with the local population. The plebescite took place in January 1935 without major civil disturbance, and the Saar voted to merge with Germany. League forces withdrew within a month of the plebescite. [26]

The United Nations international force that operated as a Unified Command during the Korean War did not conform to models for international peacekeeping forces before or since that time—nor was the peace kept. The UN force ''... never operated under the direction of any United Nations body, nor was it financed in any way from United Nations funds. In effect the Security Council resolution [authorizing military assistance] served to legitimate the reality of the American intervention on the side of South Korea....''[27] However, lessons learned from the Korean experience, including the legitimizing effect of calling a military operation a peacekeeping mission or police action, were to influence the shape of future international peacekeeping forces.

The Japanese surrender to the allied forces at the end of the Second World War set the thirty-eighth parallel as the dividing line between Soviet-held Korean territory and Korean territory held by United States forces. In 1947, at the request of the United States, the United Nations accepted trusteeship of Korea under administration by a UN commission. However, UN administration was recognized only in the U.S.-occupied south, where the United States maintained a strong military, political, and economic presence, building a South Korean military force based on a U.S. Army model, with the technical assistance of a U.S. Army Military Advisory Group.

On June 25, 1950, North Korean troops crossed the thirty-eighth parallel and began an invasion of South Korea. The United States immediately came to the assistance of South Korea, and the Security Council acted rapidly, free from the threat of a Soviet veto because the Soviet representative was boycotting the Council in an attempt to stall action—a sharp learning experience for the Soviet Union. Condemning the invasion, the Council resolved to provide military assistance to South Korea, and called for a cease-fire and North Korean withdrawal. In a subsequent resolution, the Council placed all UN military forces and the South Korean forces under the leadership of the United States and, on July 7th, gave the UN flag that had flown over Ralph Bunche's mission when he was mediating the Palestine War to Warren Austin, the U. S. delegate, as a symbol of UN confidence that this mission would bring peace to Korea.

Although many member nations contributed forces and logistical support to the Korean war effort, it remained a U.S. initiative. "[C]onduct of military operations was at all times under U.S. direction...consultations were frequently held with a committee composed of the fifteen nations which contributed to combat service in Korea. Those nations, however, recognized the dominant responsibility of the United States in exercising the Unified Command...."[28] The initial success of the Unified Command in achieving North Korean withdrawal, and the subsequent advance into North Korea, brought Chinese forces to the support of North Korea, devastating defeat to the U.S. and UN forces, and an escalating international crisis that stabilized into a full-scale "war fought to a stalemate."[29]

The first true military peacekeeping force under UN auspices was mandated by the General Assembly in 1956 in response to the international crisis in the Middle East. Egypt had supported Algeria during the Algerian struggle for independence from France, and the Egyptian nationalization of the Suez Canal during the summer of 1956 was viewed by both Great Britain and France as further threat to their colonial policies as well as a violation of international law and the International Convention of Constantinople of 1880.[30] When in late October, Israel, who had been threatened by her neighbors since achieving independence, invaded the Sinai and pushed toward Suez, Great Britain and France joined the attack. Great Britain initially justified its attack as a defensive measure to protect the safety of its own nationals in the area,[31] a justification used more recently in the 1983 regional police action in Grenada. The USSR suggested to the U.S. a joint intervention strategy and volunteered to send troops to the area. At that point, Egypt requested assistance from the United Nations.

The Security Council found itself unable to act because of the veto power of France and Great Britain, and it invoked the "Uniting for Peace" resolution to bring the situation before the General Assembly. On November 5, the General Assembly passed a resolution calling for an immediate cease-fire and withdrawal of all forces behind cease-fire lines. In a second resolution, the assembly called for the creation of an emergency military force, organized by the Secretary General, to monitor the cease-fire. Once it was clear that the UN would intervene, all parties in the crisis agreed to the cease-fire.

An advisory committee and the Secretary General's emergency force were developed on the basis of principles that have remained fundamental to other UN peacekeeping operations:

• The force only could operate with the consent of the host government.
• The force should minimize assistance from permanent members of the Security Council and from interested national parties.
• The UN soldiers were prohibited from initiating the use of force.
• "[T]he authority granted to the UN group could not be exercised either in competition with or in cooperation with the host government on the basis of any joint operation. In Hammarskjold's words: 'a UN operation must be separate and distinct from activities by national authorities'."[32]

Secretary General Hammarskjold, with the assistance of Lester Pearson of Canada, who had proposed the emergency force, quickly organized the operation. Major General E. L. M. Burns, chief of the UN Truce Supervision Organization in Israel, was appointed chief of staff and began meeting with military leaders from UN member nations to determine force composition. Burns stressed the need for patrol units; a primary objective would be to police cease-fire lines.

Twenty-four nations volunteered troops immediately. Some offers were rejected: New Zealand because it supported Great Britain in the Suez attack and therefore lacked impartiality, Pakistan because of its membership in the Baghdad Pact.[33] Canada, which had mobilized a battalion of the Queen's Own Rifles, was requested to send instead a transport squadron from the Royal Canadian Air Force and staff and support elements from its ground forces. The similarity between the Canadian combat uniform and that worn by British combat troops would set the wrong image.

The emergency force would not accept civilians, nor would it accept individual military volunteers except in the case of Finland, which had decided to send individual volunteers from existing military units. For all other troops, formed, trained, and operating military units were used.

The first elements of UNEF—rifle units from Denmark and Norway—arrived in Suez on November 16, 1956. They were distinguishable as UN forces by their blue UN armbands and blue helmet liners. As UNEF patrols came into contact with Israeli and Egyptian forces, they occasionally were under fire, and within the first few months of operation they returned hostile fire received from Israeli positions. At maximum strength in 1957, the force was composed of six thousand soldiers in units from Canada, Colombia, Brazil, Denmark, Finland, India, Indonesia, Norway, Sweden, and Yugoslavia. UNEF remained active on the Egyptian-Israeli border for more than ten years, patrolling and overseeing the terms of the cease-fire. In May 1967, at the request of the Egyptian government, UNEF withdrew precipitously from its positions in the Sinai and in the Gaza strip. Although Secretary General Thant defended the withdrawal in terms of the original host agreement with Egypt, the termination of the peacekeeping mission cleared the way for the Arab-Israeli War of 1967.[34]

The United Nations operation in the Congo from 1960 to 1964 used peacekeeping principles developed by UNEF in a much more complex situation. The Suez case had shown that a multinational military force could effectively police a border, oversee the disengagement of opposing forces, and maintain an established cease-fire. The Congo, undergoing a transition from colony to statehood, was a political vacuum with widespread civil discord, ineffective military, political, and economic leadership, and a potential for intervention from power factions in neighboring nations and from the superpowers.

The colonial policies of Belgium and the superpowers in the Congo had kept the native population uneducated, inexperienced in leadership, and untrained for positions of authority in the new state. Belgians held key positions in government, industry, and the military. They made no preparations for the transition to independence, and indeed when political unrest in Africa increased in the late 1950s, the date for independence was hastily moved forward. Simultaneously, the complex social structure of the new nation encouraged the formation of many small power factions based on tribal groups, regional alliances, and special interests.

A week after independence was declared on July 5, 1960, the Army of the Congo rebelled against its Belgian officer corps. In the ensuing chaos, Katanga Province seceded from the country and requested military aid from Belgium.[35] Belgian troops were flown into Katanga and Belgian nationals throughout the Congo began to leave, vacating management positions in industry and government. On July 12, the shaky coalition government of Patrice Lumumba and Joseph Kasavubu requested military aid from the United Nations, claiming that Belgian intervention in the new state increased internal disorder and defied the international agreements that had accompanied independence. The Security Council responded by calling for the withdrawal of Belgian troops from the Congo, and it empowered the Secretary General to take steps to provide military aid to restore order.

The United Nations force in the Congo was to operate under conditions similar to those which had evolved successfully with the UNEF operation. These included a status agreement with the host government, prohibitions on the use of force except in self-defense, the independence of UN operations from those of other authorities or the host government, and nonintervention in civil concerns. As Arthur Lee Burns and Nina Heathcote note, "This was to prove a serious restriction upon a U.N. *military* force employed to restore order *within* the Congo state."[36] By this definition, reintegration of Katanga into the Congo was an internal crisis in which the UN force should not have been involved.

The composition of UNOC, as determined by the Secretary General, was similar to that of UNEF. Member nations contributed troops. Permanent members of the Security Council and other nations with major interests in the situation were excluded from contributing ground troops to the force, although they did provide logistical support by transporting troops and supplies.[37] The force was raised predominantly, but not exclusively, from other African nations.

Because the UN had been engaged in setting up a military technical assistance program in the Congo prior to the request for aid in controlling the crisis, the first units of UNOC, from Ethiopia, Ghana, Morocco, and Tunisia, were able to arrive almost immediately. Eventually UN forces totalled about twenty thousand with most units from ten African states (the four mentioned plus Guinea, Liberia, Mali, Nigeria, Sudan, and the United Arab Republic). Additional troops came from Canada, Indonesia, India, Ireland, and Sweden. Combat units were predominately African, with some from India, Ireland, and Sweden. Other nations provided support troops and headquarters staff.[38]

The mission in the Congo, as defined by early action of the Security Council, was to be "the esentially negative task of preventing escalation by (1) securing the withdrawal of Belgian troops, (2) restoring law and order, and (3) ensuring respect for the territorial integrity and political independence of the Congo."[39] Later, as it became clear that the extent of civil disorder made nonintervention an unworkable policy, the Katanga situation was addressed more directly. On Februrary 21, 1961, following the assassination of Lumumba and substantial unrest, the Security Council resolved to empower UNOC to take measures to prevent civil war, including the use of force as a last resort if necessary.[40] In September 1961, the UN forces initiated military action in Katanga. After a series of demoralizing defeats, UNOC successfully reunited Katanga with the Congo and controlled the level of internal disorder and foreign intervention.

UNOC was beset with problems, ranging from inadequate funding and disorganization to the definition and execution of its mission. It had an unusual civilian-military dual authority structure that caused communication problems among the UN, the UNOC command, and field contingents. There were problems with force composition. While a predominantly African and third-world force was politically expedient, it produced problems with "'unsophisticated military preparedness, lack of combat experience and command training, plus...lack of equipment.''[41] In addition, neighboring African nations were interested parties in the outcome of events in the Congo, rather than impartial forces. They took sides and manipulated events upon occasions such as the assassination, when several withdrew or threatened to withdraw. On the other hand, European forces aggravated hostilities in some cases. In early negotiations, Lumumba objected to the presence of European UN forces in Katanga and requested that they be replaced by African UN contingents.[42]

Some units performed admirably and worked out ingenious and effective methods for disarming and defusing the undisciplined and highly volatile National Army of the Congo, for protecting civilians and refugees, and for mediating hostile situations. Nigerian and Ghanaian riot police were particularly effective.[43] The national government was sufficiently stable by 1964 for UNOC to phase out its operations.

In the Suez and Africa, the United States strongly supported UN mediation rather than involving itself directly. By contrast, U.S. policy in the Western Hemisphere avoided UN intervention whenever possible. This was the U.S. position during the crisis in the Dominican Republic in 1965 and 1966, when the United States invaded that country and provided most of a peace force created under the Organization of American States (OAS) for the purpose of restoring order.

Political instability had become chronic in the Dominican Republic, and in April 1965, the situation deteriorated when the two-year-old government was overthrown. Supporters of the previous government attempted to reestablish power, and a military faction attempted to maintain the status quo. On April 28, 1965, American airborne units and Marines invaded the island, with President Johnson justifying the action as necessary to protect American nationals in the Republic.

At the urging of the United States, the OAS adopted resolutions on April 30 and May 1 calling for a cease-fire, forming an OAS investigating committee, and creating an international force to restore normal conditions and protect the people of the Dominican Republic. Outrage at the American intervention resulted in a bare margin to support the resolution creating the peacekeeping force. Under the terms of the resolution, the American forces already in the Dominican Republic—totalling 21,500—were incorporated into the OAS Inter-American Force, and they were augmented by forces from other OAS states. Honduras, Nicaragua, Paraguay, and Brazil supplied additional contingents. Because Costa Rica has no army, it supplied police units.

The Inter-American Force maintained a nominally neutral zone on the island, although its presence appeared to assist the military faction rather than the rebels, and there were reports that it provided support to the military junta.[44] At a meeting of the UN Security Council in July 1965, both the military and the rebel factions requested the withdrawal of the Inter-American Force. The situation became less volatile in September with the formation of a provisional government acceptable to most parties, and by September 1966, the Inter-American Force completed a phased withdrawal.

As in the Congo, the Cyprus crisis developed out of the transition from colonial status to independence and had international dimensions. In Cyprus, however, the struggle was between two clearly delineated national groups with strong ties to neighboring nations. Historically Greek in cultural and ethnic background, the island was under the control of the Ottomans for several centuries, terminating in 1878 when it became part of the British Empire. Under British control, the population became increasingly polarized into Greek and Turkish Cypriot communities, favoring stronger alliances and incorporation into one or the other of these states.

Cypriot independence was granted in 1960. The terms created a representative form of government in which Turkish and Greek Cypriots held power based on their numbers, but proportionally favoring the Turkish minority on the island.[45] A power struggle ensued, and the announcement in 1963 of proposed constitutional changes that would shift power away from the Turkish minority led to violence. The British attempted mediation, established a truce zone, and garrisoned a small peacekeeping force on the island. Britain proposed the establishment of a NATO peacekeeping force, but the idea was not acceptable to all parties. In February 1964, Britain and Cyprus requested that the Security

Council deal with the crisis. The Council endorsed a resolution recommending creation of a UN peacekeeping force organized by the Secretary General with the concurrance of Britain, Turkey, Greece, and Cyprus, and a UN mediator to act independently from the force.

Although in many ways similar to UNOC, the earlier case of peacekeeping precipitated by independence, the United Nations Force in Cyprus (UNFICYP) differed in several significant ways and reflected lessons learned in the Congo. The relationships between civilian and military contingents of UNFICYP were clearly defined, and a separate mediator was designated by the Secretary General to act independently of UNFICYP so that some of the communications problems experienced by UNOC could be avoided. A more realistic policy on the use of force was set: UN troops could defend themselves during engagements in which they were positioned between hostile forces, but such "interposition" could be authorized only by the UNFICYP commander, not by unit commanders. The staff organization of UNFICYP also addressed administrative problems experienced by UNOC, and it more clearly defined relationships between staff and field units.[46]

For the first time, a UN military force included contingents from a permanent member of the Security Council: some British troops on the island, were incorporated into UNFICYP; the British troops on the island, retained by agreements at the time of Cyprian independence, became staging areas for the UN forces. Major power noninvolvement in peacekeeping forces was a matter of UN peacekeeping doctrine prior to Cyprus, a position later reinforced by Moskos and Fabian.

Because of objections from the host government, African contingents were excluded from UNFICYP.[47] The first contingents to join the UN forces on the island were Canadian units: a standby battalion of the Royal 22 Regiment and an armored reconnaissance squadron from the Royal Canadian Dragoons.[48] They were reinforced by units from other UN member states: Austria, Denmark, New Zealand, Australia, and later Finland, Ireland, Sweden, and others.

The composition of the contingents committed to UNFICYP varied by country. Canadian units were all from regular components such as the Dragoons, the Queen's Own Rifles, and Lord Strathcona's Horse.[49] These, and the British units, were organized along regimental lines. Contingents from the Scandanavian countries were composed of volunteer reservists and were formed specifically for short-term UN peacekeeping duty. Irish units were volunteers taken from regular units and attached to the peacekeeping force.[50] The size of UNFICYP peaked in 1964 at close to 6,500 soldiers, dropped during the late 1960s and early 1970s, and increased again to almost its peak strength at the time of the Turkish invasion in 1974.

The UN mission in Cyprus, as mandated by Security Council resolution, was to prevent the recurrence of hostilities, to maintain order, and to assist the country to return to normalcy. The forces attempted to do this by keeping major roads throughout the island open to all traffic, mediating and monitoring localized incidents, patrolling hostile lines and maintaining neutral areas, and serving as a negotiation channel between the opposing forces. Turkish gestures in the mid-1960s and the Turkish invasion in the mid-1970s inspired more aggressive UN tactics, which included interposing the peacekeeping units between hostile forces, protecting neutral areas, protecting the civilian population, arranging cease-fires, and defending the neutrality of the international airport on the island against offensive action.

UNFICYP experienced many of the organizational problems that beset UNOC, although never to the same degree. Interactions between military and civilian staff personnel were occasionally problematic, as were differences in organization and orientation between national contingents. The tedium and boredom that accompanied the routine of observation patrols seemed to be a universal problem[51]—one that received considerable attention later, in the Sinai. In practice, national contingents seemed to function equally well as peacekeepers whether they had received specific peacekeeping training prior to deployment (as did the contingents from Canada, Sweden, and Denmark), or had received no training specifically for the UNFICYP experience (as was the case for the British forces).[52] The British units performed their duties well, made a valuable contribution to the operation, and opened for debate the principle of major power exclusion from such operations. As the situation in Cyprus has remained unresolved, although usually controlled, UNFICYP has also served as a peacekeeping force in being, providing the nucleus of the second UN peacekeeping force in the Sinai and contingents of British troops for the ill-fated Multinational Peacekeeping Force in Lebanon.

International mediation in the Middle East has been a constant objective of the United Nations and other alliances in modern times. Small states, shifting boundaries and alliances, changing governments, and antagonisms dating to biblical times characterize this geographically and politically significant area. The creation of the state of Israel in 1948, resulting from the partition of Palestine into separate Arab and Jewish states as mandated by the United Nations, is the source of continued disequilibrium among Israel, neighboring Arab states, and displaced Palestinian refugees. Since 1949, the United Nations has monitored national boundaries in the area. The United Nations Truce Supervision Organization (UNTSO) has operated in Palestine, Israel, and Suez. The command for the first UN military peacekeeping force in the Sinai in 1956 was pulled from UNTSO, as were the support elements of the United Nations Observer Group in Lebanon (UNOGIL), authorized in June 1958 to monitor internal disorder and possible international intervention in the civil war in Lebanon. The United Nations Emergency Force that operated on the Egyptian-Israeli border from 1956 to 1967 was the first of several international military peacekeeping efforts in the Middle East.

Following the hasty withdrawal of UN forces in 1967 at the request of Egypt, hostilities between Israel and her Arab neighbors increased, and war broke out in 1967. In 1973, Israel found herself at war again, this time attacked simultaneously by Syria and Egypt. Within three weeks of the attack, the U.S. and USSR jointly sponsored a resolution in the Security Council calling for a cease-fire. Egypt requested the formation of a new military peace force to be created by the two superpowers. This proposal was unacceptable, but three days later, the Security Council authorized a new UN Emergency Force.

Drawing upon national contingents already serving with the UN mission in Cyprus (and demonstrating thereby the importance of forces-in-being in a peacekeeping era) and on unarmed military observers from UNTSO, Secretary General Kurt Waldheim organized the new force quickly. Within weeks, 4,500 soldiers from Austria, Canada, Finland, Ghana, Indonesia, Ireland, Nepal, Panama, Peru, Poland, Senegal, and Sweden were in place along the cease-fire lines. The mission of the new force included observing activities of hostile forces on both sides of the cease-fire lines, patrolling neutral zones, and monitoring the terms of the cease-fire. The disengagement and cease-fire proceeded relatively smoothly, and it became clear that the major problems for the UN troops would not be mediating crisis situations or intervening between hostile combatants, but rather would be boredom and avoiding buried land mines left from previous wars. Following renewed negotiations between Israel and Egypt in 1975, the area of operation of the UN force was expanded to include a new buffer zone from the Mediterranean to the Gulf of Suez.

Although the UN intervention curbed the Israeli-Egyptian antagonisms of the 1973 war, hostilities continued between Syria and Israel until May 1974, when they accepted a disengagement plan that had been negotiated through the efforts of the United States. In late May

1974, the Security Council resolved to create a UN military force—the United Nations Disengagement Observer Force (UNDOF)—to monitor the implementation of the disengagement plan. National contingents for UNDOF came from the year-old United Nations Emergency Force already monitoring the Israeli-Egyptian agreement. UNDOF numbered 1,200 soldiers from Austria, Canada, Peru, and Poland, and maintained a three-mile buffer zone in the Golan Heights area along the Syrian frontier. Complicated by internal disorder in local nations and by the claims of Palestinian refugees, implementation of the border agreements here was rockier than elsewhere. UNDOF has also been caught in the area's invasions and civil wars.

In 1979, Egypt's President Anwar Sadat, Israel's Prime Minister Manachem Begin, and U.S. President Jimmy Carter signed a peace treaty that included the withdrawal of Israeli troops from the Sinai and the Sinai's return to Egypt. In keeping with the principle of major power noninvolvement in military peacekeeping missions, these Camp David accords specified, in Article VI, section 8, that the UN Force and Observers supervising the transition would have no troops from nations that were permanent members of the Security Council.

On May 18, 1981, the president of the Security Council indicated that the Council was unable to reach agreement over the UN Force and Observers called for by the treaty. Egypt, Israel and the United States agreed to substitute a Multinational Force and Observers (MFO), serving under unified command. It, of course, could not represent the United Nations without Security Council authority.

In a letter to the Israeli and Egyptian ministers of foreign affairs, Secretary of State Alexander Haig committed the United States to contribute an infantry battalion, a logistical support unit, and a group of civilian observers to the MFO. In the months that followed, it was decided that the initial American infantry unit would be drawn from the 82d Airborne Division, to be replaced after six months by a battalion from the 101st Airborne Division, with battalions from these two elite combat divisions to alternate every six months thereafter.

The Sinai MFO consists of over three thousand soldiers, civilian observers, and support staff. It is under the supervision of a director general, located in Rome, and a Norwegian lieutenant general as force commander in the Sinai. Infantry battalions are provided by Colombia and Fiji as well as by the United States. A coastal patrol unit is provided by Italy. The Netherlands sends signal and military police units. There is a transportation company from Uruguay, a headquarters support unit from Britain, and aviation units from Australia, New Zealand, and France. In all, eleven nations are involved in the force.

The assignment of elite combat troops from a superpower to a peacekeeping mission generated some controversy.[53] However, the mission in the Sinai has been successfully executed since 1982, suggesting, in agreement with Moskos and Janowitz, [54] that effective peacekeeping is a consequence of military professionalism. As in earlier studies of peacekeeping, boredom has been shown to be a major problem.[55] Soldiers trained to engage and defeat an enemy have some trouble adapting to a mission of observing, verifying, and reporting. Moreover, boredom to the soldier in the Sinai connotes more than simply an absence of activities to fill time; time vacuums can be filled with constant training. Boredom in the Sinai has emotional components. The soldier in the desert not only has time on his hands, his boredom involves cultural deprivation, a lack of privacy, and isolation from friends and family back home.[56]

The history of Lebanon since the Second World War is one of political instability and foreign intervention. Numerous attempts have been made to mediate a lasting agreement between the many ethnic and religious groups within the country, and between the government and the neighboring states of Syria, Jordan, and Israel. Three attempts involved multinational military forces: one chartered by the Arab League, one by the United Nations, and one that originated in the mediation efforts of the United States and negotiations involving Israel and the Palestine Liberation Organization (PLO).

Following the partition of Palestine in 1948, Palestinian refugees added to Lebanese instability. In the early 1970s, more Palestinians entered Lebanon to escape the civil war in Jordan.[57] Israel accused the Lebanese government of harboring Palestinian guerrillas and supporting PLO activities, and tensions increased between the countries. The PLO presence aggravated the 1975 and 1976 civil wars. By late spring 1976, it became apparent that Palestinian-controlled factions were gaining control of the country, to the alarm not only of the Lebanese but also of the international community. The Arab League then mandated the Arab Deterrent Force (ADF) to deter Palestinian participation in the civil conflict and to maintain order in the country while the national government reorganized and strengthened its position.

Syrian troops, with the agreement of Lebanon, Israel, and the United States, had entered Lebanon slightly earlier in the spring of 1976. They became the nucleus of the ADF and were subsequently joined by small national contingents from other nations of the Arab League: Libya, Saudi Arabia, Sudan, United Arab Emirates, Egypt, and South Yemen. The force initially was commanded by Major General Mohammed Hassan Ghoneim of Egypt; in late 1976, the force was placed under the nominal control of the Lebanese government and was commanded by a Lebanese army colonel. The Arab League extended the mandate of the force at six month intervals. The first ADF mission was to isolate and control the PLO in Lebanon. The principal mechanism was to create and maintain a neutral buffer zone between the combatants in Beirut, and particularly to defend the neutrality of the international airport. Following the Israeli invasion of southern Lebanon in 1978, the ADF purpose became the aggressive containment of the Israeli advance into Lebanon. With this redefinition, support from League member nations decreased. South Yemen and the United Arab Emirates withdrew their contingents. By the end of 1983, about thirty thousand Syrian troops remained in Lebanon in control of most of the eastern section of the country.

The south of Lebanon had continued in civil war even after the stabilization of internal relations elsewhere in the country, and on several occasions in 1977, Israel engaged in hostilities with Palestinians and Lebanese forces. In March 1978, Israel invaded southern Lebanon with 25,000 troops and occupied most of the area. In mid-March, Lebanon appealed to the United Nations for help. The Security Council called for Israeli withdrawal, for the restoration of control by the Lebanese government, and for a new United Nations peacekeeping force. Israel accepted the UN resolutions and withdrew from southern Lebanon. However, local militias and an Israeli-supported Lebanese army unit commanded by Major Saad Hassad moved into the vacuum left by Israel.

Major General Erskine of Ghana commanded the United Nations Interim Force in Lebanon (UNIFIL). It initially included contingents from ten United Nations countries: Canada, Fiji, France, Iran, Ireland, Nepal, Nigeria, Norway, Senegal, and Sweden. By December 1983, Nepal, Nigeria, France, and Iran were not part of the force, but troops from Finland, Ghana, Italy, and the Netherlands had joined it. The force totalled about 5,800 troops. Although UNIFIL was unable to fulfill its mandate to restore internal order to southern Lebanon, it was successful on a local level in negotiating with forces in the area and in establishing communications with the Palestinians who controlled Lebanese territory to the north of the UNIFIL buffer zone.[58] The problems of UNIFIL are similar to those experienced by UN peacekeeping forces elsewhere:

inconsistencies between national contingents, conflicting loyaties between UN and national authorities and policies, poorly trained and
equipped contingents, particularly from some of the developing
countries, isolation of staff headquarters from field units, and bias, in
this instance among some African contingents toward the host populations.[59]

In June 1982, ostensibly in reaction to the attempted assassination
of the Israeli ambassador to Britain, Israel invaded Lebanon again. Its
announced intention was to create a larger buffer between its border and
PLO strongholds. Once that objective was attained, however, Israeli
troops advanced on Beirut, sweeping aside UNIFIL contingents. They
surrounded Palestinians and leftist guerrillas in West Beirut and,
through American diplomatic channels, Palestinian-Israeli negotiations
began. Arrangements were reached to evacuate the PLO and other
forces, including three thousand members of the ADF.[60] As part of the
agreement, a new multinational peacekeeping force was to be sent to
Beirut to monitor the evacuation and protect Palestinian civilians who
remained behind. The new NATO-based Multi-National Force (MNF),
consisting of eight hundred U.S. Marines and contingents of French and
Italian troops, was positioned in Beirut to carry out the first part of the
mandate. After the PLO force left, the U.S., French, and Italian forces
were withdrawn.

Five days after their withdrawal, Lebanon's president-elect,
Bashir Gemayel, was assassinated. Two days later, the Lebanese Christian Phalangist militia moved into two Palestinian refugee camps behind
Israeli lines, massacring as many as eight hundred Palestinians. The
MNF, which was not under UN auspices and had no unified command
structure, was reassembled and reintroduced into Beirut in late September 1983. In addition to the French and Italian soldiers and an
increased U.S. Marine contingent, British soldiers joined the force,
many on reassignment from UNFICYP. In support of the troops was a
multinational naval force that by the end of the year included fifteen
thousand U.S. military personnel, two aircraft carriers, and the battle-
ship *New Jersey*.

The national contingents displayed important differences in style
of operation and in apparent outcomes in the short run. The Italians, with
the largest unit of almost 2,200 men, played a very visible cop-on-the-
beat role. They patrolled the streets in the slums of southern Beirut.
They maintained a high profile at the Sabra and Shatila refugee camps,
where the Phalangist massacre took place. They ran an around-the-clock

field hospital that treated Lebanese civilians free of charge. They kept to a posture of neutrality, siding with none of the opposing factions. By the end of 1983, they had taken about a dozen casualties and one fatality.

The U.S. Marines, on the other hand, remained in heavily fortified but not very secure positions at the Beirut International Airport until their withdrawal in February 1984. Between November 1982 and August 1983, the marines mounted symbolic patrols in Christian East Beirut, and they set up a small number of outposts. However, after eleven months of relative noninvolvement, the marines' outposts began to exchange fire, in self-defense, with the warring factions. Patrols were cut back and sniping at the marines' positions increased. In September 1983, President Reagan ordered a naval bombardment in support of the Lebanese Army, clearly defining the American diplomatic and military posture as aligned, rather than neutral. France also used warplanes against insurgent groups.

On the morning of October 23, 1983, a large truck filled with explosives smashed into the marines' headquarters building at the airport and exploded with a force equal to twelve thousand pounds of high explosives. Over 240 marines billeted in the building died. A simultaneous terrorist attack on the French contingent killed 56 paratroopers. In the United States, the House Armed Services Investigations Subcommittee faulted the military chain of command for lax security at the headquarters building, and it also criticized the Reagan administration for the policies that put the marines in such an vulnerable position. The Long Commision, appointed by the Joint Chiefs of Staff to investigate the bombing, also faulted the chain of command for lax security. No reports, however, argued that there could be perfect military safeguards against terrorist attacks aimed at peacekeeping units.

Ultimately, the NATO forces withdrew, and in March 1984, at the urging of Syria, President Amin Gemayel abrogated the treaty between Lebanon and Israel that had led to the formation of the MNF. One political lesson of the Beirut tragedy is that the superior firepower of a NATO peacekeeping force in contrast to the more pedestrian equipment of third-world contingents cannot offset the danger in peacekeeping of deviating from a position of neutrality.

Two days after the terrorist attack in Beirut, the United States launched a two-pronged airborne and heliborne assault on the Caribbean island nation of Grenada. There was no relationship between the two events. Involved in the operation were both of the army's ranger battalions, a marine amphibious assault unit that was en route to relieve the unit in Beirut, most of the units of the 82d Airborne Division, and other

American units: it was the largest American military operation since the Vietnam War. Ostensibly the American operation had been encouraged by the Organization of Eastern Caribbean States, which was concerned about the leftist military government of General Hudson Austin after the assassination of Prime Minister Maurice Bishop. Following the precedent of the 1965 invasion of the Dominican Republic, the mission was called an "evacuation action" to rescue American medical students on the island. Also similar to the Dominican case, upon discovering more Cubans on the island than intelligence reports had indicated, the mission was redefined as an operation to stop the spread of communism.

A joint Caribbean force of three hundred soldiers and police from Antigua, St. Lucia, St. Vincent, Dominica, St. Kitts, Jamaica, and Barbados followed U.S. troops to the island. All of America's major military objectives were accomplished by October 28, and combat units were withdrawn, leaving a Caribbean Peacekeeping Force (CPF) consisting primarily of police from several Caribbean nations, furnished with U.S. equipment, trained by U.S. military advisers (including one hundred personnel sent to Grenada for that purpose after the major withdrawal of combat troops), and supported by some three hundred American soldiers who will be in Grenada indefinitely.

## Conclusions

Peacekeeping as an element of the military mission is not new. Since its founding in the early twentieth century, the motto of the U.S. Army War College has been "Not to Wage War, but to Preserve the Peace." This is usually interpreted as deterrence: peace through strength. Peacekeeping, however, is evolving into a concept posed as an alternative to deterrence, frequently manifested through international forces rather than national armies.

It is clear that the use of military forces for peacekeeping is not as ubiquitous as war itself, but neither is it a rare event. Generally spawned by armed conflict, there still is not a standard scenerio from which it evolves. It may be precipitated by internal conflict, international conflict, the establishment of international jurisdiction resulting from the resolution of international conflict, problems associated with emergence from colonial status, or refugee problems requiring international action, to name the most common. If there is no standard situation behind peacekeeping operations, there is also no standard formula for their execution. Some are small. It is difficult to imagine a lower-key operation than the Caribbean Peacekeeping Force. Others involve formations and events of much larger scale. Regardless of the impetus, the political and military dimensions of peacekeeping are inextricably intertwined. This fact probably calls for more intensive political education of soldiers than is common in the democratic nations of the West. Soldiers should see the implications of their activity and should recognize that, even for military forces, victory is not always the ultimate goal.[61]

We should expect terrorism to be a regular feature of peacekeeping. The FBI Forensic Laboratory described the bomb used against the marines in Beirut as the largest conventional blast its experts had ever seen.[62] Four months later in Rome, Leamon Hunt, the civilian director general of the Sinai MFO, was assassinated. Sniping and larger scale attacks seem an increasingly common affliction of peacekeeping. Peacekeeping operations clearly are a form of conflict: lower intensity than a nuclear confrontation between superpowers to be sure, but conflict nonetheless. The February 1984 decision to award the Purple Heart medal to military personnel wounded while on peacekeeping duty underscores this fact.

The experience of UNFICYP and MFO Sinai suggest that on the basis of perfomance criteria, major powers and superpowers might not be excluded categorically from peacekeeping duty. There is a common-sense logic to suggest that elite action-oriented combat troops would experience trouble adjusting to the constabulary role, but the accumulating evidence suggests the opposite: the best soldiers very well may be the best peacekeepers. At the same time, the liabilities of elite troops should not be discounted. Peacekeeping missions have large doses of boredom, and troops accustomed to high levels of activity in readiness training may feel peacekeeping boredom more rapidly and intensely than regular troops. One young soldier in the Sinai reported that the training for that mission was more realistic than the mission itself, and others (all young soldiers, none experienced in combat) expressed a desire to be in Beirut rather than the Sinai. Boredom can dull a unit's cutting edge. One cannot help but wonder if the laxity of the marine security in Beirut was influenced by inactivity that made it natural for them to let down their guard.

It should be remembered that, while elite combat troops may be effective as peacekeepers, they also are attractive targets for terrorists. One cannot tell whether terrorists attacked the American and French contingents in Beirut but not the Italians because the former were elite combat troops—marines and paratroopers—or perhaps because the latter went into the host community and maintained a position of neutrality.

Still, it seems an obvious opportunity for a force seeking to establish itself in the politico-military arena to show its mettle by setting out to destroy a company of United States Marines.

Fabian argued for *rapprochement* between the United States and the Soviet Union as a necessary predicate to effective peacekeeping under UN auspices. This has not occurred, as demonstrated by the difficulty of replacing the Beirut MNF with a United Nations force. The three most recent multinational military peacekeeping operations were executed independently from the UN: MFO Sinai, MNF Lebanon, CPF Grenada. The apparent success of two of these, and the failure of the other, suggests that broad-based participation may be an alternative to organizational sponsorship in establishing the legitimacy of such operations. Receptiveness of host governments (Sinai) or people (Grenada) is also crucial. The need for absolute political neutrality is also empirically questionable now. The Sinai experience suggests it is important. The Beirut experience suggests, at a minimum, that a multinational constabulary force cannot support an incumbent government that lacks clear support from it own people without the force losing its credibility. Beirut also indicates that multinational peacekeeping forces, having several national contingents but not even a hint of unified command, are likely to be less effective than truly international forces.

The Grenada operation, assuming it is properly regarded as a peacekeeping mission, suggests that a multinational force can overthrow an incumbent government if that government is not popularly supported. One may ask, however, whether Grenada really was a peacekeeping operation. In years past, the force left to reestablish a political and economic system after an invasion and conquest would have been called an occupation force, not a peacekeeping force. The Grenada operation may teach that peacekeeping legitimacy and credibility may by this time be so entrenched in the international lexicon of what is good and noble that in the future a wide range of military operations and adventures will be so labelled to take advantage of the value placed on the term. The Korean Police Action hinted at this wordplay. More frequently during the past two decades, the use of armed forces to rescue civilian nationals has been labeled "peacekeeping." Recall that the United States used this justification in the Dominican Republic in 1965. The British used it in Suez in 1956, the United States in Lebanon in 1958, the Belgians in the Congo in 1960, and more recently the United States in Grenada in 1983. In the Dominican Republic, the United States later justified intervention on the basis of a communist conspiracy to control the new government.[63] The 1983 Grenada operation obviously had historical precedent.

Military doctrine and training in the major nations emphasize the less likely but more devastating end of the combat-intensity spectrum, nuclear confrontation in Western Europe. While we do not propose a sudden switch from the deterrence strategy, we do point to the devastating consequence if it should fail: a nuclear World War III and the end of civilization. Peacekeeping assumes conflict and aims at controlling it at the lower end of the combat-intensity spectrum. If nations learn about and prepare for peacekeeping now, they not only may then achieve more Sinais and avoid future Beiruts, but they also may open an important way to reduce the risk of single-minded reliance on peace through strength.

# Reflections
# On Social Justice
# And Migration

RONALD S. SCHEINMAN

From birth, bonds of social justice tie the citizen and the state. Those bonds will break under the weight of official tolerance for prejudice, economic conditions that erode hope and pride, and an appetite for authoritarianism. Elie Wiesel described his moment in history when the bond snapped:

> When did I become a refugee?...Was it when I was still in my town, 1944, and the last Jewish families of my town were led into the courtyard of the last synagogue?...We thought, people then in Hungary, that we would not leave Hungary because Hungary would protect its citizens. Then we came to a table where the Hungarian gendarmes simply took the papers that we handed them. When my turn came, as anybody else's, to give my citizenship papers, he did not even look into them. He simply tore them up. That is what he did with all the papers. Is that when I became a refugee?[1]

## Passivity, Revolt, or Emigration

When the confidence and trust that form the citizen's relationship to his state collapse, the citizen faces three choices: passivity, revolt, or emigration. My reflections concern the choice of emigration, particularly forced migration. Forced migrants are people who are uprooted and compelled to move, within their country or across international borders, against their will. Refugees, asylees, and displaced persons are forced migrants, as are people who have moved because of natural disaster or the necessity of basic economic survival.

An estimated ten and one half million people are known and acknowledged to be refugees today.[2] More important, there are countless others who might join them if the obligations of states to their citizens and noncitizens, as well as to other states, are not met. History and the foreseeable future make it clear that forced migration is a fundamental issue for international peace.

Of all the things that could and should be said about forced migration, I believe four themes stand out:

*First.* Social justice questions have been a part of political dialogue at least as far back as fifth century B.C. Athens. Social justice addresses the equilibrium between the citizen and the state, and political thinking teaches that social justice is a necessary condition for peace and progress. These ancient political ideals have remarkable durability, weaving in and out of the history of political thought. They are urgently with us again on the edge of the 21st century. Their staying power and the fact that, in one form or another, they are espoused by thinkers across the political spectrum suggest that there is nothing soft-headed about attention to social justice. The dialogue over peace must have social justice on its agenda, despite difficulties of definition and inherent disputes over values.

*Second.* Certain social justice violations are recognized in laws that protect those commonly called "political refugees." The laws were drawn to protect victims of a very special kind of injustice, namely persecution. The integrity of the definition in those laws must be maintained. In addition, we must find ways to respond to other types of forced migrations.

*Third.* Breach of bonds of confidence and trust between the citizen and the state concerns not only the most blatant and ultimate wrongs. It also occurs through state action, like corruption or indifference, that results in such serious harm or deprivation that people are forced to migrate. This is not tolerable.

*Fourth.* We have nurtured a myth that the refugee problem, which is part of the broader question of forced migration, is temporary; this conforms with our *wish* that it be temporary. Consequently we have not organized internationally on a permanent basis to deal with refugees and other forced migrants, despite repeated evidence that whatever causes war and civil upheaval also creates refugees, and in spite too of the fact that "mass asylum," thought to be a contemporary phenomenon, is a very old one. Such short-sightedness is all the more astonishing when we consider that refugees move not only *out* of one territory but *into* another, and that such movements more and more often are large-scale and accompanied by social disruption at both the points of origin and arrival. Every new refugee flow is a direct affront to the mistaken notion that if you deal with this issue refugee by refugee, you can count on finally mastering the whole problem. It is not in the interest of the international community or of refugees themselves to treat refugee movements as a transitory phenomenon. It is time to stop such misguided attitudes.

The incongruity in addressing social justice and migration is that, while there is bound to be disagreement on what social justice is, it is less arguable that when social justice fails, one consequence is migration. We know this because, whatever our beliefs about the substance and procedures that constitute social justice, men create and submit to authority in expectation of some positive return; when the state fails them, one of their options may be to leave it.

In the history of political theory [3] there are two central views of the purpose of law and social institutions that reappear in one form or another. One sees law principally as a device for regulating conflict among men in a neutral and disinterested way. The other vests law with values that have origins outside, and above, the mere need to conduct business and prevent intra-societal violence. Even utilitarian models of the state, such as Plato's *Republic* or Hegel's conception of freedom as that which permits us to perform socially useful work, contain notions of harmony and justice that depend on some definition of self-realization. What follows is a discussion of persecution and lack of economic sufficiency—the two chief obstacles to self-realization—and the ways in which they are regarded by contemporary law.

## Forced Migration and Basic Rights

In 1952, when the Economic and Social Council of the United Nations was considering one of the first reports of the newly established Office of the United Nations High Commissioner for Refugees (UNHCR), the delegate from China found occasion to mention that his country had been confronted with refugee problems as early as 206 B.C.[4]

There is no record of the cause of that refugee flow, but one would not be hard pressed to find religious intolerance, generally mixed with ethnic and social factors relating to the struggle for political or economic power, as a source of persecution and exodus throughout history. There is ample historic evidence of what Nicholas Murray Butler called the "lingering zest to persecute" the non-conformist.[5] The story of the

Jewish people is one such saga; that of the Armenians, another. Early Christians were persecuted by the Roman state; Catholics were martyred under Henry VIII, Protestants under Mary Tudor. Between 1681 and 1685, an estimated two hundred thousand Huguenots, members of the French Protestant church, fled France as a result of continual religious persecution which had attained a pinnacle of savagery in the previous century with the St. Bartholomew Day Massacre of August 24, 1572, in which some twenty thousand of them lost their lives. In the American colonies, Massachusetts banished Roger Williams in 1635 for having challenged the authority of its magistrates to enforce religious conformity. And anti-Catholic sentiment in colonial America was so general at the beginning of the 18th century that it could be said that Catholics enjoyed a semblance of full civil and religious rights in only one state, Rhode Island.

In our own century, we have witnessed the expulsion of Armenians from the Ottoman Empire in 1915; then Russians, Jews, Spanish Republicans, Palestinians, Algerians, Hungarians, Rwandese, Cubans, Angolans, Sudanese, Ethiopians, Cambodians, Afghans, Chadians, and yet others up to this moment in history. Many of these movements have numbered well over one hundred thousand persons. In the case of Afghans, it exceeded 3 million; Indochinese, 1.6 million; Ethiopians, 1 million.[6]

We call these people "refugees," but in fact they belong to that broader class of persons whose basic rights have been violated, whom I call "forced migrants." The word "refugee" has specific content in law, even though the application of the definition is often less than clear. "Forced migrant" is a term that has no legal meaning, and this is both a symptom and a cause of our present difficulty.

To understand the difference between the refugee and the forced migrant, it is useful to repair to the idea of basic rights—a not insignificant concept if one considers social justice to be a condition of peace, and the satisfaction of basic rights to be a condition of social justice. "Basic rights," in the words of Henry Shue, "are the morality of the depths. They specify the line beneath which no one is to be allowed to sink."[7]

From the standpoint of logic alone, certain rights are the foundation for the guarantee of others: without basic rights, the guarantee of nonbasic rights is nugatory. Defining a basic right is done not by judging which are more "valuable" or intrinsically satisfying than others, but by determining whether the enjoyment of a particular one is indispensable to the enjoyment of another. For example, one would have some difficulty exercising the right to vote, otherwise participating in the political process, engaging in productive economic activity, or being creative, if a minimum physical security and sustenance were lacking. When one's whole being is consumed by finding the day's meal or keeping free from predators, then other activities are simply not imaginable.

Economic security must be considered a basic right in the same sense as physical security because its enjoyment is a condition for the exercise of other rights to which a state has subscribed in the social contract. In endorsing this argument, one needs to be clear about two things. First, there is a difference between asserting a requirement for minimum conditions of health and economic security in order to be able to exercise other rights and contending that everyone has a "right" to good health and a particular quotient of clothing and other forms of shelter. I am not making that case.

Second, economic security is sometimes confused with economic equality. Beyond a personal belief that opportunity should be equal, I do not assert this as a "right" either. But there is considerable evidence on the record, and in the history of ideas, that gross economic inequality (generally deriving from an underlying social inequality) stimulates violence and ideologies focused on violence as a means for achieving their ends. We find such an assertion in thinkers as antithetical as Edmund Burke and Karl Marx. Richard Sterling concludes that the tendency to violence that lives in all situations of inequality can be quelled only by the development of those sentiments of trust, loyalty, and community that characterize the family. He argues that it is "justice" that creates and sustains those sentiments because it is the function of justice "to make individuals secure in their social existence."[8] This idea strikingly resembles the Roman law basis of man's relationship to the state, and it is fundamental to contemporary concepts of citizenship.

Translating the theory of basic rights into positive international law or declarations of principle can imply that certain kinds of rights are somehow superior to others. This is shown in the handling of the ideas that probably represent the broadest accepted content of social justice in contemporary times, the 1948 Universal Declaration of Human Rights. For the purpose of creating international law, these principles are set forth in two treaties: the International Covenant on Civil and Political Rights and the International Covenant on Economic, Social, and Cultural Rights. Civil and political rights, but not economic and social rights, are the foundation for the most broadly accepted definition of a refugee, people commonly called "political refugees," contained in the

1951 United Nations Convention Relating to the Status of Refugees. Some find that the Declaration has distinguishable layers of assertion.[9] The most basic pertain to personal security, such as the right to be protected from slavery, torture, and arbitrary arrest and imprisonment.[10] A second layer deals with civil rights such as fair trial, freedom of speech, and freedom of assembly.[11] A third has to do with political rights (voting and participating in government).[12] Finally come economic and social rights to fulfill such needs as food, shelter, clothing, education, health, employment, and social security.[13] These rights are a scale of commitment, in which the security, civil, and political rights are negative: the state is obliged only to protect against threats to personal safety and social intercourse. In other words, the first layer exceeds, but by little, the Hobbesian concept of the state, whose purpose and principal obligation is to end the "war of every man against every man." Only then comes recognition of the social and economic needs which place the state in a different posture of obligation to the citizenry.

With the concrete expression of international concern for refugees came the problem of defining who they were and thereby the boundaries of official responsibility. Political and financial consequences of eligibility guided refugee designations.[14] Nominal definitions instead of abstract ones favored naming both the country of origin and the time frame as the conditions and limits of eligibility. Nine arrangements and conventions adopted between 1922 and 1946 used this procedure, resulting in a cumulative, but always group-specific, roster of acceptable refugees.[15]

In 1951, the United Nations Convention Relating to the Status of Refugees created for international law an abstract and universally applicable definition of a refugee, taking into account not only external factors such as race or nationality, which had been a basis for earlier determinations, but also subjective elements such as a person's perceptions and evidence to prove that his fear of persecution was well-founded. The Convention states that a refugee is:

> any person who…owing to well-founded fear of being persecuted for reasons of race, religion, nationality, membership of a particular social group or political opinion, is outside the country of his nationality and is unable or, owing to such fear, is unwilling to avail himself of the protection of that country.[16]

The significance of this treaty is that it elevated international protection, and the obligations of those states which ratified it, above the plane of political expediency and caution on which earlier international protection and assistance had rested. When the United States in 1968 ratified the Protocol Relating to the Status of Refugees, it became a party to the UN Convention, thereby accepting this definition. Congress also wrote that definition into domestic law by passing the Refugee Act of 1980. The keystone to protection is the principle of *non-refoulement*, contained in Article 33(1) of the Convention, which prohibits the forcible return of refugees to places of persecution. Similarly, section 243(h)(1) of the Immigration and Nationality Act prohibits the attorney general from deporting an alien to a place where his life or freedom would be threatened for reasons of race, nationality, religion, membership in a particular social group, or political opinion.

Thus it would appear that the question of who is a refugee has been settled for over thirty years. Until recently that has seemed true, in part because the very concept of refugee derived from western philosophical precepts concerning individual liberties and limits on the power of the state. But the feeling of certainty over who is a refugee is taking on illusory qualities, born of the passing of a relatively simple political past and the post-war reconstruction period which welcomed able-bodied refugees for their commitment and skills.

Today, questions about who is a refugee and who is an economic migrant still dominate American debate over immigration reform, five years after the Refugee Act became law on March 17, 1980. They increasingly are a subject once again of international concern, as American questions are mirrored in European and other industrial countries that feel enormous pressure from outside for asylum, and counterpressure from inside to halt what is perceived as a relentless flow of asylum seekers. The practice of using nominal categories to reflect our political interests of the day is gradually eroding the 1951 success in setting forth an agreed-upon generic definition of refugee.

One indication of the extent to which confusion reigns is expressed in a 1983 article by Atle Grahl-Madsen,[17] one of the foremost scholars of refugee case law. He identifies seven internationally accepted *legal* definitions of refugee which serve different purposes:

• *Convention refugees* are covered by the definition above or by the 1967 Protocol to the Convention, which removed geographic and temporal limits to eligibility.

• *Mandate refugees* are like Convention refugees but receive protection through the statute (''mandate'') of the UN High Commissioner for Refugees in the event a state on whose territory a refugee is has refused him protection.

• *OAU refugees* fit the broader terms of reference of the 1969 Organization of African Unity Convention Governing the Specific Aspects of Refugee Problems in Africa which, in addition to persecution criteria, includes those who have fled their country because of warfare or other man-made disasters.

• *"De facto" refugees* are not recognized by the Convention, but face a similar predicament.

• *"Refugees in orbit"* are any one of the above who have yet to be accepted by any state and therefore find themselves continually shunted from port-of-entry to port-of-entry.

• *"Contingent"* or *"quota" refugees* are members of a group collectively recognized by a national law, such as one passed in 1980 by the Federal Republic of Germany,[18] or a bilateral treaty.

• *"Prima facie" refugees* are recognized by the UNHCR categorically and without individual determination.

Each state, of course, is free to apply the Convention definition in its own way. Sweden, for example, has created a two-tiered system of Convention and "B-refugees." The latter cannot go home for political reasons and therefore benefit from residence permits on humanitarian grounds. They come close, Grahl-Madsen reminds us, to the 19th century meaning of asylum which was "non-extradition for political offenses."[19] The United States practices this through the device of "extended voluntary departure." The UN High Commissioner is not fond of either the Swedish or the U.S. practice, or of other systems which are temporizing solutions that have the merit of not sending people into potentially dangerous situations but the awkwardness of granting them less than full civil rights and the protection a recognized refugee has.

Sometimes circumstances inhibit people from meeting their fundamental subsistence needs, and the responsibility of the state varies according to conditions. For example, the state will normally not be held responsible for a natural disaster resulting in the deprivation of food, shelter, normal health care, and other essential services, although most people would agree that the state has the duty to help restore necessary administrative structures; temporarily feed, shelter, and clothe the victims; help remove citizens from a danger zone to one of safety; repair the ecology; and take other measures to enable the people once again to exercise the activities through which they enjoy their rights.

Suppose, however, that the events obstructing people's ability to exercise the activities necessary to enjoy their subsistence rights could be traced in part to a failure to take measures generally agreed to be within the scope of government. Suppose, further, that the failure were not merely a function of incompetence or lack of expertise, but could be shown to be either a deliberate policy directed against a broad class of the populace or a by-product of corruption. Would it then be correct to charge government responsibility on the ground that the political system had failed to assure minimal conditions under which acknowledged rights could be exercised?

Stephen Young finds analogies in principles of criminal law on the relationship between intent and responsibility. He argues that ''an omission to act of large magnitude such as failure to develop a society is willful neglect of one's obligations as a ruler and comes close to being actionable intent when redress for the suffering caused is sought.''[20] Like Shue, he argues that a right is something to be asserted, an inescapable obligation formed as part of the contract between the sovereign and the people. He goes on to say:

> The law does not always require that intent be overt and fully conscious. The criminal law will punish for willful neglect of others....Thus we have the possibility that the intent necessary for a finding of persecution can be imputed to a government. Persecution would thus arise not only from a conscious intent to harm (malfeasance), but also from misfeasance and non-feasance.[21]

The way the state is organized to provide the distribution of goods and services and the manner in which the state intervenes in the process of creating wealth are very much factors in understanding why people migrate. No Marxist would tolerate the analytic divorce of political from economic facets in the social contract. Nor could any advocate of free enterprise conceive of a right to participate in a free market economy without the underlying protection afforded by the democratic political system. In short, an economic system cannot be interpreted in isolation from the political framework in which it functions.

What we see here is the opening that many legal experts and policymakers in the refugee field fear and reject: the one that leads to the case for an ''economic refugee'' whose status derives from being part of a group or class that bears the brunt of failed, mismanaged, or simply nonexistent development programs.

The term ''economic refugee'' has come into use in recent years signifying different things to different people. Earl Huyck and Leon Bouvier speak of ''economically motivated *refugees*'' who differ from "economically motivated *migrants*"; the latter "could subsist at home but, dissatisfied with their lot in life, are pulled to another region by the perceived ability to secure a better job and thereby an improved life-style."[22] The economically motivated refugee, on the other hand, as a point of fact cannot survive in his homeland through employment or growing enough food to sustain himself.

Grahl-Madsen believes, as do I, that the term "economic refugee" is a misnomer: "Strictly speaking, if a person leaves or stays away from his home country for well-founded fear of persecution, that fact over-rides all other considerations, and that person is a refugee, full stop." He notes that wealthier countries often are democratic and poorer countries have "oppressive regimes of the kind that produce refugees."[23] The more or less constant flow, and sometimes mass exodus, of people from the poorer countries has given rise to the term "economic refugee." Not all these people are victims of persecution, but the usual reactive policy finds that as a group they are job-seekers and therefore should be returned home. This, Grahl-Madsen says, courts the statistical risk that in this group is a small number of genuine refugees who will be persecuted.

Grahl-Madsen's approach is close to the meaning of the Convention, while Huyck and Bouvier are concerned with what we earlier referred to as a "basic right." Both assessments of the movement of people from poorer to richer countries deserve extended comment in considerations of relationships between social justice and migration.

Let us take the case of Haiti to illustrate not only the principles involved, but also the passions and social tensions in other countries that are ignited by a neglect of basic rights. As in most pre-industrial societies, the greater part of the Haitian population, 80%, is concentrated in the countryside and depends on agriculture for its livelihood. But Haiti has not been endowed with an abundance of natural resources; two-thirds of the country consists of steep, largely eroded mountains not suitable for cultivation. Furthermore, it lacks a basic infrastructure, "including even the most elementary system of roads."[24] With such a topographic and economic profile, it is not surprising that Haiti has an unenviable combination of the world's highest infant mortality rate and lowest nutrition standard and literacy rate in the Western Hemisphere.[25]

But its poverty, Gilbert Loescher and John Scanlan write, is not only the result of "...demographic pressures, soil erosion and natural scarcity. It also derives from deliberately maintained patterns of economic inequality and abuses of political power."[26] While interpreting

Haiti's political economy, Matts Lundahl coined the word "kleptoc-racy" for systems of this type:

> In spite of the compelling fact that agriculture has always consti-tuted the very backbone of the Haitian economy, the Haitian governments have traditionally done next to nothing to improve the lot of the peasants. The gulf between the peasant and his govern-ment is abysmally wide. Haiti has never possessed a government with a broad popular backing. The country has always been gov-erned by a small clique who in no way have identified themselves with the peasant masses. The history of Haiti is the history of clique infighting for the spoils of presidential office. Economic develop-ment has never been a political goal in Haiti. Instead, a never-ending stream of kleptocracies who could think of little else than filling their pockets have squandered the available funds in their attempts to gain or retain the presidency.[27]

Larceny, while not always fatal to a society and hardly a precondition to persecution, can contribute mightily to conditions in which the basic right to subsistence cannot be exercised. Haiti's illiteracy, infant mortality, inadequate nutrition, and other indicators stand starkly in the light of the government's failure to exercise its social responsibilities.[28] The following examples represent conclusions reached by a wide variety of experts on the matter of Haiti's governance, particularly with respect to revenues and expenditures:

• The 1979 State Department report on human rights in Haiti remarked that "corruption is traditional at all levels of society, and significant amounts of domestic revenues useable for development continue to be diverted to personal enrichment."[29]
• The Congressional Research Service, in a 1978 report, estimated that "50 percent of Haiti's income was in unbudgeted accounts, which were presumed to end up in private hands."[30] As an indication of what this means, Haiti in 1978 managed to have an excess of revenues over expenditures on the order of $74 million.[31]
• A World Bank report of 1979 noted that approximately "40 percent of all expenditures and revenues were channeled through special checking accounts held at the National Bank that made it virtually impossible to determine their source or eventual disposition."[32]

• Lundahl concluded that the tax structure "has been concentrated on products which are either produced or consumed by the peasants, while products consumed by the urban elite groups have largely escaped taxation."[33]

This economic picture is rounded out by the "tontons macoutes," the ubiquitous unofficial police force of the country which is unpaid below officer rank, thus reinforcing their predilection for violence and extortion as a means of survival. (Several years ago, the "tontons" were nominally replaced by an official organization called the VSN, or "volunteers for national security." Little but the name has changed. Like its predecessor, this group systematically ignores the rule of law.)

Whether or not Haitian boat people are likely to be refugees in the sense of the 1951 Convention, Haiti clearly illustrates how the movements of forced migrants arise from social justice failures and are reflected in basic distrust of the citizen for the state. There, the driving force is the struggle of the elite to preserve its position at any cost. The consequence is that people seek safer and more hospitable environments. They cross international borders to reach a place where the state-sponsored or state-tolerated inequities to which they are subject do not exist.

The point is not to suggest that such persons must be called "refugees" in the strict Convention sense. There are probably few specialists in the field who would defend that conclusion. Rather, it is to illustrate that the state may take measures—or fail to take necessary measures—which, even in the absence of direct persecution, result in vitiating the right of subsistence, one of the basic rights for those the state must protect. People who migrate under the impulse of such disruption to their lives have a strong claim on international attention for humanitarian reasons alone. They also must be paid attention because their movement across international borders, especially in large numbers, is often a serious and immediate threat to the stability of the receiving state and a future threat to peace.

## The Passing of Simplicity

The distinction between the direct victim of persecution and the more opaque case of victims of corruption or neglect ought to be simple to maintain. Unfortunately, it is a lot easier to state in principle than to put into practice through laws and regulations that are applied uniformly. In fact, it is clear that an era of relative simplicity has given way to one in which categorization of international migrants is becoming extremely complex. There are at least four clearly identifiable reasons for this confusion and ambivalence:

• The number of independent states has grown, roughly tripling since the time the UN Convention was written. Since it is a requirement of the Convention that a person have crossed an international boundary to be considered for refugee status, proliferation of the number of countries alone has transformed certain population movements into refugee events.

• Even more than at the time when ideology, law, and policy coincided, granting or withholding refugee status has become a politically accepted instrument of the receiving state's diplomacy toward the sending state. What was originally an east-west issue is now an east-west and a north-south problem, in which the wealthy countries of the northern tier seem very reluctant to consider those from the poor south as refugees. Indeed, the geopolitical angles of refugee status cross-cut in another sense, too. External intervention in Third World conflicts generally prolongs them by building up the strength of one or more of the parties. It also causes more and more people to become refugees. This has happened in Ethiopia, Afghanistan, Angola, El Salvador, and other places around the world where the superpowers arm and support their surrogates.[34]

• The world-wide recession of the past several years provides new significance to population pressures and strains on resources, considerations which were obscured in earlier decisions by receiving states to admit refugees.

• Increasingly hard cases present themselves. A showing of persecution, the distinguishing mark of a refugee, cannot be made easily, but a human rights denial, often with an economic element, is more clearly present.

These issues are more prominent today because the growth in numbers of refugees has tended to parallel limits on the ability of industrial and developing societies alike to absorb so many people. They also pose the question of whether large refugee movements are dangerous to the process of democratization. Emerging democracies may feel that their efforts to extend due process to aliens in applying their laws of asylum are jeopardized by uncontrollable population movements. The impact of these trends raises the stakes of categorizing international migrants, particularly for the industrialized countries, to a point where ability to control movement into a country starts to outweigh the original purpose of protecting victims of persecution. Such resistance recently prompted the UN High Commissioner for Refugees to editorialize, in an unusually direct way for an international secretariat, on the legal and moral implications of the problem:

> In certain regions of the world, despite their well-known humanitarian traditions, we find States turning inwards upon themselves, setting up obstacles to the entry of persons seeking asylum, and applying restrictive criteria to avoid recognizing those who have nonetheless managed to enter. The only objective in view would appear to be to reduce the number of persons requesting asylum.[35]

One conclusion I would not wish to see drawn is that Haitians, or the victims of poverty-stricken countries, corrupt regimes, and every person of whatever description unfortunate enough to live under madmen or criminals like Equatorial Guinea's Macias or Uganda's Amin, are *necessarily* refugees. Rather, attention must be paid to the two systems of eligibility determination toward which we have been moving for some years, both equally unsatisfactory.

One, reflected in the burgeoning of refugee definitions illustrated earlier, when carried to its logical conclusion, so enlarges the meaning of the word "refugee" as to nearly empty it of the special content it had in 1951 with respect to persecution. Persecution, for all the legal niceties that surround it, is a particularly ugly phenomenon because it is either sanctioned or perpetrated by the state; and it is to the state that we look for protection of last resort. Persecution comes in many forms, subtle and brutal, massive and nagging. Persecution is Cossacks carrying out pogroms and the legions of Pol Pot destroying people who wear glasses because glasses are evidence that they are literate and therefore a threat to the state. Persecution is the free thinker in the totalitarian society who loses job after job because he will not give up his religion, or the idea someone or some book has planted in him that he has a "right," of whatever provenance, to speak freely and associate with those whom he chooses. Not all these experiences are life-threatening, but what they have in common is that the state is behind them and the actions are directed against people either because of political views they hold or because they belong to a group or class of targeted people. This is why I could not conclude that all Haitians, as a class, are refugees; but I could so conclude in individual adjudications, given reasonable evidence of persecution.

We are moving toward another system, particularly in the industrialized nations that have highly developed legal structures, a growing sensitivity to the number of asylum requests, and an eye to the ethnic balance of their nations. It is one in which the applicant for refugee status must bear the burden of proving, in something very much like an adversarial proceeding, that he personally will be subjected to persecution if he returns home.[36] This restrictive interpretation of Convention standards comes close to requiring that the event take place, that the damage be done to oneself or a close family relative, in order to satisfy a receiving state that the risk to life or liberty is genuine. This is why I find the opening quote from Elie Wiesel so moving; there could be no more graphic way of removing protection than for an agent of the state to destroy evidence of citizenship. We can't expect a person to wait until something like that happens before acknowledging that he has a well-founded fear of persecution.*

Yet certain attitudes, events, and policies had to be in place before Wiesel, and millions like him, found themselves herded into lines where a system preparing to destroy them—the ultimate denial of social justice—ironically paid tribute to the significance of the social contract by breaking it. These may be thought of as steps preparatory to persecution. The time during which conditions are brewing is a time when personal violence may not yet have been visited on an individual, but there are unmistakable signs of threat. Whenever particular social groups are singled out as a cause of national malaise, failure, or internal stress, as frequently occurs in authoritarian systems and in the

---

*People become refugees in different ways, marked by violence, or callousness, or indifference, but always by some breach of social justice. In international law, the point in time at which a person begins qualifying as a refugee is generally that moment when he crosses an international border. United States law, through the Refugee Act of 1980, makes a small but significant modification by allowing the President to designate certain people still within their country of origin as refugees. This approach is more sensitive on three counts. First, it stems from a pragmatic as well as a humane concern to permit one country to offer its protection to a citizen of another, if the second government will allow that protection to be exercised. Second, it recognizes that a victim of persecution may not be able to flee across a border. In all likelihood, there is not a single prisoner of conscience or political detainee on an Amnesty International list who would not be a refugee, were he physically able to escape and willing to choose exile over the high risk of protesting social justice violations at home. Third, it acknowledges that it is no simple matter to fix in time the moment when the necessary conditions for persecution and absence of protection have fallen into place. This last point, of course, along with the principle of sovereign immunity expressed in Article 2(7) of the UN Charter, is why the multilateral norms on refugees take effect only after a state boundary has been crossed.

nation-building process, a refugee situation is in the making. The question of when and under what conditions a person belonging to such a group could make a claim to international protection is difficult to settle, especially when substantial numbers are involved, but it need not be made impossible.

So, if a recognized expert in refugee case law deliberately or inadvertently demonstrates the growing imprecision of the term "refugee"; and if a conference, co-sponsored by the State Department and the leaders of Christian and Jewish organizations involved in domestic and international refugee aid, on "ethical issues and moral principles" in U.S. refugee policy is unable to reach any cogent, policy-relevant conclusions to guide a leading country of the international system, then where do the observations on basic rights and migration really lead us?[37]

They tell us that understanding and creating the conditions for peace are the foundation for controlling forced migration. Over the long term, foreign policy must take account of its direct and indirect effects on migration, before forced migration becomes the dominant issue of the next phase of history. When foreign policy closes one eye to corruption, mismanagement, or human rights abuses because of overriding military or ideological considerations, the groundwork is laid for future problems that could have military consequences of their own (revolution, insurgency) or domestic fallout (mass migration). To the extent that foreign policy emphasizes economic development and trade on equitable terms, comes down hard on corruption, demands respect for human rights, helps others to become more conscious of the relationship between population size and resource management—along with an appropriate stress on security—it can and should directly affect future refugee demand in a positive way.

I mean this in two senses. First, over the very long run, forced migration would be reduced, at least within regions such as the Caribbean in which the gaps between the wealthiest and the poorest are less marked and where economic complementarity is matched by appropriate political compatibility. It has been said more than once that the United States forms with Mexico, Central America, and the Caribbean one vast market. To the extent that is true, immigration policy is an extension of foreign policy. Since the developing world is going to have an impact on us one way or another, it is not just a matter of morality that we aid development: it is the national interest. Second, if migration that is economically motivated were reduced, the pressures on present-day refugee decision-making structures might also be reduced to a point where we could once again recognize a refugee as international law originally described him.

## Migration Forces in the World of Tomorrow

To appreciate the significance of the relationships we are discussing, it is helpful to work from assumptions about the world of the next twenty years. Using reasonable projections from the state of today's political, social, and economic conditions, six areas have particular interest: population, food, world economy, science and technology, terrorism and conventional warfare, and international organizations.[38] Certain assumptions can guide our thinking:

• *Population*. The more population grows, the more economic development slows: there is a demonstrable inverse relationship between population growth and economic development, and it is strongest at the lower ends of the economic spectrum. In recent years in black Africa, for example, population growth has outpaced per capita food production by about 1 percent a year.[39]

• *Food*. Food supplies will be badly distributed, with the wealthier and technologically more advanced societies producing ever greater quantities of food, and the reverse in poorer countries. Natural catastrophes such as flood or drought do not discriminate between the rich and the poor. But their effects are less drastic in countries that produce more, can buy more, can successfully protect crops against disease, can design and install effective irrigation systems, and have strategic stockpiles. The political economy also affects food production, with market economies generally resulting in lower consumer prices and greater variety of basic foods than centrally planned and controlled economies.

• *Investment*. The banking crises of the early 1980s and the policy of the United States government to exercise a restraining influence on soft loans to developing countries through the International Monetary Fund and the World Bank suggest a future shortage of capital for economic development. Private industry is counseled to limit its capital exposure through investment in such regions as Latin America, an important source of illegal migration to the United States, and to concentrate on fast and reliable profits from sales.[40] Such advice may be appropriate for business in an unstable area, but it is likely to contribute to a perpetuation, if not a worsening, of the sources of instability. It is a short-sighted business strategy that seeks only to market its products without looking to create jobs so that people may earn the money within their own national economy with which to buy those goods and services. Its profits will be equally short-lived. Reductions in both public and private capital available to developing countries may have several disagreeable consequences: default on loans; externally-imposed austerity plans, which inevitably wind up being translated into budget cuts in the public sector, thus creating the potential for even greater social unrest;[41] failure to develop industries that can furnish jobs for a growing population increasingly concentrating in the capital cities and other urban areas. Any of these results would have direct implications for migration, whether prompted by economic factors or created by social violence.

• *Technology*. Problems in the transfer of technology will persist. Developing countries will seek "appropriate" technologies for such areas as energy and agriculture, but private business is reluctant about such uncertain investments. Needed are greater public guarantees for private investors and more readily available hard currency. For the benefits of innovative and inexpensive products of appropriate technology to reach broad areas of the population of developing countries, bilateral aid programs and public international organizations must take responsibility and risk. Appropriate technologies might improve yields in food production, energy, and other areas which raise the quality of life even at very modest levels. Failure to act will be a continued stimulus for economically motivated migration.

• *Armed conflict*. An upsurge in terrorism and conventional warfare, whether declared war, guerrilla action by clients of the superpowers, direct involvement of the superpowers, or civil disturbances with or without demonstrable proof of external involvement, is already plain and likely to continue. This is a function of more cautious nuclear strategic doctrines which leave a great deal of room to maneuver between first provocation and ultimate recourse to nuclear weapons, and it is stimulated by the widespread sale and availability of arms, from small-caliber weapons to airplanes and other highly sophisticated instruments of war. The type and level of violence ranges from direct superpower action (the Soviet Union in Afghanistan; the United States in Grenada; the United Kingdom in the Falkland-Malvinas Islands); to third-party struggles with distant superpower involvement

(El Salvador, Nicaragua, Chad, Ogaden); to internal factional strife with religious or ethnic rationales (Lebanon, Northern Ireland, Sri Lanka). Nearly all these situations have resulted in forced migrations with international implications. Those that have not are characterized by massive internal displacement. Societies in which conflict resolution takes place by peaceful means seem to be increasingly rare. The outlook concerning forced migration based on civil disturbances is thus not optimistic.

• *International organizations*. Finally, the next twenty years will probably see increasing resort to international organizations for coping with these issues. It is less clear whether global or regional organizations will dominate. Although the problems themselves tend to be fairly constant in nature, regional interests are more easily perceived than global ones. The evidence of the European Communities (in the area of the economy) and the Organization of Eastern Caribbean States (in the area of collective security) indicates that fast action with a minimum of fundamental philosophical disagreement is greatest at regional and local levels.

Obviously, it would be mischievous—and missing the point—to hold one literally to such projections. However inaccurate they may turn out to be, it is important to recognize that responsible policy development and planning for the use of resources must make reasonable assumptions about the future. The picture that emerges has hopeful elements, but they are outweighed by more sobering ones. Population growth in political-economic systems that produce inadequate quantities of food and numbers of jobs and cannot count on private capital to make long-range investments is especially volatile when combined with the easy availability of arms and apparent casualness about resorting to violence for political ends.

Even if this picture is only partially accurate, one prospect is certain: forced migration will increase. There will be greater numbers of people crossing international borders as a result of some kind of compulsion, be it the search for subsistence jobs, food, escape from violence, or flight from persecution resulting from new upheavals in the nation-building process. Many others will probably move simply because now it is physically easier and more attractive than in earlier generations. Modern communication has brought the enticements of the rich countries tantalizingly close, enhancing the expectations of those who do not live so well but have been told that they can. Cheaper and faster means of transport have made the economically motivated decision to move easier to carry out, even between continents.

The relationship that links population and resource questions with political stability and migration deserves a closer look.[42] That a causal relationship does exist is hardly a scientifically proven assertion, but it is a strong common-sense formula. Let us consider some indisputable facts and discuss their ramifications.

The astonishing rate of population growth is the first element in this volatile mixture. It took thousands of years to reach the one billion mark in 1830. Then it took one century to reach two billion, and another thirty years to reach three billion, which was the world population of 1960. The growth time to the fourth billion was seventeen or eighteen years (1977 or 1978). Projections based on the 1980 growth rate show that by the end of this century world population will exceed 6.35 billion.[43] 1982 recorded the largest twelve-month population growth in history: the United States Census Bureau reported a one-year, world-wide increase of 82,077,000 people. As the *Washington Post* remarked, this was equivalent to adding "…the entire populations of both Mexico and Somalia to the world, or populating Switzerland again each month, or the Bahamas each day."[44]

The distribution of this population is important. In 1940, approximately 65 percent of the world's population lived in developing countries. Today that figure is about 75 percent, and by the end of this century it will be over 80 percent.[45] (It is worth remarking that, as a group, the developing countries also produce and receive over 90 percent of the world's refugees.) This trend creates social and demographic facts. Even in the face of declining birth and fertility rates, now appearing in certain Latin American countries, the data imply political minefields through which the governments of developing countries, and the United States, will navigate over the next twenty-five years.

One feature of the combination of population growth and the unrealized promise of industrialization is the gravitation of masses of people to the capital cities and other urban centers of these countries. The population of Lagos, for example, rose from 100,000 to 1.5 million in thirty years; some say the actual population of the city is closer to 3 million,[46] which would approximate 4 percent of Nigeria's estimated 1982 population of 85.2 million. Guatemala City is an even more dramatic example: its projected population for the year 2000 is over 2 million,[47] close to 16 percent of the total projected population for Guatemala for that year.[48]

These people come in search of jobs, while unemployment rates in developing countries hover around 40 percent. The International Labor Organization estimated that in 1982 the number of unemployed in developing countries, exclusive of China, stood at about one-half billion.[49] In the five Central American countries of Nicaragua, Costa Rica, El Salvador, Guatemala, and Honduras, the total population grew from 11 million to 21 million in the period from 1960 to 1980, and unemployment presently ranges between 25 and 50 percent. The combination of population growth rate, age distribution, and unemployment rates is such that the annual increase in the Central American workforce will be 300,000 by the year 1990. Testifying before the National Bipartisan Commission on Central America, historian Loy Bilderback illuminated what this portends for the region by inviting us to consider what a proportional increase in the workforce would mean for the United States, even in the best of circumstances:

> With an economy 40 times the size of the Central American, we have never achieved the creation of over 3,000,000 jobs in a single year....Hence, the annual formation in Central America of 75,000 jobs (1/40 of 3,000,000) would be laudable, but that is only 25 percent of what is needed every year for the foreseeable future.[50]

One of the outcomes that can be anticipated when large numbers, scarcity, and unemployment mix, is political violence. Another is migration. The likelihood of migration grows when one considers that nearly half the Central American population is, and will continue to be, under age fifteen. [51] Worldwide, in developing countries, at least half the population is under age twenty, [52] and there is a positive correlation linking youth, activism, and violence: "...social discontent, political violence and open warfare are simply to be expected."[53]

Maxwell Taylor, a former army chief of staff and chairman of the Joint Chiefs of Staff under President Kennedy, recently turned his attention to the security implications of these factors in Central America. After reviewing the same elements, Taylor wrote:

> What do these figures tell us? First, they remind us that at least until the turn of the century, the present forces and conditions adverse to our objectives in Central America will sharply increase. In the various countries, mounting misery awaits the poor, the result of greater crowding, poverty, hunger, unemployment and ill health. Their hopelessness may be expected to express itself in domestic

turbulence, frequent overthrows of government and expanded migration to greener pastures beyond national boundaries. It is also predictable that many governments, overwhelmed by the mounting burdens of governance, will often be replaced by dictatorships of the right or left that will quickly prove equally inadequate to their tasks.[54]

The most vital and sobering feature of this picture is that the demographic facts are already in place, despite the fact that for Central America, birth and population-growth rates have actually been *falling* for some years. The ironic combination of declining fertility and dramatic increase in absolute numbers results from the juxtaposition of two other trends: past demographic behavior in these countries, characterized by high fertility, and declining mortality—in Harry Cross and Leon Bouvier's felicitous phrase, a "death dearth." The fact that two presumably desirable social goals—improvements in public health and a more conscious control of births—fail to cancel one another out is testimony to the power of past demographic behavior to project its effects far into the future. Cross and Bouvier explain with respect to Guatemala:

> Dramatic increases in the proportion of children and young adults...are the first impacts of a population explosion that began at least two decades earlier. Unfortunately, that impact will be felt for many years to come....Assuming a decline in the birth rate from 44 [per thousand] in 1975 to 24 in 2025, the Guatemalan population will still grow from 6.2 million to 21.7 million during that 50-year span....The large proportion of children and young adults in the Guatemalan population means that the number of women of child-bearing age will nearly double between 1980 and 2000 (from 1.7 to 3.1 million)....In sum, Guatemala's near-term population future as it relates to a number of key development issues [employment, land use, housing, migration] *is fairly well fixed and cannot be altered. The country's population momentum and present age structure will exacerbate socioeconomic and political problems for years to come.*[55]

Moreover, the dynamics at work in Guatemala are present in all five Central American countries, whose total population will grow from 21 million in 1980 to 37 million by the year 2000.[56]

General Taylor makes it clear that there are military and security implications for the United States that grow directly out of the unhealthy mix of elements to which we are pointing. It should be equally evident that there is nothing softheaded about placing high on a list of foreign policy objectives our ability to influence other countries to exercise their domestic responsibilities more conscientiously; these forces jeopardize nascent democratic institutions, and they create a fortress mentality in the developed world.

With these population trends and the reasonable assumption of more migration, it may seem unimportant whether we call those people refugees or migrants such as undocumented aliens seeking economic opportunity. Yet it does matter, because once we apply the label, those we call refugees are entitled to a measure of protection that the other migrants cannot claim. And once our foreign policy addresses the forces that create both kinds of flows, there may be less reason for people to leave their countries as forced migrants under either kind of compulsion.

## Institutional Responses to Forced Migration

Since the end of the first world war, governments have recognized that refugee problems are inherently international, that the means for dealing with them in a purely national frame of reference are limited, and that cooperative mechanisms are necessary.

Beginning with the first League of Nations High Commissioner for Refugees, eleven international organizations were created. These are:

• The League of Nations High Commissioner for Refugees (1921-1930 and 1939-1945);
• International Labor Office Refugee Services (1924-1929);
• The Nansen Office(1930-1938);
• The High Commissioner for Refugees Coming from Germany (1933-1938);
• The Intergovernmental Committee for Refugees (1938-1945);
• The United Nations Relief and Rehabilitation Administration (UNRRA) (1943-1945);
• The International Refugee Organization (IRO) (1946-1952);
• The United Nations Korean Reconstruction Agency (UNKRA) (1950-1960);
• The United Nations Relief and Works Agency for Palestine Refugees (UNRWA) (1950-    );
• The Intergovernmental Committee for European Migration (ICEM) (1950-    ), now called the Intergovernmental Committee for Migration (ICM);
• The United Nations High Commissioner for Refugees (UNHCR) (1951-    ).

UNHCR and UNRWA are still in existence and serve refugees. ICM serves migrants more generally. An important and effective network of nongovernmental agencies in the field of refugee and migration assistance supplements and complements these governmental efforts.

The ability of international organizations to respond to the current magnitude and ambiguity of large-scale population movements is under challenge. International organization mandates are limited; in pre-planning and coordination, they suffer in greater or lesser degree the ailments of most large bureaucracies, magnified by the fact that they are multinational. Because they depend on voluntary contributions to fund their programs, they are often in direct competition with one another for money. These liabilities are a direct outgrowth of their histories and the assumption that refugees would be a transitory phenomenon.

As the number of organizations alone demonstrates, no single institutional form or composition has proven adequate. With the exception of UNHCR, all organizations either had restrictive mandates that allowed them to deal only with specifically designated groups of refugees or displaced persons for the duration of a particular problem or they had limited membership which likewise affected their potential impact on global problems. Most had both handicaps, and only four (UNRRA, IRO, UNKRA, and ICM) escaped serious financial constraints because they were composed solely of western countries and were strongly backed by the United States. Moreover, of all these organizations, only ICM has a permanent statute, and it is an agency with strictly defined technical tasks wholly outside the area of legal protection.*

Countries directly involved in the IRO up to its conclusion in 1952 became jaded by the magnitude of their effort; this directly contributed to the international community's failure to organize itself on a

---

* Legal protection means the rules and practices under which asylum is granted and steps are taken to normalize the civil status of the refugee. The refugee is not a "normal" alien, even if legally admitted to his country of asylum, because he can neither return to his country of origin nor, usually, obtain documentation from its government. His liability to accidental discrimination by the everyday functioning of the law where he is needs recognition and compensation. The standard sought in international protection is for refugees to have the same treatment as nationals of the host country or at least treatment no less favorable than that given to non-refugee aliens who come from the same country. The 1951 Convention seeks this by spelling out the host country's obligations in such matters as the right to work, public education, transfer of assets, entitlement to social security, and the issuance of travel documents and other papers necessary for daily life. UNHCR seeks to secure the widest possible adherence to the Convention, or, failing that, observance of its most basic norms. It also seeks to help countries improve the structures and rules by which they deal with refugees.

permanent basis to provide refugees legal protection and material assistance. In addition to the sense that the general refugee problem was solved, the huge expense and number of refugees and displaced persons that the succession of wartime agencies dealt with left a residue of lassitude. Indeed, the IRO was an immensely expensive exercise. Between 1947 and 1951, it provided various forms of aid to 1,620,000 persons at a cost of $428,505,335.[57] In its most intense period of activity, its international staff numbered close to three thousand, not including locally recruited officials estimated to be in the thousands. By comparison, UNHCR's total staff in 1980 numbered around 1,600. Moreover, IRO maintained its own fleet of ships.[58] The United States, in particular, had no wish to repeat such an experience; nor did it want funds of any successor organization to be under the control of the United Nations which, in the 1950s, was already less than wholly trusted. Consequently, UNHCR, the tenth in the string of agencies, was created in 1950 with the temporary mandate it continues under today. Its predecessor IRO began operations with 712,000 people on its rolls; assisted 1.6 million people and left 410,000 to the High Commissioner.[59] Although the statute of the UN High Commissioner for Refugees permits it to assist governments and private organizations in their own efforts to help refugees, even its capacity to appeal publicly for funds to carry out that task was subordinated to the approval of the General Assembly until 1957.[60]

The history of these organizations' mandates, authority, and composition points to three major conclusions about international recognition of refugee problems and, by extension, of the more inclusive problems of forced migration.

The most positive conclusion is that nations agree that forced migrations which involve movements of people across national borders require international cooperation. This is not an insignificant observation. It illustrates the rule that international organizations are created not out of altruism but out of mutual self-interest.

International organizations date from the last century. They began from the understanding that certain kinds of issues are inherently transnational in nature. The precipitating forces that cause people to flee their own countries as refugees have rippling effects that hit many other nations, whether contiguous or distant neighbors. Refugee flows are a sign of instability as well as a cause of it. But organization around refugee issues has not yet reached the legitimacy associated with the regulation of international radio frequencies or waterways. In part this is because efforts to prevent human rights abuses depend on overcoming the barrier of state sovereignty, which no international organization has achieved. In addition, heavy responsibility for this temporizing rests with the myth that the source of refugees will one day disappear.

Futhermore, refugee organizations are largely ineffective in dealing with the root causes of refugee problems; nor were they designed for that purpose. The failure to resolve root causes lay with the parent bodies, the League of Nations and the United Nations, to which political matters were assigned. Even the more narrowly based refugee organizations, which enjoyed ideologically homogenous membership, never sought to do more than repair the damage brought about by refugee-producing situations.

A final observation is that, with the single exception of the IRO, all international bodies concerned with refugees and migration have depended on voluntary contributions. The practical effect of this constraint is to deprive them of long-range planning capability and to force them to respond to crises as piecemeal, *ad hoc* events.

In recent years, the categories of migrants and types of assistance have started to broaden. Through successive resolutions of the UN General Assembly, as well as some quiet diplomatic initiatives, the mandate of UNHCR expanded to encompass assistance to groups clearly beyond its original scope. Categorically, these groups include displaced persons, victims of man-made disasters, repatriates, and people still within their country of origin. As well, there is international interest in linking refugee resettlement projects and economic development programs, both to encourage countries to accept more refugees for permanent residence and in recognition of the fact that lack of development is itself one source of international migration with refugee characteristics.

Neither trend is firm and both buck heavy tides of resistance. The United Nations Fund for Durable Solutions, a U.S.-sponsored device within UNHCR to serve as a resettlement-development bridge, is moribund without having had an opportunity to prove itself. When the United Nations commissioned Sadruddin Aga Khan, a former UN High Commissioner for Refugees, to produce a study on mass migration, it recognized the anomalies and dangers of sudden population movements. But it took no subsequent steps to respond to the study by repairing the identified legal, institutional, and programmatic gaps through which forced migrants fall. With that experience, initiatives are beginning *outside* the UN system to broaden the terms of reference under which international action can be taken. In June and July 1983, for instance, steps were taken in Geneva, Switzerland to create the

"Fridtjof Nansen Centre," named for the first League of Nations High Commissioner for Refugees, to "...improve the conditions of refugees, displaced persons, and other(s)...in similar predicaments"[61] and to establish an "Independent Commission on International Humanitarian Issues" with very similar objectives.

## Forced Migration and Social Justice

Just as refugees are caused by violations of social justice, we can classify solutions to refugee problems in terms of four social-justice concerns: repatriation, citizenship, resettlement, and rejection.

From the outset of organized intergovernmental refugee programs, repatriation was a chief objective, for material and symbolic reasons. Materially, countries of origin often wanted to recover the lost manpower and citizenry drained by a refugee outflow, particularly if large numbers were involved. This, for example, was virtually the only interest the Soviet Union had in post-World War II organizations dealing with displaced persons and refugees (defined by them only as persons who had fled Naziism and fascism).[62]

Overall, however, it is probably fair to say that the symbolism of repatriation far outweighs material gain from the return of exiles. Voluntary repatriation is a form of reconciliation, much like what Lincoln meant by "binding up the nation's wounds." It is a mutual act of forgiveness on the part of the state and a man. Perhaps because of the underlying persecution or fear of persecution, it more accurately is repentance from the state and forgiveness from the man, although the historical instances of public acts of contrition by states are exceedingly rare, even when one regime has replaced another. The Argentina of Raul Alfonsin is a happy and courageous exception to this rule.

Repatriation is a special act of faith for the refugee. With his being, he states that whatever drove him from his homeland will not occur again. Perhaps one measure of its difficulty is that, like anything in the material world where value is determined by demand or availability, repatriation is relatively rare. For a well-founded fear of persecution to disappear, fundamental alterations need normally to occur in the basic political orientation of the state, its policies, its dominant political figures, and sometimes even in its formal or unwritten constitution. Changes of that magnitude are generally called "revolutions," and they generally create refugees of their own.

The political battles waged over repatriation carry unusually high stakes, whether for a whole group or, in the case of prominent figures, a single individual. Of the estimated European refugee population of 1.6 million at the end of World War II, about half were originally displaced persons from the Baltic region and other East European countries which had fallen under Soviet domination. Most of these 850,000 people were unwilling to be repatriated by the United Nations Relief and Rehabilitation Administration (UNRRA). UNRRA was succeeded in 1947 by the International Refugee Organization (IRO) which operated until the end of 1951. In its lifetime, it assisted between 1.4 million and 1.6 million people, but only some 72,000 of these ever repatriated, of whom 60,000 were from East European countries. The vast majority of those repatriations took place during the IRO's first six months of operation, in the latter half of 1947. It was during this period that the Soviet grip began to tighten in Eastern Europe, although not as evidently as after the Czech coup of 1948. Eventually, the waning rhythm of repatriation was counterbalanced by a rising number of new refugees from Eastern Europe. When UNHCR succeeded the IRO, for many years the Soviet bloc saw it simply as a tool of western imperialism because it respected the wishes of those who did not want to be repatriated, while the Soviet Union and its allies considered repatriation to be the only legitimate function of a refugee organization.

More recently, refugees increasingly come from former colonial areas and are victims of right-wing regimes as well as of communism. The proportion of contemporary refugees repatriated to those for whom no solution outside their countries of origin have been found is roughly 1 to 10, better than double the earlier ratio. The total number of refugees who repatriated under the auspices of UNHCR, the only ones for whom accurate figures exist, is approximately 1.8 million for the eight-year period 1975 through 1982. These people are reported to have repatriated to fourteen countries.[63]

These figures—heartening to some, disappointing to others—have the usual unreliability of refugee statistics. Caveats are necessary: the figures above suggest peaceable and durable solutions to those particular refugee situations, but voluntary repatriation as a widespread resolution remains a most elusive goal. For example, the second largest national group in those figures consists of 300,000 Angolans reported to have repatriated in 1975, plus another 50,000 in 1979. The first group fled events associated with the struggle against colonialism. They repatriated on independence from Portugal. They returned to a three-way struggle among liberation movements, which very quickly degenerated into ideological and physical warfare between the two largest. While 350,000 Angolans repatriated, 200,000 Angolans are refugees in Zaire,

37,000 are in Zambia, and a small, indeterminate number are in Botswana as of 1982.[64] Such continuing imbalance unfortunately is more characteristic of refugee situations than the rare cases of genuine reconciliation and repatriation. One large repatriation which may prove to be more stable involved approximately 30,000 Equatorial Guineans who voluntarily returned home after the overthrow in 1979 of the Macias dictatorship, one of the more murderous and medievally oppressive in modern history. The disappearances, systematic use of torture, arbitrary arrest and imprisonment, and other human rights violations that were characteristic of the overthrown regime were reported to have ceased at the end of 1981.[65] The new government, however, still includes many who held office under Macias, and it seems premature to say an enduring ''reconciliation'' has taken place.

In sum, there are three respects in which voluntary repatriation is the best balanced solution to refugee problems. First, if people are willing to return home and have full and accurate information available on political conditions, it logically indicates sufficient improvement to suppose an acceptable level of social justice. Second, the fact of returning whence one came resolves many of the dilemmas associated with resettlement. There is no need to adjust to new cultures and languages; reintegration takes place among those of the same ethnic group, or one with close social ties. Finally, repatriation reinforces the dynamic concept of asylum as a temporary condition.

It must be borne in mind, however, that for the relationship between repatriation and social justice to work, the repatriation must be voluntary, and the perception of changed conditions to which the refugee returns must be accurate. For a person to return voluntarily to an environment in which he once felt threatened is like the dove leaving the ark in search of land. The underlying principle of voluntary repatriation is an exercise of free will leading to the reestablishment of those bonds of trust and confidence between man and the state that Cicero saw as the essence of justice; but once broken, the bonds rebuild only agonizingly and slowly. An element of doubt persists, to be tested only by risk. No external body can fully guarantee the safety of a returned refugee.

The grant of new citizenship is an act of rebirth and a symbol of failure in attempts at reconciliation between the refugee and his homeland. It is the antithesis of repatriation and, short of repatriation, is one of the goals toward which the 1951 Convention aims by requiring, in Article 34, that contracting states ''shall as far as possible facilitate the assimilation and naturalization of refugees.'' In addition, all major human rights instruments on the subject of nationality either provide specifically for or set as a goal the acquisition of stable citizenship.

As fear of persecution abates and people once again feel safe under the protection of the government of their country of origin, they return and "make room" in their temporary host country for others to take their place as refugees. This "kinetic" conception of asylum is particularly important where a host country's consciousness of numbers outweighs its sense of justice or compassion. Repatriation simultaneously may reflect improvements in social justice at home while facilitating social justice in the host country by making it easier to welcome others. The obverse of repatriation is assimilation through citizenship, itself a social justice remedy for the refugee. In the United States, this idea is acknowledged in the provision of the Immigration and Nationality Act that allows for up to five thousand asylees per year to adjust status and become lawful permanent residents of the U.S. on their way to citizenship. This theoretically cleans the slate for the admission of new victims of persecution.

Of all the ethical models of public obligation to refugees, conferring citizenship springs from the most liberal: Richard Feen calls it "shared humanity."[66] To love thy neighbor is to make him your equal. In law, this is done through citizenship.

Between repatriation/reconciliation and new citizenship/non-reconciliation lies long-term exile, existence that is neither a return home nor a new home with full socio-political participation. When repatriation is impossible and citizenship is barred, social justice is still an issue for the host country, whether it continues to extend itself on behalf of the stranger or it forces the asylee to go elsewhere, seeking third-country resettlement.

In local settlement (remaining in the country of first asylum) or third-country resettlement, material aid from the international community is vital. The first UN High Commissioner for Refugees, G. J. Van Heuven Goedhart, headed a new organization with full responsibility to protect refugees legally, but without authority to aid them. He believed that protection was next to meaningless without the possibility of materially assisting the refugees directly or through support to their country of asylum. Otherwise, his office was reduced to "administering misery."[67] He understood that, if the international community expected to hold its members to a moral obligation with respect to asylum, it had to offer appropriate forms and levels of assistance to those whose geopolitical circumstances resulted in unusually heavy burdens. From 1955 on, the UNHCR budget devoted significant amounts of money to programs involving permanent solutions to refugee problems, programs which aimed at refugee self-sufficiency so they would cease being a drain on the economy of the host country and begin, instead, to become a net economic asset.

Most people understand emergency aid and temporary mainte-nance, but longer-term aid presents risks as well as opportunities. Risks include dependency and the appearance that refugees are a privileged population, because of the extraordinary attention sometimes given them by an eager and well-meaning network of organizations. This is upsetting to host country nationals, and is one reason receiving countries have difficulty admitting to their own population that refugees might be there permanently. Since the mid-1970s, Thailand has experienced a long-term massive influx of refugees. Ultimately, Thailand tied its continued willingness to accept refugees to resettlement commitments from other countries.

Proportionality of aid needs careful balancing when refugees may remain in their country of first asylum. Appearing to trade the needs of the stranger against those of the citizen is neither pleasant nor politically palatable. There remains opportunity, however. Investment in refugee self-sufficiency linked to national development goals is an important consideration when one notes that roughly 90 percent of today's refugees are either in or from developing nations.

One suggestion for an intermediate system providing both flexibil-ity and protection is the concept of "safe havens": regional centers, preferably under international authority, which would be reception and processing areas for asylum claimants, including those whose refugee status is not clear but whom we are or should be reluctant to treat as undocumented aliens.[68] Persons in safe haven would have a temporary legal status sufficient to provide international protection and to make them eligible for assistance programs.

Some view the idea of creating any kind of center with great misgiving. Safe havens are intended to be long-term institutions for temporary residence. Those passing through would be in transit long enough to benefit from protection, respite, and sustenance while finding a more durable solution outside the center. Critics point to the refugee camps in Europe, where hard-to-settle cases still languished more than a decade after the end of World War II. They rightly note that the High Commissioner has no wish to become the world's innkeeper. They point to the Palestinians, where a new generation of refugees grew up in camps without citizenship or homeland and were nurtured on a diet of revanchism that has proven a very real threat to peace. They conclude that safe havens would inevitably translate into institutions with analogous problems; that even though the intention is to create a place for temporary stay, very soon no other solution would be on the horizon for people in safe havens; that the havens themselves might wind up being an instrument for states to wash their hands of a problem.

There is no denying that risks, perhaps not as drastic as these, do exist. Proponents, however, consider the alternative and believe that safe havens would be more like hospitals or jails—also permanent institutions, but not ones we expect people to remain in forever. They would be way stations from which longer-range solutions, like repatriation or determination of *bona fide* refugee status, would emerge. Safe havens also could tie into the UN Fund for Durable Solutions.[69] This fund was originally launched by the United States to fill two gaps in existing UN programs: to provide the financing vehicle to link refugee relief with development projects, and to be broadly enough conceived to include displaced persons and forced economic migrants. It would help developing countries that wish to accept refugees for permanent resettlement, thereby relieving pressures on countries of first asylum and providing the human capital for development projects. The principle was approved by the UNHCR Executive Committee in 1979, but the program remains unfunded and untested.

Perhaps the most useful observation about safe havens at this point is that the idea is inadequately formulated, but is worthy of development and study because it has social justice implications and, especially if the critics are right, is a real peace issue. It is precisely the kind of question for the agenda of a national peace institute.

If acceptance by the old state or by a new one signifies one end of a refugee journey, rejection lies at the other end of the scale. This, of course, is no solution to a refugee problem. But rejection unfortunately has become a "solution," sometimes by default, more often as a deliberate reaction to expressions of fear as countries see themselves as targets of mass migrations. Rejection is to forced migration what appeasement was to Naziism. Appeasement represented, first of all, complicity in evil. But it also was futile. The problem grew and ultimately engulfed those who had sought to escape it.

The Palestinians illustrate rejection by default. The situation is *sui generis* and I make no pretense of treating it adequately. Its political and analytic complexity derive from the intense emotion it arouses and the fact that at its source is a dispute between two peoples concerning sovereignty over one area.

By definition, no solution to a refugee problem is possible so long as repatriation or new citizenship is excluded. The sovereignty issue cancels out the first solution to the Palestinian question. As to new citizenship, the numbers and status of Arab Palestinians are far from agreed, but three distinguishable situations are clear:

• At the end of 1982, an estimated 366,500 Palestinians, who had once lived in Israel, lived in Lebanon, Syria, and Iraq, outside the historic territory of Palestine.
• Another group, estimated at 83,500, first were refugees from Palestine living on the West Bank where they were given Jordanian citizenship; they fled the West Bank to Lebanon, Syria, and Iraq after the 1967 war.
• A third group, numbering 217,000, lives in Gaza, part of the historic territory of Palestine, and is stateless.[70]

Citizenship is not in sight for the first group, which has been subject to political manipulation by the host countries in the name of non-recognition of the state of Israel and maintenance of the myth of the return of the *status quo ante*. Citizenship was a solution for the second group, but once again they are refugees, outside the territory which offered them protection. And citizenship as a solution for the third group is wrapped up in the sovereignty question.

The Palestinian refugee problem signifies rejection in other senses too. The United Nations agency created especially to deal with it has only an assistance mandate. UNRWA is like a department of health, education, and welfare; it cannot offer legal protection. UNHCR for its part does have a protection mandate which it interprets to include some Palestinians, but it has never taken an active role toward Palestinians and is unlikely to because the problem is a diplomatic, financial, and political quagmire.[71] As the responsible international agencies thus effectively cancel each other out from the protection issue and a group of host countries remains unwilling to consider citizenship, the Palestinians are the model of a rejected refugee group. Unlike any other in the world today, there will be no conclusion to their dilemma until there is a satisfactory political solution in the country of origin. That remains a very distant likelihood.

The second meaning of rejection is more deliberate and physical. The past several years have witnessed some particularly unedifying spectacles of people being forcibly turned away or ejected from places of asylum, flagrant violations of the 1951 Convention. In 1982 alone, the government of Djibouti was reported to have forcibly repatriated an unknown number of refugees back to Ethiopia on three separate occasions. In the summer, officials of Thailand forcibly repatriated hill tribe refugees to Laos. In October, some two thousand refugees from Guatemala were attacked in Mexico and thrown out of a camp by what were described as "local authorities" acting without the knowledge of the central government. Also in October, a mass "displacement" of about eighty thousand people in Uganda, including some refugees from Rwanda who had been settled for over two decades, was carried out with the full complicity of the central government.[72] A particularly graphic instance of rejection in 1983 and 1984 is presented by reports that the Thai government has a policy of "pushing off" boats of Vietnamese refugees which land on their shores. With supplies replenished, the Thai navy and marine police tow boats out to sea. In January 1984, twenty-three people lost their lives when a refugee boat was rammed and sunk during such a pushoff.[73]

In addition to such expulsions, efforts to prevent massive immigrations have included other means which, although apparently legitimate, indicate protectionist and fearful attitudes toward refugees. They are all the more striking when taken by countries which historically have been most generous and supportive of the principles of refugee protection. For example, the United States government concluded an agreement with the government of Haiti in 1981 allowing U.S. Coast Guard vessels to interdict Haitian boats in international waters, conduct interviews on the spot regarding the passengers' destinations and reasons for leaving Haiti, and return them to Haiti. And the 1982 Asylum Procedural Act of the Federal Republic of Germany contains provisions that restrict the employment, residence, and freedom of movement of asylum applicants.

## Numbers and Attitudes

Granted there is a great difference, however we measure "civilized" behavior, between forcible repatriation and policies of deterrence, what explains this restrictionist attitude? The most obvious answer is simply numbers: more people moving across international boundaries in search of asylum makes asylum a scarce good.

The phenomenon called "mass asylum" is imagined to be a peculiarity of contemporary times. But the activities of Renaissance Spain, for example, show that this belief is historically mistaken. Beginning in 1492, Spain expelled between 120,000 and 150,000 Jews who refused conversion to Catholicism; they accounted for about 2 percent of Spain's population. Between 1577 and 1630, Spain eliminated Protestants from the Low Countries, which it then occupied, resulting in a total emigration of some 14 percent of the population of what is today Belgium and The Netherlands. Spain relegated its population of Moslem extraction to North Africa over a five-year period beginning in 1609; approximately 275,000 people were involved.[74]

Because mass migration is thought to be a modern phenomenon but really is not, some commentators believe that numbers alone cannot account for the newly restrictive attitudes. Gilbert Jaeger observes:

> The estimated 10 million refugees the world over...is a large number, frightening if we realize that it results from so many infringements of fundamental rights and freedoms. Relatively speaking it is not larger, however, than the 3 to 4 million refugees of the early twenties, all concentrated in the Northern Hemisphere, at a time when the population of the world numbered about one-third of its present figure and when the standards of living were considerably lower than they are in the early eighties.[75]

Raw numbers, however, very well may account for present attitudes. The public is generally unaware of either the numbers or proportions of refugees in movements that took place five centuries ago or of the growth of their own populations. Nor does the public distinguish accurately between refugees and immigrants as a general class, or more specifically, between refugees and undocumented aliens, as public opinion poll data show. Although the data vary, by and large they are unfavorable to immigration, and this attitude is accentuated by poll-takers not providing a legal definition of refugee when asking questions, thereby reinforcing the public tendency not to distinguish among types of migrants. While Jaeger and others may be right about the relatively unremarkable impact of today's numbers compared with those of earlier decades or centuries, what the public *perceives*, and what lawmakers respond to, is growing numbers of people regardless of legal classification seeking entry into a shrinking, and therefore select, number of wealthy countries.

Numbers are not the only variable behind restrictive attitudes. Numbers take on distinctive meaning in the economic context of a receiving nation. There have been periods in history, and will be others, when refugees are positively desired for resettlement because they supply manpower and creative force. The post-World War II period was one such time: over one million emigrated from countries of first asylum to new homes in the Americas, Scandinavia, Australia, New Zealand, the Middle East, and Western European countries rebuilding their economies.[76] But in a period like today's of generalized recession, it is not propitious for asylum seekers to come to countries with high levels of unemployment. Furthermore, the whole point about mass asylum is that the receiving nation does not choose whom it wants; it is put face to face with a direct moral and legal obligation, instead of having the luxury of selecting, from afar, the numbers and types of refugees it will accept for permanent resettlement. There is as well what some have called "compassion fatigue," others "psycho-historical" fatigue.[77] Our senses are repeatedly assaulted by images of starving, drowning, or tortured people whom we are asked to take into our hearts, if not our homes, so we feel we have reached an emotional limit on what we can do for others.

Policy toward immigrants in general, and refugees in particular, is formulated partly in response to a legitimate need to "maintain the integrity and security of the existing culture."[78] This can be translated into a restrictive admissions policy and is more likely to be so interpreted in periods of economic hardship. If the "general welfare" theory of obligation resembles a sum of individual wills, then what Richard Feen says about the ambivalence of American attitudes is a sobering and frustratingly inconclusive commentary on how we treat the stranger:

> Americans as a whole vacillate between "minimal altruism" (which entails that one help others when it can be done without great cost) and "heroicism" (which calls for major personal sacrifice). While the Judeo-Christian ethic obligates the American citizen to assist the less fortunate, the Social Darwinist streak prevents compulsion towards heroic behavior. Thus there is no consistent ethical norm which would obligate the surrender of an individual's high standard of living to come to the aid of the poor. That is to say, no national consensus exists which would accept the curtailment of individual welfare in order to allow the millions of oppressed persons a homeland in the U.S. The dialectic between the rights of the individual and his obligation to others will always remain, offering no solid guidelines for U.S. refugee policy.[79]

## Conclusion

Everything we know about the direction of political, economic, and demographic trends points to more movement of large numbers of people across international boundaries met by efforts of states to protect their sovereignty. This phenomenon will be a major issue over the next generation. The legal and aid apparatus currently in place carries burdens that can only become more of an impediment to peaceful social development. The existing classification of categories of international migrants leaves large numbers of people without legal status. We call people tourists, business visitors, permanent resident aliens with their "green cards," refugees, foreign students, temporary workers, and citizens. Anyone whose situation places him outside such categories, we call an "illegal alien." When you cannot classify a stranger in law, it becomes even more difficult to treat him with dignity and attention to his personal needs.

The hard truth is that there is no hidden answer to "the refugee problem" that a researcher or diplomat will discover one day. Forced migration is a product of the same sources of injustice and competition for power that produce breaches of the peace, and it cannot be solved without answering the ultimate issues of peace and justice. In the meantime, and it will be a long meantime, we resort to our ingenuity and material resources to manage and control the demands of forced migration. This requires innovative forms of assistance and legal measures.

In at least three areas, the United States created and still has opportunity to encourage initiatives that can have substantial positive effects on the management side of the forced migration dilemma:

*Honesty.* Bilateral aid, as well as multilateral aid to which we contribute, should include more visible and serious efforts to prevent the worst cases of official corruption. Questions of economy and justice aside, there is pragmatic justification because, sooner or later, corruption leads to violent reactions, and that creates population movements. Moreover, development money that doesn't accomplish even a fraction of its programmatic objectives fails to create the trade and employment opportunities that give us a return on our investment. To believe that corruption is so deeply embedded in certain political systems as to make any effort to control it laughable, is defeatist and wasteful of our diplomatic credit.

*Participation.* Involving refugees in economic development projects has been a subject of conversation reaching near mystical character for years, yet almost nothing significant has been launched. In 1983, the World Bank worked with UNHCR for the first time in a labor-intensive infrastructure project in Pakistan aiding both Pakistani nationals and Afghan refugees. This kind of cooperation, tying refugees and host-country nationals together in a project of lasting developmental importance to the host country, is long overdue. The unwillingness in the past of any single organization to take the lead and the tendency of each to exercise its territorial imperative have hindered the evolution of such relationships. This is classic, but it is neither foreordained nor need it be a permanent condition. International organizations are complex and very much subject to the vagaries of international politics. Nevertheless, they can be moved by a combination of compelling events, executive leadership, and the diplomatic and economic muscle of principal state actors. The United States can provide that leadership, and it should because it advances the national interest on both domestic and foreign fronts.

Concrete benefits will demonstrate the direct relationship between refugee resettlement and development programs. Some will object that the economic motive is somehow not in keeping with the humanitarian purpose of the act. They should know that economic considerations have historically played a role in some third-country resettlement, nearly all of which has been "successful" when measured by the criteria of saving lives, creating opportunities, and giving net long-term economic benefits to the refugees and their hosts.[80] Where there is abuse, it should be rooted out. But genuine mutual benefit is hardly abusive. Moreover, when people claim refugee status with mixed political and economic motives, it at least is a symmetrical answer when programs to help them also spring from mixed motives. This is one reason that the concept of "safe havens" merits serious examination.

*Planning.* Refugee agencies are starting to focus on preplanning. This needs encouragement and funding. Social justice issues are at the source of refugee problems. They are also evident in the impact of refugee problems, especially of mass movements into areas poorly equipped to meet immediate needs because of their own poverty. There are relatively few unforeseeable refugee events, in the past or today. Particularly now, there is little excuse for failing to project not only the event and the approximate numbers and demographic characteristics of people likely to be affected, but also to plan for the aid that will be needed. We should support such techniques as pre-positioning of stocks and advanced inter-agency planning.

Finally, the Convention definition of refugee should be kept. As asylum pressures grow and economic considerations become more prominent in asylum claims, there are corresponding movements to contract and expand the UN definition. For all its ambiguity in interpretation, that definition is specific in protecting victims of persecution. Such people are a distinct and unique category within the list of human rights abuse. This at least the law makes plain. Even if it continues to be difficult to adjudicate claims of persecution, the definition, which took some thirty years to elaborate, is a monument in the human rights structure that should not be toyed with.

The other side of this coin is that protection must be assured to migrants fleeing insufferable economic conditions or random violence. Modest protection already exists, but it is only lightly acknowledged or practiced and therefore does not bridge the legal gap between refugees and undocumented aliens. For example, the OAU refugee convention, in addition to incorporating the 1951 Convention definition, covers "every person who, owing to external aggression, occupation, foreign domination, or events seriously disturbing public order...is compelled to leave his place of habitual residence."[81] This kind of definition would protect large numbers of Salvadorans, for example. Jaeger and others have pointed out, too, that General Assembly resolutions authorizing the High Commissioner to include displaced persons within his mandate have, for all practical purposes, broadened the scope of UNHCR.[82]

But General Assembly resolutions and *ad hoc* acts or authorizations do not have the force of law; because these statements and practices remain uncodified and not part of customary international law, no state can be said to be obligated to respect them. Among the useful propositions Grahl-Madsen has advanced is one that is particularly apt in the interests of legal protection. A "slight amendment" of the High Commissioner's mandate would enable UNHCR to "establish the individual's character as a 'United Nations protected person,' thus playing down the political overtones of refugee status and at the same time assisting governments in their task—without infringing on their prerogative—of determining Convention eligibility."[83]

It bears repeating that forced migrants are those who are compelled to move, that refugees are a special subset of forced migrants, and that peace and social justice are equally indispensable to the realization of our national goals. Many forced migrants cause anxiety simply because the legal and administrative systems do not recognize them. In the face of such anxiety, we do regrettable things like manipulating definitions and procedures to meet numerical targets and making refugees the issue when in fact they are symptoms of more fundamental social and political problems.

If we keep in mind why we committed ourselves to protect refugees, it may become easier to focus on the practical task of creating the means to respond constructively and humanely to the forced migrant. When there are refugees, there is no peace in corners of the world whence they came. When there are forced migrants, there is no social justice.

# PART TWO

# Themes
# From the Legislative
# Debate

## JENNINGS RANDOLPH

Having just left the Congress after more than forty years in public life, there is particular satisfaction in recalling those successful measures I guided to passage from a leadership position. I remember well the thirty-year effort to win the vote for eighteen-year-olds through what became the Twenty-Sixth Amendment to the Constitution, the long and continuing fight for the rights of handicapped Americans, the struggle to create and sustain the Appalachian Regional Commission, and the less controversial but equally complicated process of establishing the Air and Space Museum within the Smithsonian Institution.

My most important unfinished project was completed in the final weeks of the Ninety-eighth Congress when we established the United States Institute of Peace and provided it with an initial appropriation of four million dollars. This happened as the Senate adopted, through an amendment to the Defense Authorization Act, the national peace academy bill (Senate bill number 564) as reported out of Labor and Human Resources Committee. Because the House version of that act did not include the peace academy, the issue went before conferees from the Senate and the House. Despite opposition, it survived in excellent form. Conferees changed the name from ''academy'' to ''institute,'' modified the board of directors, and limited the institute to rented facilities rather than its own site. With a name change from ''center'' to ''program,'' conferees kept the Jennings Randolph Program for International Peace. I am deeply honored. That part of the institute is for scholars and leaders in peace from the United States and around the world to pursue scholarly inquiry and other appropriate forms of communication on international peace and conflict resolution.

Creating this peace office within the United States government has involved my entire career. The debate over a national peace academy has been intriguing and gratifying. My experience in launching other institutions convinces me that the proper beginning of this new national institute of peace requires an appreciation of the history of the idea and particularly of the themes that have marked the legislative debate.

## National Security

The idea of a national peace institution has roots in the time of the drafting of the Constitution. The peace academy debate thus assumed an appropriate historic dimension, particularly over the proper role of the federal government in education. There are those who assert that education should be solely, not just primarily, the responsibility and privilege of the private sector. A national peace institute, they say, would represent a deviation from that principle. Those who support a national peace institute say that this argument misses the mark. It is a non sequitur, for it misapprehends the nature of education in the United States as well as the institute proposal itself. We see a national peace institute in terms of the nation's security, which clearly is a preeminent federal responsibility. We recall that in 1789 the architects of our republic conceived the federal government's most important role as that of protector of the collective security. The question, we believe, is not so much "is education a federal responsibility?" as it is "does national security require federal participation in some types of education?"

National security in the modern age has assumed new meaning, posing unique and demanding challenges. National security includes maintenance of military might: We must be vigilant and prepared to protect ourselves and our interests even onto the battlefield. National security also includes the ability to avoid armed conflict whenever possible; in the world of the late 20th century, the consequences of failing to avoid armed conflict and the potential eradication of God's earth cannot be grasped by human imagination. With stakes so high, I have long believed there is a strong case for our national will to direct the establishment of a national institute of peace. The private sector alone is not asked to prepare for military approaches to conflict, nor should we expect the private sector alone to develop nonmilitary approaches to conflicts which affect the nation's security and well-being.

## Learning about Peace

Opponents claim that establishing a national peace institute will set an "unhealthy" precedent by encouraging federal meddling in what should be a private matter: research, information services, and education and training on international peace. Precedent shows the fallacy of that contention. The United States government has not hesitated to inject itself into educational matters where there was a national interest in doing so. There are many examples of federally created institutions that demonstrate the active and important role the national government has taken in research and education: the Department of Agriculture Graduate School, the Uniformed Services University of the Health Sciences, the Federal Executive Institute, the Naval Postgraduate School, the National Institutes of Health, the Air Force Institute of Technology, Howard University, Gallaudet College, and, of course, the entire land-grant college system. This federal presence has always complemented and supported, rather than harmed or overshadowed, private activities. It is a selective perception, too, that discounts the Congress's creation of military academies. They emphasize military training along with liberal arts and science education. They help create the effective military so necessary to our national security. Although the model is different, the peace institute responds to the same national interest; it, too, is part of the search for national security and peace among the nations.

Because the idea is untested, some see the institute as outside the norm. Since it does not replicate what we already have, that is understandable. When the Matsunaga Commission designed the national academy of peace, there was no exact model to draw upon. The commission, therefore, examined many public institutions and was pleased to find that its vision could actually be put into practice by taking certain tried and true programs and institutions and applying them as an ensemble for this special purpose. Following the commission's design, the institute will function as a national endowment for peace, with strong similarities to our national endowments for the arts, the humanities, and the sciences. In fact, we expect that the national peace institute will learn much from these institutions and will collaborate closely with them. The Jennings Randolph Program for International Peace, which will house portions of the institute's research and be a sabbatical home for scholars and leaders from around the world, drew its idea substantially from the Smithsonian Institution's Woodrow Wilson International Center for Scholars. The specialized resource center—the public information part of the academy—is a significant component of many federal institutions, from the Library of Congress to the Departments of Agriculture, Commerce, and Health and Human Services. The graduate and mid-career emphasis is central to the National Defense University and other war colleges, and the education and training function is at the heart of the FBI Academy, the Foreign Service Institute, and the National Fire Academy. The structure may be new, but the components are well-known.

Some detractors charge that the national peace institute would threaten the principle of pluralism so important to American education; this is far from the truth. The strength of the American educational system is its variety—its pluralism—in method, ideas, and even purpose except for the overriding concern for responsible citizenship. Free exchange of ideas, openness of expression, and individual paths of inquiry help make American education the best in the world. These values were uppermost in the thoughts of the commissioners and of those of us who have participated in this effort for decades.

Because the commission was so concerned about pluralism, it built into its design for an academy the mandate for outreach. Educators and institutions around the country, and around the world as well, should have access to and be served by the academy. Refinement in legislative language, particularly the markups at subcommittee and full committee levels, included efforts to dilute this in the academy proposal. We resisted strenuously all attempts to move the institute toward being a monolithic, Washington-based, elitist "think tank." The institute must belong to the American people quite beyond the Potomac.

The Senate Labor Committee, on which I served and which considered the proposal extensively before approving it and sending it on to the full Senate, emphasized this theme. In our committee report, we stated our "expectation that the Academy's primary role is to coordinate its own program with and enhance the efforts of existing institutions with programs in peace studies and conflict resolution." Pure and simple, then, the institute is meant to be a catalyst. Grounded in respect for pluralism in education, the institute, through the national imprimatur of Congressional enactment and presidential endorsement of its founding legislation, will accelerate the process begun privately to develop the field of peace and conflict resolution.

## Peacemaking

A nonissue caused a major confrontation that boiled up during congressional attention to the bill. It was the question of the academy granting academic degrees. In the late spring and early summer of 1983, the Senate Labor Committee took up the bill. There was a significant amount of testimony, particularly from the schools of foreign service, indicating that the academy was seen as competition to the extent that section 5(b)(6) authorized the academy to seek accreditation in order to grant academic degrees. It was gratifying to see the skills of conflict management put to the test, as the parties to this dispute came to understand that what actually was agreement had been obscured by misconceptions and stubbornness on both sides.

When the members of the commission drew up their proposal, they saw the long-term importance of the academy. The legislation, for which Senators Mark Hatfield and Spark Matsunaga and I were principal Senate sponsors, and Representative Dan Glickman was principal House sponsor, was drafted by the commission, which saw the bill as a charter for an institution that would be around well into the 21st century. S. 564 used language that gave room for growth. The commissioners and those sponsors most involved in promoting the bill knew from the start that the academy, through its board of directors, would have to pick and choose where to begin the work, which parts of the institution's scope would have to wait, and the best ways to ensure that the academy evolved properly. In short, the legislation was broad and durable, and it anticipated that many critical decisions would be made by the directors, a much more refined and expert forum than the Congress as a whole or even a committee with its large and pressing agenda.

From the outset, the authority in section 5(b)(6) to seek degree-granting power was considered as something for the future, which some day might be appropriate. Few called for the academy to open its doors and immediately prepare a master's degree program in conflict management. And those who had such an institution in mind did not come out of the commission or the congressional sponsorship. We understood that this decision would have to wait years and would depend on guidance from existing academic institutions.

Specialists in diplomacy and administrators from schools of foreign service concluded that degree granting would intrude on their turf, and on that basis, they voiced their opposition to the academy in letters and testimony. Congressional and ideological opponents of the academy idea in general seized on degrees as their issue to cloud and perhaps defeat the measure. The perception of the academy competing with the private sector became ominous and even threatened to sink the proposal. Fortunately, we could see that a drawn-out fight loomed over a point that was marginal. Once we understood that the provision that allowed the academy to seek accreditation was a serious bone of contention involving real concerns, it was easy for the sponsors to omit it. True interests became the focus of negotiation: for the schools, avoiding competition; for academy proponents, getting started. We dropped the troublesome language, and the committee moved on to other matters.

## Independence

The most important question, in my judgment, is the institute's independence. Virtually all other issues have touched on this one, whether the concern was content, procedure, program emphasis, or funding. When the federal government creates a new institution, it is a national act done in the name of the people of the United States. How can a national institution created by government have intellectual freedom and administrative independence while not posing a potential threat to the very government which gave it life? What components must such an institution have for it to gain and keep the respect of people holding divergent political views? Because its reason for being is the international condition of the world, how can it maintain the allegiance of the American people, be an American institution, and at the same time engage the interest, perhaps the participation, and the emulation of people of other nationalities? The institute should be important to them, too, for the issues it is concerned about clearly cross national borders. Simply put, the institute must be an institution of our nation, a national institute of peace, and must have and be regarded as having independence from government and special interests. It must also be considered relevant and a place of purpose and importance.

Autonomy and control are the core of governance. The composition of the board of directors, particularly the first board, may be the single most important factor in establishing the institute's direction and credibility. The key is balance. We expect the board of directors to include persons experienced in international affairs, democratic politics, and the nonviolent resolution of conflicts, as well as eminent scholars, teachers, and diplomats with keen awareness of the strengths and weaknesses in education and practice concerning issues of peace. The political right must know that control is not with the political left, and vice versa. By limiting a bare majority of the board to one political party affiliation, much more than label is involved; we certainly understand that political views are not captured by party membership. The point, rather, is to try to keep the institute separate from partisan politics. Stature, integrity, and commitment are required, as is some sophistication in working the shoals of politics and public opinion and the spectrum of interest group pressures.

These concerns were on the minds of the members of the Senate Labor Committee when we charged the board with responsibility to ensure that, "for the purposes of balance, a wide vareity of viewpoints in relevant areas be represented among those individuals and entities receiving assistance from the academy. A balanced board is prerequisite to a balanced program. In addition, we expressed the hope that the academy would become "respected as a scholarly institution which in its own...activities maintains a healthy balance and diversity of responsible approaches and viewpoints." And that, too, will emerge from the composition of interests and politics on the board.

Still, such expressions remain hortatory — a challenge, if you wish—until we see what really happens in the process of appointing directors. Selecting a responsible board is the single most important step now that Congress has established the institute. To that end, the Senate Labor Committee suggested to the president—who is directed to appoint, with Senate advice and consent, a majority of the board — that his nominees be men and women of "eminence in the issues of peace and conflict resolution." The breadth of the board is important, and it should represent a mix of "eminent academicians, lawyers, corporate figures, labor leaders, and others who have contributed to the resolution of conflict throughout the world."

Supporters of the institute review the experience of the Arms Control and Disarmament Agency with fascination and gratefulness. In a number of ways, the ACDA is the direct ancestor of the national institute of peace. When it was created in 1961, it had many of the same expectations and responsibilities, particularly the conduct of independent research and analysis. But it had day-to-day responsibilities, as well. Situated in the State Department, its mission directed it toward involvement in tactical and strategic policies in its mandated area. Soon it became controlled, administratively and bureaucratically, by whatever administration was in power. Wholly dependent on the Departments of State and Defense, it never became the independent advocate for arms control within in the government that many of us who created it had hoped it would be.

The ACDA experience shows that policy and education are uneasy companions, and under the roof of a federal department, the practical demands of policy will dominate because they are immediate. In reviewing this experience, I have no intention to slight the ACDA performance; over the years, I have consistently supported a strong and dynamic ACDA. But the fact remains that its reasearch and education functions were pushed aside. The lesson for the national institute of peace is that the ACDA is not an institutional model. The institute's board and staff must be permitted to operate on a daily basis free from government demands, control, or interference. The legislation contains directives and safeguards. The institute should not interject itself as a party in active disputes nor should it be involved in federal decisionmaking. If, for instance, its president is asked to sit on the National Security Council, the answer should be "no." In image and reality, it must project thoroughness, evenhandedness, and integrity. Across the board, the password is "nonpartisan."

## A Symbol of Peace Among Nations

There is one other matter to place on the record here, and it raises real passion in the peace institute debate. Often lurking below the surface, it has dogged national peace academy legislation since its inception: the possible symbolic impact that establishing a national peace institution could have at home and abroad.

Let me be as plain as possible. I would never advocate creating a national peace academy, or any other institution, solely because of its symbolic impact. A solid justification, based on real need and likely performance, is prerequisite to congressional approval and to the expenditure of public monies.

It is useful to consider the impact our national peace institute could have in other countries. Visualize for a moment the announcement of the institute's launching. It will be joyful. We show the world that the United States is devoting important resources, particularly its intellectual capacity, to examining as a nation, as well as a government, fundamental questions of international peace. We set forth a challenge similar to the Peace Corps' challenge that the world should work together to develop and establish an interpersonal foundation for peace; that challenge, as we well know, was greeted with enthusiasm in many nations. Here the challenge is our common survival at the most basic level, coupled with serious questions over qualities of life that encourage creativity, productivity, and harmony among peoples.

Opponents worry that establishing a national institute of peace will signal weakness to adversaries and friends abroad. It will, they say, encourage unfavorable Soviet perceptions. Myopic, fearful men have even taken to questioning the integrity and patriotism of the bill's sponsors. Behind such frustration is the opinion that military strength is the only reliable, tested, and reasonable resource in international politics for the remainder of this century. This is dangerous thinking. I am not an advocate of unilateral disarmament, and I support a strong and ready military defense. It is regressive, however, to refuse to recognize dynamic and hopeful realities in the affairs of men and nations. Establishing the United States Institute of Peace signals to the world the large vision for which Americans are known. I am confident that, as it proves its mettle, the national peace institute will be seen by millions here and abroad as a tremendous source of hope.

Time and again I have heard from people from all parts of the globe. In one way or another, they have said: "What a demonstration this would be to me and my countrymen about the values and priorities of the United States! What a statement of resolve and sincerity about your commitment to work for peace!" Power, security, and international prestige clearly mean more than guns and the ability to use them. In fact, true security rests most firmly on the capacity to reach one's goals without resort to guns. Former Assistant Secretary of State Harold Saunders said it well:

> [A] strictly military or strategic approach to the problems of the world does not meet the full challenge to the U.S. interest in building a more stable world. My purpose is to assert that, if the United States is actively engaged in the pursuit of peace and in dealing with the causes of conflict, the U.S. ability to influence the course of events in the world and its position in the world in relation to the Soviet Union is strengthened, provided we do not neglect the continued development of our own military power.

He went on to observe that 'peacemaking' is an instrument of power, because it puts the U.S. on the side of the highest aspirations of mankind, and not just the pursuit of its own self-interest."

To those who argue that the national institute of peace will signal our lack of resolve, I ask: Which is the real sign of weakness—and I mean not just military, but intellectual, cultural, and moral weakness—creating the national institute of peace, or not creating the national institute of peace? I submit that the national institute of peace will not say to the world "We are weak." Rather, it will speak loudly and clearly, "We are strong. We are imaginative. We are dedicated to the most penetrating analysis and incisive action to bring peace to the world. We are putting our money and talents where our mouth is."

It is fascinating to observe opponents of the institute agree that the idea is excellent, but cavil over delivery. The need to be more prepared and knowledgeable on questions the institute will consider is almost universally accepted. But the rocks in its path have made skeptics of some. Perhaps it is the old difference between optimists and pessimists. I see them as pessimists, unwilling to move ahead, always saying the glass is half empty, so don't drink. As for me, I am an optimist. I am confident that we are capable of doing this well. And once we do, many nations will follow our example.

## In Conclusion

The legislation creates an oversight process for the Congress of the United States to assess the institute's successes and failures, and to provide guidance on federal funding levels. I will not be in Congress for that first oversight hearing two years from now. Therefore, I take this opportunity to suggest important questions for that hearing, questions to help reveal whether the institute has started properly:

1. How well has the institute integrated itself into the existing community of institutions and individuals, both in and out of government, involved in the study of international peace and conflict resolution?
2. Drawing data as well as anecdotes from witnesses, has the institute served the American people?
3. Has the institute been a catalyst for the work of other institutions?
4. Has the institute avoided an elitist mentality and image?
5. Is the board balanced, ideologically and politically?
6. Has the institute's administration developed an innovative, nonpartisan, and balanced program?
7. Has the institute insulated itself from undue outside influence?
8. Is the institute being run with fiscal responsibility and have directives about outreach been met?

The answers to these eight questions will guide evaluations of whether the institute has adhered to the vision its proponents hold for it.

Is it at the cutting edge of international peace and conflict management? Is its future sound? And what additional guidance, through funding, participation, and the experience of public life, can Members of Congress provide? Positive answers to the questions that I would ask will show that the institute is on the road to becoming an institution of profound importance that merits continued backing by the American people as represented in the Congress of the United States.

I am certain that our decision to establish the United States Institute of Peace will be regarded by those who come after us as one of the best investments in the future that our nation ever made.

# The
# National Peace Academy
# And the Conflict
# Over Peace Research

KENNETH E. BOULDING

The creation of the United States Institute of Peace is an outcome, in large part, of the development over the last fifty years or so of what has been called the "peace research movement" within the scientific and scholarly community. It goes back to the 1920s to Quincy Wright of Chicago and Lewis F. Richardson, the English meteorologist. It emerged as a more self-conscious movement in the 1950s, with the founding of *The Journal of Conflict Resolution* at the University of Michigan in 1956 and the establishment of the International Peace Research Association in 1965. Its North American affiliate, the Consortium on Peace Research, Education and Development, was founded in 1970, and the Peace Research Section of the International Studies Association was created about the same time. This is a worldwide movement. The meeting of the International Peace Research Association in Hungary in August 1983 attracted more than three hundred scholars from forty-six countries and virtually every corner of the world, except China.

The motivations of the scholars who formed this movement—and it is still a small group—are no doubt varied. A powerful underlying concern is that the institution of war and national defense is a deep threat to the continued existence of the human race and even of the whole evolutionary process on earth, coupled with the belief that the only way of avoiding this catastrophe is the human learning process. Other scholars who may argue with these assertions have joined in supporting the establishment of a national peace institute, even though they would not identify themselves as part of the peace research movement.

It is a little hard for any member of the human race to come out against trying to save itself; surely, the scholarly community should seek ways to lessen the threat of world destruction. Nevertheless, the peace research movement has aroused antagonism. In the United States, for instance, this appeared in a column by George F. Will (*Newsweek*, November 21, 1983) and in a article by Emily Yoffe, entitled "Peace of Mindlessness: The Moral Equivalent of Basket Weaving" (*New Republic*, March 12, 1984). There is also a certain amount of covert opposition in some schools of international relations, though this does not seem to have surfaced very much in the International Studies Association, which would be the logical forum for such debate.

## Conflict Management

I have argued that the title "peace research" was perhaps unfortunate, and that "conflict management" might have been a better term for the peace research movement.* Perhaps it influences some critics, like Emily Yoffe, who seem to think that the peace research movement denies the existence of the reality of conflict; this is sheer misunderstanding. What interests the movement is the management of conflict in ways that make it less costly to the human race. Nobody will deny the existence of conflict. The problem is how to make it cheaper, not only in the crude terms of economic measures, but in terms of human suffering and anguish. If we believe in conflict management, then we certainly should be interested in how to manage the conflict between the peace research community and its critics, so that, if possible, both parties benefit and learn from it.

---

* Unfortunately, there is no good name for the study of conflict management. The French call it "polemologie," but that is too much of a mouthful in English. The word "polemics" in English has too narrow a meaning. I once suggested we might call it "irenics," from the Greek word for peace, but that has never caught on. In American colleges and universities, it is frequently called "peace and conflict studies," but that seems rather clumsy. Still, no matter what we call it, there is no question that the study exists. Whether we call it a discipline or not is just a matter of semantics. If we define a discipline as "any body of knowledge which has a large bibliography and in which one can give an examination," then certainly conflict management stands up very well. I have given an examination in it, and it has a large bibliography, enough to make a substantial volume.

There also is intramural conflict that arises in part because the study of conflict management has two aspects. One is the "pure" study which tries to form an image of the phenomenon of conflict, especially, of course, on this planet as it exists in the biosphere, in the record of the human race, and in experiment. The other is the study of conflict management as an applied field, with a body of professional practitioners, arbitrators, mediators, diplomats, politicians, and so on, which also has a wealth of practical knowlege useful in ordinary daily life.

Some of the antagonism toward the study of conflict management arises because, as a pure field, it must follow the ethic of the scholarly and scientific community: This involves placing high values on curiosity, veracity, and testing while always applying the fundamental principle that people should be persuaded only by evidence and never by threat or bribery. This principle is also found in legal systems, particularly in the tradition of common law, where the rule that the judge should be influenced only by the evidence presented in court and not by external threats or bribes legitimates the whole structure. These ethical principles are not always observed, but violations of them are really quite rare, and if found out, are subject to severe sanctions.

Yet this ethic of law and scholarship stands in sharp contrast to an ethic held by national defense and military organizations, irrespective of nationality, wherein the belief that "might is right," especially about property, can be established by superior threat, and evidence has only secondary relevance. Military ethics have many other values that are by no means to be despised, such as courage, self-sacrifice, patriotism, and so on, values shared by the scholarly and legal communities. The love of country, indeed, is to be preferred to single-minded selfishness; but love of country is not the same as hatred of others. The love of good is often confused with the hatred of evil, yet these completely different emotions have very different consequences: The love of good usually leads to more good, the hatred of evil nearly always leads to more evil.

There is a real ethical conflict here, which I suspect can only be resolved by presenting enough evidence that the existing dogma of national defense is a guarantee of human destruction, not to mention national destruction, so that the basic military beliefs on might and threat change by persuasion. It is rather strange that, whereas no one will argue for the use of threat in science or in legal decisionmaking, we believe profoundly in the use of it in politics. That is why the politicization of the search for truth has been so disastrous. We saw it in the Spanish Inquisition, which excluded Spain from the scientific revolution; in the destruction of scientific genetics in the Soviet Union by Stalin's legitimation of Lysenko's genetics; and even in the relatively mild threat to scientific education presented by the politicized creationists in the United States.

Nevertheless, both the study and the practice of conflict management recognize the existence and even the necessity of threat systems. The judge must not be influenced by threats, but we hope the criminal will be. The very concept of property implies some sort of legitimated threat system. The question is, of course, what threat system? And how is it managed? We could not have taxes without a threat system, as we can easily see by asking ourselves, how much would we pay tne federal government if it were financed by a "United Fund"? Economists have always argued that the very existence of public goods, which cannot be supplied through the market because they are in a sense common property, demands a legitimated threat system and the sanctions of the law to prevent a "tragedy of the commons," as we have now in ocean fisheries. We must, by legal and legitimated threat of sanction, regulate what is not suitable for private appropriation.

We do not have to agree with Proudhon that "property is theft" to recognize that a good deal of property originates in theft—that is, an appropriation through some kind of threat-submission system. Thus, the United States may have bought the Louisiana Territory, though it could be argued that it was stolen property in the first place, but we certainly stole what is now the southwestern part of the United States from Mexico. Ancient theft, however, becomes legitimate property, and it is just as well, for continued attempts to establish who owns what by threat often have the effect of destroying the property in question. The careful study of threat systems along many different lines—the historical record, psychological experiments, and so on—and the study of the relation between images of conflict in the human mind and the relation of this to redistributions of human welfare in the real world are a very important part of conflict management, both pure and applied.

## Paradigm Shift

Another source of the antagonism toward conflict management comes from the fact that, especially in its applications to the international system and to war and peace, it represents what Thomas Kuhn called a "paradigm shift," a new way of structuring and organizing the image of reality. Any new paradigm is always a challenge to the old and may indeed be perceived as a threat, even when it is presented as evidence. We see this even in the scientific community. A new way of looking at things, like the theory of relativity or plate tectonics, always produces reactions of defensiveness, especially on the part of older scientists who have been following and teaching the old ideas. As evidence accumulates, however, and as older and more rigid people retire, the new ideas gradually spread and even those who originally held the old ideas become convinced by the evidence and change their minds.

An essential part of this paradigm change is a shift between what in the psychology of perception is called the ''ground'' and the ''figure.'' Among psychology's famous examples is one drawing, called the ''Rubin figure,'' which can either be seen as a goblet or as two human profiles facing each other. It is very hard to see both patterns together; they tend to switch. Another drawing appears either as an old lady or as a young one, depending on how the perceptual apparatus interprets it. In the military and national governmental cultures, war and organizations designed for war are nearly always seen as the figure, and peace as a rather vague white background. War is regarded as the active, vigorous, dynamic pattern, and peace is regarded simply as the absence of war, a kind of nothing. The paradigm change that is involved in conflict management is quite complex. So was the change involved in the theory of relativity! The world itself is very complex, and a change of paradigms often represents a shift from a simple image of the world to one that is less simple but closer to the real world.

It would be too simple to say that conflict management sees war as the ground and peace as the figure, though there is a tendency to see war as merely a disturbance, an interruption, a very confusing dark background against the light and colorful figures of peace. It would be more nearly accurate to say that conflict management tries to see peace and war as a single system comprising, in effect, the activities and dynamic of the whole human race. This activity can be divided fairly sharply into war activity and peace activity. That does mean that peace is simply what is not war and war is what is not peace. Peace is not seen just as a vague background, but as all non-war activity — that is, plowing, sowing, reaping, the whole great realm of economic production, the making of goods and the means of production of goods, being born, loving, living, raising children, pursuing an occupation, singing, acting, dancing, making music, art, and sculpture, building, praying and worshipping, laughing and weeping, and dying. In this sense, peace is and always has been much larger than war.

There is a problem in that this large concept of peace, which I sometimes call "inclusive peace," can have very different qualities, some better than others. Peaceful activities can be carried on in an impoverished, oppressive, tyrannical, and miserable society, or they can be carried on in a prosperous, tolerant, relaxed, and democratic society. Whether Ben Franklin believed what he said, that the worst peace is better than the best war, is beside the point. There is no doubt that the best peace is much better than the best war and that war activity involves destruction and the development of means of destruction, rather than production and development of the means of production. It is very hard to have war without denying humanity to the enemy and without deterioration in human decency. The holocaust of the Jews under Hitler was part of war, and the roasting of children alive in Hiroshima, Nagasaki, and Dresden was also part of war. It is not a facile matter to determine which was worse. Peace is seen, then, not just as a background to war but as including all the rich variety of human activity that is not war; this is not a negative concept at all.

## Taboos

Another concept very important in conflict management in the international system is that peace is a set of taboos. This, again, can make peace seem just a negative concept, but taboo is a very important human organizer. We are all surrounded by what economists call the "possibility boundary," which divides everything that we can think of doing into what we can and cannot do. The actual description of these limits is very important; otherwise, we may try to do what we cannot do, and we will probably be much worse off. Within the possibility boundary, however, there is another line that might be called the "taboo line," which divides what we can do and do, from what we can do and do not do. It is no accident that most of the Ten Commandments are "thou-shalt-nots." Without taboo, all social life would fall apart. The law is a body of legalized taboo, and criminal justice is very largely a matter of trying to deal with people who violate these taboos. There is also a great deal of taboo that does not involve the law—matters of politeness, courtesy, respect, obedience to consensus, and so on. Any organization or human community would fall apart overnight without these things.

The difference between peace and war is very largely in the position of the taboo line. In peace we refrain from doing things like invading people, throwing fire bombs or nuclear weapons on them, that we do not refrain from in war. War always begins with a shift in the taboo line in terms of doing harm, like the assassination of an archduke, which began the First World War. Once the line shifts, it is hard to stop it from shifting further. We see this in the Second World War. It began as an internal war in Germany against Jews and dissenters and became an international war when Hitler invaded Poland. It had several months of "phony war," in which the Germans, the British, and the French at least did not bomb each other's civilians. This broke down and civilian bombing started, ending in genocidal attacks on Dresden. This is why the concept of limited nuclear war, now proposed by some people in the United States, seems to violate all that we know about these systems, for there is no political or structural apparatus whatever to limit it, once war is accepted as legitimate.

## Stable Peace

On the other hand, one of the encouraging things about the world is that we have now developed a large area of natural security through stable peace among at least eighteen sovereign states, in a triangle between Australia and Japan, and across North America to Finland. This, again, rests on taboo, on the absence of plans for invasion, on disarmament of frontiers, like the frontier between the United States and Canada. It does not mean the absence of conflict. Indeed, the real conflicts between the nations at stable peace are probably considerably larger than they are between, say, the United States and the Soviet Union. This, again, may be a paradigm change. It involves the recognition that conflict is a relatively minor and arbitrary cause of war, though there may be exceptions, and that we have to look at the dynamics of action and reaction in the threat system, which often has very little to do with the underlying conflicts. Who has been allied with whom throughout history, for instance, has practically nothing to do with economic conflicts. Who fights whom has a very strong random element in it; the enemies of one generation become the allies of the next, and vice versa. The conflict structure remains much the same. A case can be made that ideological conflict is an exception to this rule, but the historical record certainly suggests that war is just as likely or even more likely among nations of the same ideology as between nations of different ideologies. At the moment the biggest war is going on within Islam. One of the greatest dangers of war is between the Soviet Union and China.

This point of view is a severe challenge to what might be called the conventional wisdom in these matters, yet the evidence for it continues to accumulate. The evidence is now overwhelming, for instance, that empire and even hegemony are severely injurious to the economic development of the imperial or hegemonic power. The British and French empires crippled the economic development of Britain and France in the nineteenth century. Since they got rid of them, they have done much better. The United States's image of itself as a hegemony power could well mean that we are about 25 percent poorer today than we might have been had we minded our own business like the Swedes. China would be much better off if Tibet were an independent country, and the Russians would be greatly benefitted by the breakup of the Soviet Union, which now drains their economy, gobbles up their resources, and even prevents the achievement of their professed ideals. This is a view of the world contrary to what is usually taught in history books. It is certainly different from that possessed by the critics of conflict management. And an important thing to be said for this view is that the evidence continues to pile up in its favor.

## Why the Institute?

In all this dispute, why have a national peace institute? The principal case for it is not that it will help the cause or study of conflict management, which will go on anyway, although it may be helped a little by the legitimation that a national peace institute would provide. Political legitimation, however, has a dangerous side, when such legitimation is used or seen to make something true. While truth can help politics—and it is obviously dangerous for a political leader to believe what is in fact in error—truth transcends politics. As the search for truth is part of the human purpose and dilemma, the main justification for a national peace institute must lie in the contribution it can make to that end, and in concrete terms to the welfare and security of the United States. There is a great deal of evidence that the traditional paradigm of national defense, in contrast to more complex concepts of national security, has simply broken down with the development of the long-range guided missile and the nuclear weapon. Even if there were only the smallest possibility of this being true, it would pay to have it studied along with other critical issues, especially at a cost of some five cents per American per year.

A great deal depends, of course, on the leadership and quality of the institute, something that cannot be guaranteed. One wishes there were a larger field of leaders to draw on. Perhaps the most important quality to look for is sensitivity to managing the conflicts with which the institute undoubtedly will be surrounded. The institute must be a voice in dialogue, not a voice in preaching or confrontation. It should be a living embodiment of the concepts and practices it espouses. This should include not only conflicts that are likely to arise with the military and the Department of State, where other paradigms may be held, but it should also be sensitive to the conflict, often latent, between the academic and the scientific view of the world and what might be called the "folk knowledge" of people in the ordinary business of life. The view that the ordinary American citizen has of the world may be very different from that of the specialist, and it is the responsibility of the specialist to understand this and, in some sense, to bring ordinary citizens into a larger, participatory learning process to which they can contribute. This, too, should be a major objective for the national institute of peace.

# Why Establish A National Peace Academy?

MILTON C. MAPES, JR.

**News Flash:**
**U.S. Air Force, Navy Clash in Nuclear Exchanges**

Several task units of the Navy's Seventh Fleet and at least four major Air Force ground installations were destroyed yesterday in a series of nuclear exchanges involving planes of the U.S. Air Force and the Navy's Air Wing.

Officials in Washington were reported frantically trying to prevent any repetition of yesterday's nuclear violence, which apparently resulted from an escalation of recent air battles between fighters of the two branches of the Armed Forces. Tension between the two branches has been mounting over a period of several months, including armed clashes between small groups of officers and men in shore leave and liberty status.

The inter-service conflict broke into the open with press reports of serious confrontations in the Pentagon at levels up to and including the Joint Chiefs of Staff. The situation has been exacerbated by the well-advertised fisticuffs between the Secretaries of the Navy and Air Force at last month's hearing before the House Appropriations Committee.

This quite imaginary news flash is drawn to emphasize a point. Our problem is not simply the existence of nuclear weapons. The threat lies in what the humans who control such weapons are likely to do. The actions they take are largely controlled by the effectiveness with which they manage the many conflicts always present on the international scene. Professor Roger Fisher of Harvard Law School and the Harvard Negotiation Project has made the point on many occasions that the U.S. Army, Navy, and Air Force all have nuclear weapons, yet they constitute no threat to each other because they have learned to manage nonviolently the conflicts that exist among the three services. It is not that the services do not have conflicts, but that they have learned to handle their conflicts in nonviolent ways. But handling some conflicts nonviolently does not necessarily imply the ability to manage others effectively, creatively, or constructively. There is some evidence that the armed forces are as handicapped as many lesser groups and organizations by their incapacity in the finer arts of conflict management.

Early in the history of the National Peace Academy Campaign— in fact, shortly after I made my initial public presentation on the national peace academy proposal—I spoke to my old friend, Captain Chan Swallow, who had recently retired from the United States Navy. I asked his reaction to the peace academy idea, and his reply startled me. He said he had discussed the subject with his wife, Edie, just the preceding evening after my talk, and he had commented then that the peace academy would do more for our national defense than any idea he had heard of in the past twenty years. Caught off guard by this unexpected response, I asked him how he came to that conclusion.

"Very easily indeed," he responded. "The four years before I retired, I was assigned to the Office of the Joint Chiefs of Staff. There I saw dozens of issues—some important, many not too important, but almost all involving strong conflicts—come up for decision by the Joint Chiefs. For the minor issues we usually were able to work out solutions at the staff level and send up agreed positions to the Joint Chiefs for action. But in that four-year period, I don't think I ever saw a major issue get satisfactorily resolved so that action could be taken. All the important issues were strongly contentious, with at least two and often three positions being held and vigorously expounded. Without exception, decisions were argued over, fought over, and finally put aside for later consideration, with no conclusion. If we had had one or two members of that staff who had been trained at the national peace academy and who really knew how to go about resolving conflicts, it would have made all the difference to the proper progress and planning of our national defense."

The national peace academy that I had talked about would have three basic functions —*research, education and training, and information services.*

In *research*, the United States Academy of Peace would perform and assist research about peace and conflict resolution through work by its faculty, students, and visiting scholars, some of them in residence at the Center for International Peace to be established at the academy, and through grants and contracts for research at other institutions. Not only will this research capability greatly accelerate the development of knowledge about peace, but it will very possibly produce results we can not even imagine. Every culture has well-developed systems and methods of resolving or avoiding conflict. Bringing together experts in the field from many different cultures may produce exciting intellectual cross-cultural fertilization and synergistic effects that are impossible to foresee.

The *education* and *training* programs at the academy will be at graduate and post-graduate levels. Short- and long-term programs will educate and train persons from government, private enterprise, and voluntary groups in peacemaking skills and conflict resolution. Much of this activity will take place across the country with academy financial support. A critical element of these programs, envisioned since the earliest days of the National Peace Academy Campaign, could be the involvement of a substantial number of foreign scholars, students, and trainees. This will greatly expedite the global reach of both the issues and mechanics of conflict resolution and will hasten the day when other nations follow the United States and establish their own national institutions.

The academy's *information services* will inform citizens about the field of peace learning and will disseminate the carefully selected products of academy-funded research. The nation's network of libraries and academic institutions are central to successfully fulfilling this mandate of the academy.

## National Security

Since the Romans first said *si vis pacem, para bellum* ("If you wish for peace, prepare for war"), that dictum has been the basic assumption applied in the relationships among nations. It animates policy in foreign and military affairs of every nation in the modern world, with the only possible exception being Costa Rica, which has police but no armed forces. For two thousand years we have been wishing for peace, yet gone right on preparing for war with almost slavish devotion to the most demonstrably false assumption in history. Millions upon millions of human beings have suffered because of this one totally irrational and clearly wrong idea. Our folklore tells us: "Don't listen to what he says—watch what he does!" Yet for two thousand years, humankind has *said* it wanted peace and *done* preparations for war and wondered why it kept getting war for its efforts!

A by-product of the proper establishment and development of a national peace academy would be an eventual change in the definition and use of the term "national security." Throughout most of two centuries, national security has been defined as the capability to resist and repel attack either on ourselves or our interests abroad. But in a most basic sense, it has been equated with national defense. Today, military experts and leaders tell us that, in the thermonuclear age, defense in the traditional sense is no longer possible.

Faced with such a basic change in the factual framework of our national security, one would think we might have reevaluated our responses to the challenges of survival. Unfortunately, no major power has done so. We all keep right on wishing for peace and preparing for war, which in the nuclear era translates directly into a policy of deterrence.

There is no question that deterrence can have a temporarily stabilizing effect on international relations. But as General Andrew J. Goodpaster, the then Superintendent of the U.S. Military Academy at West Point, pointed out to me five years ago, deterrence is essentially a negative approach to peace based on the threat of unacceptable violence. In clinging to it as the structuring element of our national policy, we have neglected almost completely the development of affirmative approaches to peacemaking and peacekeeping. That, General Goodpaster explained, was the reason he believed that a national peace academy would be a rational and essential addition to our national educational structure. It dawned on me only sometime later that what General Goodpaster was suggesting was a change in our basic attitude. If we wish for peace, we should prepare for peace, although presumably not at the expense of our military capability.

It is worth mentioning here that the preceding discussion echoes in part the judgment of the early sociologist, William Graham Sumner, who wrote in 1903: "A wiser rule would be to make up your mind what you want, peace or war, and then to get ready for what you want; for what we prepare for is what we shall get." As Sumner realized, either form of preparation could prove to be a self-fulfilling prophecy. By concentrating our "defense" efforts under the category of deterrence, we limit the development of our conflict resolution capabilities to violent means of settling disputes and we neglect the improvement of approaches not based on violence. The danger is that one-sided preparation will seriously limit the options available to national leaders and policymakers responding to crises that could threaten the survival of civilization.

The point here is not that deterrence cannot be an effective form of peacekeeping in the short run; clearly it can and has. The point is that the peace produced by mutual deterrence is an unstable form of equilibrium that offers only a negative approach to peacekeeping. It is essential that, if our efforts to achieve peace are to have any balance and stability and offer real hope of long-time success, we study and teach affirmative peacemaking and peacekeeping. Yet in this area we do not have even a ghost of a national policy.

Peace needs and is constant preparation. Today it is now or never. And the exciting thing is that *we can do it!* We know how; and even better, we know how to learn to do it better. The human method is institutionalization, and the specific institution is the United States Academy of Peace.

Roger Fisher concluded his analysis of the Falklands episode in the Sunday, August 22, 1982 issue of the *Boston Herald American* by advocating a national peace academy:

> Today, professional training in negotiation and mediation is lost among a welter of government institutions dominated either by day-to-day events or military concerns. What is everybody's business has become nobody's business. We need a central, active body to focus, stimulate and conduct first-class training in the skills of dealing with differences. More than 50 Senators have jointly introduced legislation to do so. Without further delay, Congress should establish the United States Academy of Peace and Conflict Resolution.

## History's Longest Running Paradigm Shift

In 1962 Thomas Kuhn described a *paradigm shift* as a basic change in the framework for thinking about a problem. It is my firm belief that what was effectively launched with the founding of the National Peace Academy Campaign on July 4, 1976, was a concept that is the latest and the most dynamic current element in the longest-running paradigm shift in history: the evolving change in the framework of the way we think about and deal with conflict.

Kenneth Boulding wrote in *Stable Peace*:

> There is a long, painful, slow but very persistent historical movement from stable war into unstable war into unstable peace into stable peace. The main object of peace policy is to speed up the transition by deliberate decision.

A national peace academy, quite simply put, is an institution designed to speed up that transition from stable war to stable peace by deliberate decision.

The paradigm shift referred to is the long-term context of history as it relates to the handling of conflict, and we can go back five thousand or two million years in considering it. It began with the age-old law of fang and claw, when, in the words of Langdon Smith,

> We lived by blood and the right of might,
> Ere human laws were drawn;
> and the age of sin did not begin
> Till our brutal tusks were gone.

Ancient primitive societies institutionalized the blood feud and a scrupulous *lex talionis*, the law of retaliation, which was enforced by and among tribes and families.

The Code of Hammurabi in 1750 B.C. and the Mosaic Code about 1200 B.C. made "an eye for an eye and a tooth for a tooth" into both state law and holy writ. That continued as the most forward-looking law until about 1,950 years ago, when Jesus Christ produced the truly radical breakthrough, a total revolution in thinking about conflict. He said humans should do not as they were done unto, but as they would like to be done unto.

"An eye for an eye" is clearly lose/lose conflict resolution, and the less structured conflict of war maintained the win/lose context of winner-take-all. But the Golden Rule was the birth of win/win thinking. Perhaps it is regrettable that it was presented in a religious context rather than merely as a highly pragmatic social art with a very high benefit-cost ratio. That way, it might have shown up sooner on our social and financial profit and loss statements.

Whether the Golden Rule was divine or human inspiration is moot for this discussion, but it is probable that the breakthrough was in part the product of the cross-cultural fertilization of East and West—the East of the Essenes and the West of the Roman Empire. But Christianity went west into the cultures of Rome and northern Europe, where there was no cultural basis for accepting its dictates, and Christians proceeded to spread some of history's most nonviolent teachings by force and violence. Thus there were religious wars of unprecedented violence; history-bending crusades of bloodshed; and the crushing cruelty of the Inquisition, all in the name of the Carpenter from Nazareth. History has seldom witnessed greater incompatibility between the means and the end.

But the concept of win/win conflict resolution did make progress and, in the context of Christianity, gradually permeated Western culture. The spread of empire brought continued cross-cultural contact, and after World War II Mohandas Gandhi removed the British Empire from India by nonviolent resistance. What he did, of course, was attack the British at their Achilles' heel: the inconsistency between their methods of violence and their ideals of peace. It took the genius of Martin Luther King, Jr. to take Gandhi's techniques and show us how to apply them in America so as to conform our methods to our goals and to strive for a nonviolent society by nonviolent means.

When we examine world society in the past two decades of the twentieth century, it appears self-evident that the peaceful resolution of conflict is the most crucial challenge of our time, and perhaps of all time. It is difficult to emphasize that point enough—to say it as forcefully as it deserves to be said. It is a simple fact that, if we do not learn to handle conflict far better that the human race has ever handled conflict in the past, then we and our civilization, the product of thousands of years of humankind's best efforts, shall not survive. In 1946, Einstein said it neatly: "The splitting of the atom has changed everything save our modes of thinking, and thus we drift toward unparalleled catastrophe."

In a Toynbeean sense, the single dominant challenge of current history is the suddenly desperate nature of mankind's management of conflict. This has always been a major challenge, although the response has not been all that critical; but suddenly, since 1945—the blink of a gnat's eyelash on the historical timeline—our response to this challenge has become the question of our age and, in a real sense, of all history. An inadequate answer will allow unparalleled catastrophe, while an adequate answer will require a total change in our "modes of thinking" about conflict. The peace academy is merely and importantly the next step in the flow of history. It is a critical step, for it would commit history's most powerful nation to a long-term program of research and training in the ways and means of peace.

## The Reality of Violence and Conflict

Conflict is both endemic and epidemic in society. That it is so often so harmful and so terribly threatening cannot fail to make us wonder why. I believe the answer is that we do not have the clear ability to manage conflict constructively and creatively.

In answer to a letter from Albert Einstein, Sigmund Freud responded to the mathematician's inquiry concerning the nature of man by writing that, although *conflict* might indeed be a natural and essential element of man's nature, *violence* was not a necessary result. The challenge was to find ways to resolve and manage conflict constructively without it becoming unacceptably violent.

Dr. Israel Charny argues, in the January 1980 issue of the *Journal of Marital and Family Therapy,* that conflict is a built-in structure within every living organism: "[Life] itself begins with a basic and immutable conflict between the two fundamental givens of our existence, LIFE and DEATH." He goes on to point out that the basic conflict of humankind is that man wants to live but must also yield to the awareness of his inevitable death, and he concludes that illness results either when people seek life too much and yield too little to the inevitability of death or seek life too little and yield to death too readily. In such an intellectual framework it is hard to quarrel with his comment in summation: "What a fascinating and difficult balance we humans are asked to develop and maintain."

Dr. Charny's superb summation of the inevitability of conflict compels inclusion of one paragraph of his description in this discussion. Referring to "life's fundamental contradictions as they derive from and elaborate on the original awesome polarity of life and death," Dr. Charny writes:

> There is no alternative to experiencing these fundamental conflicts within ourselves and between one another. These conflicts are much more than a trite statement that people clash because of "differences" in personality, in ideas or even of wills, nor are these the same as powerful political conflicts or struggles over

power at every level of human relationships. The conflict process about which we are speaking is all of these, but it is still more. For we are referring to the ultimate substrata where man's aliveness is counterpointed against death, a contradiction that is so enormous, and forever unresolvable, and yet requires of us throughout our lives reconciliation and integration. We live our lives faced with the inevitability of death and incompleteness as the context of our aliveness and efforts to fulfill our potential. It is an enormous struggle that leaves its mark on each of us. So that there should be no wonder at all that when we come together in the intimacies of family life, it proves to be enormously difficult to live with one another.

It is probable that in another context Dr. Charny would have been the first to add that what is difficult at the family level may appear almost impossible at the international level when all the problems of distance, semantics, and cultural diversity are added to the picture.

If we start from Dr. Charny's description of the philosophical and psychiatric basis of conflict in discussing the peace academy, it is apparent that developing and maintaining that "fascinating and difficult balance" he speaks of is the essence of conflict management. Dr. Charny makes the point that it is not the right ways and wrong ways of being a human being, the good or bad behaviors, that lead to peace, health, and emotional stability, but rather it is the effective processing of either good or bad behavior patterns.

This attention to behavior patterns, I suggest, fits very closely into the distinction one might draw between *conflict resolution,* which seems to imply some final solution to each conflict, and *conflict management,* which implies the ongoing nature of conflict, without denying the possibility of occasionally reaching a true resolution. It was Professor Kenneth Boulding who coined the term "conflict resolution" back in the mid-1950s, when he established the Institute for Conflict Resolution at the University of Michigan. But he confessed only a year or two ago that he now believes the term "conflict management" would have been a more accurate description of what the field properly involves, since the great majority of conflicts do not get "resolved" but are normally "managed," often repeatedly and over a substantial period of time. The challenge, of course, is either to resolve the conflicts or to manage them effectively and nonviolently to prevent them from becoming destructive and counterproductive.

The point of this discussion is that we must start by accepting the inevitability of conflict in our lives. The corollary is that this is true of conflict at all levels, from the interpersonal to the international. Our response and that of the next generation in the nuclear age to the challenge of learning to manage conflict effectively and nonviolently will be the most critical issue of all history.

We *must* understand the roots of conflict, its conditions, processes, and stages of development, and the effectiveness of specific types of intervention at specific stages. We must have answers to those and a thousand other problems so we can manage conflict effectively enough to assure our survival. And we must develop systems that permit us to apply each item of new knowledge as it is developed. We do not have the luxury of ignoring the steps while waiting for ultimate solutions. Our plight is too desperately dangerous.

The trouble is that we know so terribly little about how to manage conflict effectively: how to keep it constructive and not destructive of our values, let alone our property and lives. For almost two millennia at Christmas time, much of the Western world has sung the songs of "Peace On Earth, Good Will Toward Men," and when mixed with silver bells they sound very beautiful indeed. But the truth about Peace on Earth is that we have almost no idea of how to go about achieving it in the dynamic shove and whirl of human society—in the immortal words of Patrick Henry, "Gentlemen may cry, 'Peace, Peace!!,' but there *is* no peace!" The world has had nearly 150 wars since the end of World War II, and dozens of nations are involved in destructive conflict today.

It would seem that, if peace has been a nearly universal goal of our civilization for nearly two thousand years and is still as far away as ever, it is time we asked ourselves why. Why have we evolved in so many other areas of human society, yet remained at almost a prehistoric stage in our dealing with conflict? We have always beaten each other with clubs, and the only difference is that today we use legal or nuclear clubs, rather than wooden ones. I find it difficult to accept that as a definition of progress. We face a genuine crisis of science; analyzing how we got here may point a way toward safety.

We have done a superb, an awesome, job of applying science to the arts of destruction. Our new weapons systems are magnificent, superlative scientific achievements. But what have we done to apply the very real accomplishments of our social and behavioral scientists to the art of survival to teach us to live together on this shrinking globe in peace? The answer, unfortunately, is that we have accomplished almost nothing, at least until the last decade or two, and too little by far even now. General Omar Bradley spelled it out in Boston in 1948, when he told us:

We have grasped the mystery of the atom and rejected the
Sermon on the Mount. Ours is a world of nuclear giants and ethical
infants. We know more about war than we know about peace—
more about killing that we know about living.

It is hard to imagine a more terrible indictment of any "civilized"
society: "We know more about killing then we know about living!"

Upon analysis, the explanation of this apparent anomaly becomes
obvious and simple: *You get what you pay for.* And since General
Bradley made that statement, we have invested over three trillion dollars
($3,000,000,000,000) in a search for security through military arms,
while spending almost nothing to develop a science of peace. On any
morning in America alone, some two hundred thousand scientists will
go to work to apply scientific findings to the development and improvement of our war potential, and fewer than two hundred scientists will
report to work on funded projects to develop our capability to wage and
maintain peace. We like to think we are a peaceful people, but if the
scripture is correct in saying that where a man's treasure is, there will his
heart be also, I think we can excuse certain foreigners their doubts about
America's dedication to peace.

If ever in world history there was a need for new ideas, new
institutions, new breakthroughs in the field of peacekeeping, and new
systems of conflict management, surely, this is the time. Yet the last
great institution we and other nations created to contribute to world
peace was the United Nations. It is remarkable that after four decades the
United Nations still does not have an Office of Mediation, staffed by the
world's most skilled mediators. If there comes an urgent need for skilled
mediation at the highest, most critical level of international relations, the
task can only be undertaken ad hoc.

The same is true for the United States in international affairs. An
example of the dangers of this negligent approach was described in a
brilliant but stinging analysis by Roger Fisher in the *Boston Herald
American* of Secretary Haig's handling of the U.S. attempt to mediate
the Falklands crisis. Listing mistake after mistake in both concept and
execution, Professor Fisher concludes: "It is truly scandalous that there
was no one on the Secretary's staff sufficiently skilled in the theory and
practice of mediation to have made sure the United States avoided these
mistakes. To avoid such mistakes in the future, the government needs
far better negotiating skills among our mid-career and top level people."
Professor Fisher's point is valid, but perhaps equally important is the

fact that such an obviously partisan party as the United States never should have gotten involved — and probably never would have if the United Nations had been equipped with an effective Office of Mediation to handle just such emergencies.

My hypothesis is this: We have allowed a terrible gap to develop between the application of science to war and its application to the cause of peace. This has occurred largely because we have created the institutions to apply the systems of war and allowed them to use unlimited amounts of money. Like springs at the top of a hill, our institutions of war have gushed forth resources that have cut deep channels in our society, channels capable of handling almost unlimited resources. At the same time, we have had no equivalent institutional springs to create channels for resources in the *affirmative* search for peace, so more and more of our resources are flowing into the channels of violent conflict management and almost none into channels of nonviolence.

The solution is apparent in the analysis. We can close that terrible gap by creating institutions to direct resources into channels of peace research and education. It is a truism that humankind creates its institutions and those institutions shape its society, and go on shaping it long after the creators have passed from the scene. The need now is for institutions whose goal is peace; if a national peace academy can be kept true to that goal, it may well live up to its potential as one of the principal factors in moving the whole future toward the survival of humanity. But it should be realized that achieving that result in the years ahead will be a difficult test of intelligent leadership, for the forces seeking selfish short-term gain at the expense of the integrity of the peace academy will by many and varied, subtle and extremely powerful. It is with such erosion in mind that the academy was designed to have independence, not to be involved in the day-to-day policy decisions of government, and not to intervene in ongoing disputes.

## Needed: A New Science of Peacemaking

If society does not learn to handle conflict far better than the human race has handled conflict in the past, then our civilization probably will not survive. In conflict resolution terms, peace is not defined as the absence of conflict, but rather as the nonviolent management of conflict. While the problem can be stated with easy facility, its solution is incredibly difficult, for it will involve a fundamental shift in our entire approach to conflict, and that approach has been bred in our bones over a period of many millennia—in fact, from long before the beginning of human history.

When we analyze the problem, we become aware that what is involved in such a fundamental shift is a change from adversarial approaches to conciliatory approaches to conflict: from win/lose solutions to win/win solutions, from confrontation in every conflict to joint problem-solving, and, in a most fundamental sense, from a society bent on "winning" to a society determined to survive in the thermonuclear age on a limited planet.

There is no space here for extended discussion or analysis, but it is a fact based on innumerable examples that often the solution of a conflict may be well on the way to attainment when attitudes shift from the adversarial to the cooperative. To state the problem symbolically, if A and B are arguing over the division of 100 marbles using a confrontational approach, it is perfectly apparent that if A gets 55, B can only have 45. But if they shift to a win/win problem-solving approach, they will often find that this will so broaden the scope of their investigations that instead of 100 marbles they may have 185 marbles to divide up and both parties can obtain almost everything they were seeking.

We know a good bit about specific types and techniques of conflict management, such as mediation, arbitration, negotiation, and conciliation—perhaps 10 percent of what we need to know—but without a national commitment to devote far greater resources to the conflict resolution field than it has ever enjoyed, it will remain overshadowed by responses based on violence. We know also that unresolved conflict in any society feeds upon itself and grows stronger. There is a closed circle of conflict: Conflict unresolved and unmanaged escalates to violence; violence fosters or creates unhappiness and insecurity, which in turn generates more conflict; and the circle repeats itself in a rising spiral of unmanaged and soon unmanageable violence. When that link in the circle between conflict and violence is broken before it escalates to violence, then it may be possible to reverse the spiral into a downward course.

From the very beginning of discussions of the peace academy concept, a basic belief has been that a national academy would add emphasis and recognition to academic work on peace issues. It would focus resources, both human and financial, to programs in the field. Benefits would flow into education and research, through interdisciplinary departments as well as the traditional discipline-based departments. As an emerging social science, the field has so much to gain from other disciplines, which are so strongly interrelated in conflict resolution — history, political science, sociology, anthropology, psychology, and a dozen other fields of social and behavioral science. We must expedite the incorporation of this immense, diverse, and growing fund of human knowledge into workable ways of managing conflicts among nations.

The possibility of such interdisciplinary cooperation was dramatized early in the history of the National Peace Academy Campaign by the question of whether schools of foreign service would adopt a positive or negative position with respect to the academy concept. The identical question had been faced earlier by the several dozen schools and faculties at various universities offering specialized courses of study in peace studies, peace research, and conflict resolution. After extensive consideration, this group of broad-gauged social scientists endorsed the concept wholeheartedly through their professional organization, the Consortium on Peace Research, Education and Development (COPRED). For the past several years, COPRED has strongly supported the development of a national peace academy in the firm belief that recognition by the U.S. Government of peacemaking and conflict resolution as a valid component of our national security would have a major effect in increasing the credibility, authority, and respectability of the entire enterprise. Such a development could stimulate and bring into wide acceptance the programs in this field and allocations of resources that have been tucked away in hidden corners in the budgets or space assignments of departments of sociology, anthropology, and psychology. As one long-harassed teacher in the field commented, "It's time for conflict resolution and peace research to come out of the closet."

Peace academy proponents have always assumed that a national peace academy would complement rather than compete with existing educational institutions. It was this belief that led the supporters of the academy to agree that a degree-granting capability in the academy would be unnecessary at this time, after deans of foreign service schools expressed concern over what they saw as an invasion of their traditional turf and the possibility of competition from a degree-granting federal institution. As should be apparent by now, nothing of the sort is contemplated or expected to develop. It is hoped that the great expansion of knowledge and capability in the field of peacemaking and conflict resolution will substantially expand and enrich the curricula in those fields at all existing institutions as well as the resources available to them.

If we are to meet the challenge of improving our management of conflict on any rational scale, it is unacceptable to wait a quarter of a century for the field of conflict resolution or peace learning to mature into a complete and academically acknowledged social science. With the release of the nuclear genie, the rapid development of improved methods of peacemaking, peacekeeping, conflict management, and conflict resolution is terribly urgent. National security demands that there be new means to accelerate the development of peace learning immediately. We can no more afford to let our capabilities in this field grow unattended like Topsy than can a medical team faced with a deadly epidemic afford to delay the importation of appropriate drugs and vaccines. An immense amount of information and theory relevant to the management of peace is already available in almost every field of our behavioral and social sciences. But it is inchoate, unorganized, and thus only marginally useful.

There is debate over whether conflict management is an academic field. Professor James Laue of the University of Missouri-St. Louis, who was vice chairman of the national peace academy commission, states that it is not accurate at the present time to refer to conflict resolution as a valid social science. Too much of the necessary framework, structure, and information is not yet compiled or correlated. Professor J. David Singer of the University of Michigan reports that the data base for conflict resolution as an emerging social science is still seriously inadequate. Nevertheless, Professor Kenneth Boulding of the University of Denver at Boulder, one of the leading theoreticians in this field, has written recently that the field of conflict management is recognized as an emerging discipline that requires rapid development if it is to be adequate and timely to the human predicament. There is agreement that a great deal of good and valid information and research relevant to the field of peace learning is available, but to date the material is scattered and unstructured.

It is to be hoped that the peace academy will establish the much needed institutional memory on conflict resolution and peacemaking. We desperately need to compile and correlate past instances and techniques of effective peacemaking and to distribute such information as widely as possible through our educational and library systems. An academy would provide a research base for the development of conflict resolution into a valid social science and, in the interplay of research, education and training, and information services, it would expedite that process. By aggregating practitioners and theoreticians of the field in a fairly tight community, it would provide the critical mass to accelerate the development of this entire area of human knowledge into an accepted social science.

It is hard to overstate the potential benefit from the application of conciliatory win/win attitudes in place of the confrontational win/lose approaches currently in vogue in international circles. Name-calling and vilification of other nations and national leaders—which has sometimes characterized public expressions of national leaders and political figures—is hardly conducive to meeting at, much less working at, the negotiation table.

There is a circle of conflict that can increase tension and conflict levels until they result in violence. The process seems to be especially applicable in international relations and arises when there exists a dispute that is unresolved and poorly managed: a festering sore between the parties. When new conflicts are added in the normal course of events and they too remain unresolved, the tension level rises until it finally breaks out in violence. This violence in turn adds tension, insecurity, and misery; it contributes to the evolution of more new conflict, and what was a circle becomes a rising spiral of conflict and tension. If, on the other hand, the initial conflict or conflicts are resolved or managed peacefully, the immediate effect is a lowering of tension in the overall society and a decrease in the conflict levels between the parties. The circle turns into a downward spiral leading to decreased levels of conflict and tension as well as a structure for building permanent peace.

Most violent conflicts do not simply erupt from the conscious actions of national leaders. They follow rising levels of conflict and tension between nations. Too often escalation occurs without real attention being paid. If we developed a "tension criterion" to evaluate the actions and statements of national leaders, we might have a handy tool to prod those with most responsibility to step back and see where they are taking us. In a nuclear world, the tension criterion would label as unhelpful any statement or action by a national leader that tended to increase the level of international tension. Conversely, actions that tended to lower the levels of international tensions could be evaluated as beneficial to the public interest. If public opinion were to hold all the national and international leaders accountable by such a standard of international action and reaction, more progress toward a stable world might result.

Conflict resolution is normally described as comprising mediation, negotiation, arbitration, conciliation, fact-finding, and other less for- malized problem-solving techniques. With the improved capability in the theory and practice of conflict management which can be expected to develop from peace academy training and research, it is reasonable to expect substantially improved techniques of negotiation to be available for the training of those professional diplomats in our foreign service who are most responsible for our international well-being.

It was Richard Pipes, professor of history at Harvard University and a Russian history and Soviet foreign policy specialist, who testified in June 1980 at the Boston hearings of the national peace academy commission that we need to devote far more attention to improving the teaching of our negotiating techniques. He stated this most emphatically in reference to representatives capable of effective negotiation with the Soviet Union. Professor Pipes observed that the United States sometimes sends out people with negligible experience or training to handle very difficult negotiations with the Soviet Union and other countries. The burden of his testimony was that we need to do a far better job of training our diplomats in the art of negotiation if we expect to come out of negotiations with a reasonably acceptable solution. The Soviet Union, he reminded the commission, sends only highly trained and experienced experts to participate in such deliberations.

Professor Pipes recommended that a two-year training course in negotiation be established in Washington for diplomats. The training and the development of negotiating theory and techniques that should emerge from a national peace academy will be an important gain for the State Department whether or not a two-year program is in order. Some progress is evident at the department's Foreign Service Institute (FSI), where short courses in negotiation have been established in recent years, and at the Center for International Affairs, recently established within FSI. It is to be hoped that in time all national leaders and international diplomats will have received training in conflict resolution theory and techniques through the national peace academy, whether this training takes place at the academy itself or in courses, perhaps supported by academy funding, at the many institutions involved in training such national leaders. The long-term impact on the conduct of international relations and the prospects for international peace should be highly beneficial.

A basic concept taught to all U.S. military forces is that the use of violent armed force should be a last resort in any conflict. Unfortunately, this directive is not accompanied by training in conflict resolution techniques that could equip these officers to abide by this rule. Roger Fisher has proposed that this problem be eased by providing each class at the military, naval, and air force academies with training courses in negotiation, mediation, and dispute resolution during their final year of study. In a February 8th, 1983 letter to me, he wrote that "the relationship between military force and effectively influencing the decisions of government is something that every military officer should understand — in depth — before receiving his or her commission." And he suggested: "Conflict resolution skills should also be taught extensively at the Naval War College, the War College, the Air War College, the Foreign Service Institute, and the National Defense University. To the best of my knowledge, existing courses in this subject are wholly inadequate. It should be the responsibility of some government institution to improve training in conflict resolution skills at all these institutions." When the superintendents of the various academies met individually with members of the national peace academy commission during 1980, however, they said then that their curricula were loaded to the bursting point and there was no space for the inclusion of courses on conflict resolution knowledge and skills. It was on this basis that General Andrew Goodpaster at West Point urged that the national peace academy be established at a graduate level with courses available to military and naval officers as well as other government officials.

## Domestic Levels of Tension and Conflict

With better capacity in conflict management as the result of peace academy success, one beneficial effect will be the lowering of levels of tension and conflict on the domestic scene, on the community and national levels, and perhaps, the interpersonal level as well. Conflict management theory and techniques are broadly applicable, albeit with variations, at all levels of society from the interpersonal to the international, and improved capability at one level is likely to improve capability at the other levels.

It is of course true that even the most cursory surveillance of our society will reveal innumerable institutional and procedural devices which, under normal circumstances, provide effective resolutions of conflict. The biennial election process and especially the quadrennial president election campaign highlight substantial differences over policy and substance, let alone power politics, which in many countries have literally torn apart the social fabric. In America, the Democratic and Republican parties fight their continuing battle by methods which almost never lead to any substantial level of violence and which traditionally permit a rapid reconciliation of individuals and interests once the campaign has passed. Similarly, the members of almost any well-regulated family, in the absence of severe psychological problems, normally handle the many conflicts that arise in their relationships with a minimum of turmoil and violence, however impassioned the feelings of the moment when the issues are under discussion.

If the ability to manage conflict constructively and nonviolently is the most important challenge facing humanity in the closing years of the twentieth century, then we must consider whether a national peace academy responds to that challenge. My seven years of total immersion in this question has led me to conclude that a national peace academy is the best available response to the overall challenge. By itself it is not adequate to meet the immense needs the challenge implies, yet it is the best proposal developed to date to respond to the most critical and complex problem of our era. Because the academy is only a part, but a crucial part, of the response, there are two additional concerns that must also be kept in mind. First is that we cannot rationally expect a sudden overnight metamorphosis in our dealing with conflicts. Second is that, if the task is to be accomplished soon enough to make a difference in this generation's handling of the problem, it must be undertaken on a society-wide basis reaching from the training of kindergarten pupils to the management of international relations.

A start has been made in applying conflict resolution principles and techniques at many points in our society where they are most needed. The Society of Friends teaches win/win conflict management to primary school pupils. Marriage counseling and divorce mediation are rapidly expanding professions meeting an intense need. There are some two hundred community dispute resolution centers (a 50 percent increase from two years ago) across the nation that provide improved handling of thousands of interpersonal and community conflicts. The American Arbitration Association manages tens of thousands of business disputes each year without resort to courtroom battles. With leadership from Chief Justice Warren E. Burger, lawyers in many jurisdictions are looking to mediation as one tool to relieve court docket overloading. The Federal Mediation and Conciliation Service assists resolution of disputes ranging to the most serious labor-management conflicts. The Justice Department's Community Relations Service has kept channels open from Wounded Knee to Wilmington. And the Camp David accords stand as a shining, albeit too little understood, example of what can be achieved by the purposeful application of conflict resolution methods to a major international dispute.

It can even be argued that the development of arbitration, negotiation, and mediation techniques for labor-management relations in this country has been a principal factor in rendering much of Marxist doctrine obsolete in America. While Marx and Engels thought they saw the future in revolution spurred by the irreconcilable conflicts between labor and capital, what they did not foresee was the development of conflict resolution systems and techniques within the framework of a democratic society. With nonviolent methodologies for handling conflicts and avoiding ultimate confrontations between the two forces, there has simply not been a final violent revolution. How those two gentlemen would have reacted to labor union officials sitting on the boards of directors of major American corporations one can only imagine.

An improved level of domestic stability may very well feed into the international level, augmenting its stability. Professor John Burton, visiting professor at the University of Maryland and former Director of the Centre for the Analysis of Conflict in Great Britain, has hypothesized that there are few if any international conflicts that do not have their bases in the domestic conflicts within the states involved. If Burton is correct, then improved capability of conflict management on the domestic scene may very well provide a major benefit by improving the probability of maintaining long-term stability on the international scene.

## Peace Academies in Other Nations

As an institutional commitment by the United States government to a long-term program of research, education and training, and public information in the ways and means of peace, a national peace academy will demonstrate a determination by the American people to devote at least a part of our national treasure to improve the ancient art of peacemaking and to develop the emerging social science of conflict resolution. Time and again over the past eight years, foreign visitors to the National Peace Academy Campaign office have expressed amazement and delight at the possibility that America will establish the United States Academy of Peace. The responses of Latin American visitors, who mix delight and total incredulity, have been especially interesting to behold. They indicate that south of the border it would be hard to convince acute observers that the Colossus of the North could be serious about establishing a national peace academy, but that if it actually happened it would do more than anything to shift the image they hold of the United States.

The other response by foreign visitors to the peace academy proposal is the likely emulation of the concept by their countries. Over the years, official and unofficial foreign delegations have visited the campaign office to discuss the concept of a national peace academy and the process by which that concept had advanced in the United States, in government circles and the public view. One such visit occurred in early 1984, when the Canadian Embassy arranged an appointment for Mr. Jeffrey Pearson, son of Canada's justly famous Prime Minister Lester Pearson. On April 2, 1984, the Canadian government announced its intention to establish the Canadian Institute of International Peace as the final achievement of Prime Minister Trudeau's administration. This institute will provide many of the functions planned for a United States academy of peace. It is probable that over the years ahead both the image-making and emulation effects of the peace academy will grow progressively, and this is rendered almost certain if participation is structured to include people from foreign countries.

The important factor here is that the substance of the peace academy in the years ahead will give proof to the initial promise and will turn many of the initial doubters into believers. It will also provide an immensely impressive response to the challenge issued by the Honorable Harold H. Saunders, former Assistant Secretary of State for Near Eastern and South Asian Affairs. In a commencement address, entitled "Peacemaking Is Power," delivered in Florida in 1981, and reprinted in the *Congressional Record* of September 29, 1981, Mr. Saunders stated:

> The United States in the last two decades of this century needs to give at least as much attention to strengthening its peacemaking arsenal as it needs to give to assuring its military power. We need to agree among ourselves that peacemaking, too, is a form of power. To have power is to have a dominant role in affecting the course of events. When the United States is aggressively pursuing peace in the world, our own position in the world is strengthened. The alternative is a steady decline in our ability to influence the course of history. I believe the position of the United States as a world power in the 1990s and beyond will be determined to a significant extent by whether we play an aggressive, imaginative and leading role in helping to bring real peace to the world.

## Cost Effectiveness

In 1984, the United States was committed in a five-year program to spend $1.6 trillion on its military budget. For a population of 235 million people, this computes to approximately $1,360 per year for each man, woman, and child in the United States. These figures help give perspective to the expenditures required to provide for an effective national peace academy in the years ahead for this country.

In the middle of the campaign to pass peace academy bills through the Congress, a number of opponents protested that the peace academy would be too expensive, an unnecessary burden on the federal budget and the American people. The Senate bill proposed an authorization of $23.5 million for the first two years of operation of the peace academy. Using the same population figures as above, the cost for the peace academy is exactly five cents per year for every inhabitant of the United States. It is perhaps understandable that supporters of the peace academy felt it was not unreasonable, in light of the $1,360 each is spending for military programs, to invest five cents a year to improve the knowledge and capability of the field of peacemaking.

War in the modern era is incredibly expensive. If a national peace academy can be effective in reducing the possibility of war so that some of the preparations for it become unnecessary or less costly, it is predictable that the investment in the academy itself will prove to be the best investment ever made by the American people. The same could be said if the improved negotiation capabilities combined with lowered international tension allow agreement on effective arms control. The financial savings from reduced military expenditures could amount to hundreds of billions of dollars, all in return for an investment of twenty or thirty million dollars a year in an efficient national peace academy. This would assuredly give the peace academy the highest benefit-cost ratio of any government project in the history of the world.

In testimony before the Subcommittee on Education, Arts, and Humanities of the Senate Committee on Labor and Human Resources, Senator Roger Jepsen of Iowa stated on March, 16 1983: "To enthusiastically support the United States Academy of Peace, one need not believe either that one can negotiate away all wars or that the training given at the United States Academy of Peace will enable its graduates to prevent every war that is, in theory, preventable. Rather, if this added focus on the peace process—if this added training for our future negotiators—prevents even one small war that otherwise would have started, the Peace Academy will rank among the best expenditures ever made by government."

In its essence, Senator Jepsen stated the financial argument for the peace academy, and it would appear to be irrefutable. An example of a "small war" was the Falklands dispute between Great Britain and Argentina. In the relatively few weeks of that conflict, it cost the two parties involved hundreds of lives and more that six billion dollars, enough to finance the peace academy generously for two hundred years. Since many students of this conflict believe that an effective mediation or negotiation might very well have concluded the conflict within the first two weeks, while the British fleet was still steaming south from England to the South Atlantic, it stands as a prime example of what might have been avoided but was not because there was an absence of effective conflict resolution capability and training by the parties involved in the conflict and in the attempts to terminate it.

## Conclusion

Step back a minute and examine in general terms the response we propose to the challenge we face:

• We are a race of beings literally on the verge of catastrophic planetary self-destruction due to our demonstrated incapacity to deal effectively with conflict.
• We have an emerging field of knowledge which can prevent that disaster if it can be developed and applied soon and fast enough.
• We have demonstrated the ability to meet challenges of scientific development by the creation of specialized national institutions. When faced with the need for a nuclear bomb, we developed the Manhattan Project; when challenged to reach out from our own planet and begin the conquest of space, we established the National Aeronautical and Space Administration.
• We possess a widespread educational system that can be used to disseminate rapidly the results of research, and a government that is capable of mobilizing its resources to use such research.

In such a factual situation, what course of action would any rational social being recommend? One obvious answer is the establishment of a national center to facilitate and expedite research, development, and education in the field of conflict resolution and peace learning.

The use of applied physical science has brought us to the brink of annihilation because of the framework of thought—the adversarial win/lose paradigm—we still apply to conflict at every level of society. But suddenly knowledge and wisdom from our social and behavioral sciences are coalescing into a whole new field of nonviolent conflict management, of "conflict resolution," and there is new hope.

Conflict at any level need *not* be a zero-sum game; win/win solutions *are* possible; cooperative paradigms *can* be developed; conflict need almost *never* escalate to violence; and we *can* train peacemakers, conflict managers, crisis intervenors, mediators, arbitrators, and negotiators to give us and our grandchildren some hope of survival and a decent life on Earth. That is the challenge, and the urgently needed response is a national center for research, training and education, and public information on the ways and means of peace: the national academy of peace.

# PART THREE

Report of the Matsunaga
Commission on The
National Academy of Peace

# Creating a New Institution

## FRANK K. KELLY

The work of the U. S. Commission on Proposals for the National Academy of Peace and Conflict Resolution gave the movement to establish a national peace academy new energy, visibility, and confidence. Its balanced final report, *To Establish the United States Academy of Peace,* is now the basic statement for building a national peace institute. The commission's primary purpose was to explain why and how to create a national peace academy; its analysis remains durable and important to thinking about peace. *The Hundred Percent Challenge* concerns the idea's future. Our excerpts from the commission's report cover the academy's design; research perspectives; and negotiation, mediation, and conciliation as seen through the eyes of a diplomat seized by Colombian guerillas, an advisor on the Camp David accords, and a minister active in the Iran hostage crisis.

When you enter the Thomas Jefferson Memorial in the District of Columbia, you read his words:

> I am not an advocate for frequent changes in laws and constitutions, but laws and institutions must go hand in hand with the progress of the human mind. As that becomes more developed, more enlightened, as new discoveries are made, new truths discovered and manners and opinions change, with the change of circumstances, institutions must advance also to keep pace with the times. We might as well require a man to wear still the coat which fitted him when a boy as civilized society to remain ever under the regimen of their barbarous ancestors.

Jefferson's experience taught him that one of the hardest tasks in American life, and in the life of any nation regardless of its age, is the changing of old institutions and the creation of new ones. The ringing statements of the Declaration of Independence — that "all men are created equal," that they are "endowed by their Creator with certain unalienable rights," and that governments are instituted "to secure these rights'' — were not accepted by many Americans as self-evident. Jefferson, Washington, Mason, Madison, Hamilton, and all the other founding citizens did more than debate these truths; they set out to make them part of America's daily life.

Having experienced governance under the Articles of Confederation, Americans decided to change institutions. A stronger national government was needed, so the new Constitution did not refer to a union among the states but instead declared, ''We, the people of the United States, in order to form a more perfect union, establish justice, promote the general welfare, and secure the blessings of liberty to ourselves and our posterity, do ordain and establish this Constitution.'' The Constitution was an instrument for peaceful resolution of conflict— between the executive, the legislative, and the judicial branches of government; between the states and the federal authority; between the economic interests of the country's various regions; and between government and the individual as reflected in the Bill of Rights.

Dr. Benjamin Rush, a signer of the Declaration of Independence, and Benjamin Banneker, a mathematician, architect and designer, publisher, and black American, tried to convince Congress to add a provision on peace. In an article published in *Banneker's Almanack and Ephemeris for the Year of our Lord 1793*, they called for the Constitution to include a ''peace office'' for the United States on a government level equal to that of the War Department. Although not espousing the anti-federalist barrage of criticism of the Constitution, they wrote that ''it is much to be lamented that no person has taken notice of its total silence upon the subject of an office of the utmost importance to the welfare of the United States, that is, an office for promoting and preserving perpetual peace in our country.''

In the United States, perpetual peace was not preserved. Jefferson and others had known that the poison of slavery could tear the republic apart, but they were unable to repudiate that wretched institution of ''barbarous ancestors.'' Nor could they see how to incorporate secession into their ''more perfect union.'' The bloody Civil War—viewed by the South as the War Between the States—changed the Constitution and abolished slavery, but left deep wounds still felt today. Nineteenth-century Europe, too, was violent and events seemed to prove the maxim of Charles Darwin—''the struggle for existence goes on everywhere''—and the incompatibility of biology and religion.

Yet a poet from that time spoke to men who made decisions about violence, death, justice, and peace. In ''The Golden Year,'' Alfred Lord Tennyson wrote, ''Ah! when shall all men's good/Be each man's rule, and universal peace/Lie like a shaft across the land?'' And in 1842, his poem ''Locksley Hall'' foresaw changes in technology and institutions:

> For I dipt into the future, far as human eye could see,
> Saw the Vision of the World, and all the wonder that could be;
> Saw the heavens fill with commerce, argosies of magic sails,
> Pilots of the purple twilight, dropping down with costly bales;
> Heard the heavens filled with shouting, and there rained a ghastly dew
> From the nations' airy navies grappling in the central blue...
> Till the war-drum trobb'd no longer, and the battle-flags were furl'd
> In the Parliament of Man, the Federation of the World....

These hopes were shared by President Woodrow Wilson, whose presentation to Congress in 1918 of a fourteen-point program for durable peace included a new institution that became the League of Nations. Despite the League's collapse (heralded by its impotence in the face of Haile Selassie's 1935 plea for intervention to stop the Italian war on Ethiopia), Wilson's idealism had a strong impact on the people of later generations, including Presidents Franklin Roosevelt, Harry Truman, and Dwight Eisenhower. Truman, in fact, carried a copy of ''Locksley Hall'' in his wallet for many years, and he told a biographer: ''Now Tennyson knew there were going to be airplanes, and he knew there was going to be bombing and all of it. And some day there would be a parliament of man. It stands to reason, and that's what I was doing when I went ahead with setting up the United Nations....The UN is the first step.''

Yet for two centuries, the Rush-Banneker idea of a national institution in the United States devoted to improving the ways of peace had proponents but little success. In his 1969 booklet ''Why a Department of Peace,'' Dr. Frederick L. Schuman reported that ''the proposal was later echoed during the course of the 19th century by various publicists and legislators, [but] their efforts were without result.'' One could date the modern era back fifty years to 1935 when Senator Matthew Neeley of West Virginia introduced a Department of Peace bill similar to the Rush-Banneker peace office and Congressman Fred Bierman of Iowa proposed a ''Bureau of Peace and Friendship'' for the Department of Labor to do sociological research on peace and war. Between 1935 and 1976, more than 140 bills were introduced to establish a department of peace, a national peace agency, or standing committees of Congress.

World War II prompted a number of Cabinet-level proposals. In 1945, Senator Alexander Wiley of Wisconsin proposed creating a small high-level Department of Peace with the Secretary's responsibilities to include the position of United States Representative on the United Nations Security Council. That year, too, Congressman Jennings Randolph of West Virginia, who later became a senator and continued his constant and steady advocacy of a national peace institution, introduced a Department of Peace bill that for the first time incorporated the proposition that the international exchange of people and ideas would be an effective way to promote peace. In 1945 and 1947, Congressman Everett Dirksen of Illinois, also later a senator, introduced bills for a peace division in the State Department, and in 1947 Senator Karl Mundt of South Dakota urged a Department of Peace.

In 1955, Senator Mike Mansfield of Montana and Congressman Charles Bennett of Florida proposed the creation of a Joint Congressional Committee for a Just and Lasting Peace, and Congressman Harold C. Ostertag of New York introduced a bill that included the concept of a national peace college. One of the most significant accomplishments occurred in 1961, when President John Kennedy signed the legislation promoted by Senator Hubert Humphrey of Minnesota to establish the Arms Control and Disarmament Agency, a semi-independent agency located in the Department of State that would formulate policy, conduct negotiations, disseminate public information, and undertake research on the control and reduction of armaments.

The idea of private citizens also promoting such a national effort began with the Rush-Banneker proposal. In our time, Dan and Rose Lucey of Oakland, California persuaded members of the Christian Family Movement in the 1960s to support the formation of a peace academy, and in 1969 Thomas C. Westropp took out a full page newspaper ad in Cleveland to outline reasons for a national peace academy. In 1976, Senators Vance Hartke of Indiana and Mark Hatfield of Oregon introduced Senate Bill Number 1976, to create the George Washington Peace Academy. When the Hartke-Hatfield bill was introduced, a parallel effort to support that action developed among private citizens. Dr. Bryant Wedge, a Washington psychiatrist and teacher concerned with mediation and conciliation, Dr. Jerome Frank, a Johns Hopkins University psychiatrist, and Nachman Gerber, a Baltimore businessman, formed the Ad Hoc Committee for a National Peace Academy. This committee launched the National Peace Academy Campaign (NPAC).

NPAC set out to examine the scope of public support for a national peace academy, and it was at that point that I became involved with the movement. Dr. Wedge persuaded Henry Burnett (a direct-mail specialist) and me to develop materials about the peace academy idea for mailings to several million citizens. Burnett's work led to a special project of the Anacapa Fund of Santa Barbara. The response showed Americans from coast to coast were ready to consider such a new institution to "keep pace with the times." NPAC was poised to begin its drive that ultimately would expand membership from the initial three thousand supporters to an active constituency of more than forty thousand people. The combination of S.1976 and the establishment of NPAC marked the beginning of today's organized movement to establish a national peace academy.

Senator Claiborne Pell of Rhode Island chaired hearings on S.1976 by the Senate Labor and Public Welfare Subcommittee on Education, but the committee took no action. Senator Pell and others concluded that, although public interest was strong, the peace academy idea needed further development. The route would be a federal study commission. In 1977, Andrew Young of Georgia and Helen Meyner of New Jersey introduced a national peace academy commission bill in the House, and in the Senate the measure was introduced by Mark Hatfield, Jennings Randolph, and Spark Matsunaga of Hawaii. Hearings were held, but progress again stalled as the House measure failed in 1978. The Senate, however, amended the House-passed Elementary and Secondary Education Bill with a provision to establish the Commission on Proposals for the National Academy of Peace and Conflict Resolution. The amendment was accepted in conference, the bill became law when signed by President Jimmy Carter in November 1978, and appropriations became available in 1979. In December 1979, commission appointments were completed: President Carter appointed Arthur Barnes, Elise Boulding, and James Laue; House Speaker Thomas P. O'Neill, Jr. named William Lincoln and Congressmen John Ashbrook of Ohio and Dan Glickman of Kansas; and Senate President Pro Tempore Warren Magnuson chose former Congressman John Dellenback, John Dunfey, and Senator Spark Matsunaga, who was elected commission chairman.

The law directed the commission to study the theories and techniques of peace and to examine the existing institutions involved in resolving conflicts among nations. From these analyses, it was to determine whether there should be a national academy of peace and, if so, its size, cost, location, and relationship to institutions of higher education and the federal government. These evaluations were to be transmitted in "a final report to the President and each House of the Congress."

The commission worked for a year-and-a-half. In addition to its study of theories and techniques and its examination of institutional strengths and limitations, it held more that 50 private meetings with educators, representatives of religious, ethnic, scientific, and academic groups, and practitioners in the arts of conflict resolution. Commissioners undertook a number of special visits, including ones to military service academies and the United States Mission to the United Nations. The commission conducted "public seminars" (expanded versions of public hearings) at sites around the nation: Boulder, Portland, St. Louis, Columbus, Los Angeles, Boston, Dallas, New York, Atlanta, Tallahassee, Honolulu, and Washington, D.C. Approximately ten thousand people were specifically invited to participate in these two-day meetings. The public seminars produced over six thousand transcript pages. Questionnaires were sent to two hundred people with experience in community, national, and international mediation, and to two hundred and fifty students enrolled in peace and conflict study programs as well as their faculties. The commission also received thousands of unsolicited communications. Commissioners held two half-day and six day-long public meetings to organize their work, determine findings, debate conclusions, and develop recommendations.

The commission's principal recommendation was that "the President and the Congress of the United States of America should establish the United States Academy of Peace." In its report, the commission emphasized the appropriateness of the federal government creating this new institution, especially in such precarious times of frequent breach of peace among nations and threats to global survival. The commission pointed to the enormous resources of the United States, drawing particular attention to our democratic history and to the practical lesson from our heritage that the ways communities and nations resolve their disputes must be incorporated into any examination of peace among nations. The commission emphasized that the academy should serve people outside of government as well as those in government, that it should be structured so its independence is protected from undue influence, whether private or government, and that it should not participate in government policymaking or intervene in ongoing disputes. Finally, as part of its report, the commission included draft legislation that incorporated its recommendations. This proposal became the measure to establish the United States Academy of Peace that was introduced in the Senate by Senators Hatfield, Randolph, and Matsunaga, and in the House by Congressman Dan Glickman.

Among the many leaders who supported the academy idea, General Andrew Goodpaster—former Superintendant of West Point and former Supreme Allied Commander of the NATO forces in Europe—offered some of the strongest reasons for considering it a necessary institution.

It has long seemed to me that there is a place as well as a need for a carefully designed institution, additional to all that now exists, devoted to the serious study, both theoretical and practical, of peace and conflict resolution. From many years of service in peace and war, it is my conviction that a clearer, deeper understanding of the issues that bear on peace and the processes that support it can be of great and lasting value.

There is widespread failure, I believe, both in the government and in the population at large—including, in particular, its opinion-leading elements—to understand how peace relates to the other fundamental values, needs and aspirations of our people, and how peace together with these other values can best be safe-guarded and sustained.

# Excerpts from the Report: "To Establish The U.S. Academy of Peace"

## Preface

This report contains good news. For over two hundred years, American leaders have urged creation of a federal institution devoted to the peace education and peacemaking capacities of the American people and their government. That major step is poised to be taken now with establishment of the United States Academy of Peace. This report is about that idea and that new institution. I commend it to your attention.

The United States has no interest greater than international peace. In this century, Americans have fought and died in two world wars, in Korea and Vietnam, and in other smaller and briefer conflicts. We are experienced in the bitterness of war and its impact on our economy, politics, and ability to concentrate on serious national problems. We know the drain of preparation for war, and we know that uncertain world conditions compel such expenditures. We know that, whether from cries for justice and freedom or from natural and manmade disruptions to daily toil, international conflicts inevitably affect us. And we know that when there is war or the likelihood of war, there is no real national security; that was true before the nuclear age and is ever more true today.

That political and economic conflicts mark our days is not a cause for despair; it is, however, a cause for concern. We must ask whether or not we have done what we can with ourselves and our resources to develop ways to manage international conflict to reduce the incidence of violence, and to promote a more peaceful world. In addressing the 1963 graduates of The American University, President John F. Kennedy spoke of peace as "the necessary rational end of rational men" and observed that "the pursuit of peace is not as dramatic as the pursuit of war...but we have no more urgent task.'' He was not referring to a vague concept of universal goodwill, but to a practical and attainable peace "based not on a sudden revolution in human nature, but on a gradual evolution in human institutions.'' Because the challenge is clear and the need immediate, I am optimistic about Americans supporting the establishment of the United States Academy of Peace.

When Senators Mark Hatfield and Jennings Randolph and I sponsored legislation to create the Commission on Proposals for the National Academy of Peace and Conflict Resolution, we understood the skepticism about a federal peace institution and the need to examine the idea closely. We agreed that caution should accompany such an unprecedented move, and that a commission using academic scrutiny and political outreach and sensitivity could test and refine the proposal. The commission did precisely that. It has answered the questions in its mandate and shown the need and timeliness for the Congress and the president to establish a federal institution for international peace research, education and training, and information services.

In transmitting the commission's report to President Ronald Reagan, Senate President Pro Tempore Strom Thurmond, and Speaker of the House Thomas P. O'Neill, Jr., I urge their special attention to the opportunity presented in the United States Academy of Peace. The proposed academy will enhance the understanding of peace and peacemaking among people in government, private enterprise, and voluntary associations. The commission specifically recommends that the academy itself not engage in policymaking or dispute intervention. Members of Congress and the executive branch and the citizenry in general will recognize these limitations as important in maintaining the broadest range of inquiry and in situating the academy prominently in the eyes of the world as a major, nonadvocacy peace institution of this nation.

There is substantial debate today over the proper role of government. International peace clearly is a fundamental federal concern residing in Congress and in the Office of the President. Aspects of the quest for international peace are woven into the activities of virtually all federal departments and agencies as well as those of many state and local governments. It is equally true that issues of international peace concern all Americans and are pursued by many through international organizations, business, labor, religious groups, and educational and nonprofit institutions. Throughout this report, including the stories of Diego Asencio, Roger Fisher, and John Adams, the breadth of American peacemaking activities is made plain.

The commission concluded, and I fully concur, that there is a necessary and proper federal role in serving the nation through international peace research, education and training, and information services. These functions are complementary and best carried out in concert. Without the focus and stimulation that only the federal government can supply, it is unlikely that the promise from refinement and broad participation in peace knowledge and skill will be realized. Unless the federal government exercises its leadership in this area, peace will not flourish fully, despite its profound basis in our nation's heritage.

As rational Americans in pursuit of a rational end, we should bear in mind the teaching of the great Chinese philosopher Confucius: "There will be no peace until the individual citizen wants it, seeks it, and works for it." If peace is a risk, never won for sure but held for the day, then we must know its ways and means surely today and tomorrow. Establishment of the United States Academy of Peace will be a bold action toward the attainment of this greatest of our national goals.

SPARK MATSUNAGA
Chairman, Commission on Proposals for the
National Academy of Peace and Conflict Resolution
October 1981

## Peace and Conflict: Working Concepts

The Congress and the president set the background for the commission's inquiries by directing its attention to the national "goal of promoting peace" and to "conflict between nations ... [and] in the areas of international relations."

The commission uses "peace" forthrightly in its discussion and recommended academy title. The commission rejects emphatically any insinuation that peace—any more than love, church, justice, family, or flag—is soft and naive. The commission believes timorous attitudes toward peace do not advance the national interest or reflect the American character. Peace is neither utopian nor a sign of weakness or cowardice. Peace is not to be measured simply by absence of tension or quietude of complaint. Peace is not only a desired state; it is a process that is vigorous and includes devotion to those life-affirming values that have made "American" a cherished concept. Peace requires knowledge, judgment, and skill no less complex than what is required for war.

The commission's chairman, United States Senator Spark Matsunaga of Hawaii, makes clear the attitude the commission brings to its work:

> There is no better cause than the cause of world peace. As a rational American, I believe that mankind can create institutional safeguards to prevent nuclear holocaust and I reject the idea that war is inevitable.

The commission believes that, for the nations of the world as for the United States, the abhorrence of war and the providence of international peace and its correlate, national security, depend on an international climate that fosters economic and cultural relations and such American concerns as justice and the development of political and economic systems that serve fundamental human needs. These needs include physical and spiritual sustenance, individual expression, and the free ability to choose and then be held accountable for one's choices.

The commission was charged with looking at problems of international conflict as well as peace. Like "peace," "conflict" has many connotations. The commission highlights three propositions about conflict.

• First, conflict is a normal part of life and is neither good nor bad; the critical question is how conflict can be met constructively in the advancement of peace.

• Second, much of the conflict we face can be managed and resolved with fairness and without violence, but right and wrong are valid and necessary judgments, and there rightfully remain values that admit no compromise; when conflicts over interests concern these values, the question is how to advance and hold true to that which is right while keeping respect and dignity for self and others and using minimal or no coercion or violence.

• Third, the conflict and peace focus of this commission is international, but definitive separation between intranational and international conflicts is not possible for two reasons: (1) internal situations affect a nation's external relations and intranational conflicts spill over borders; and (2) the way a country approaches and handles its internal disputes may bear upon its international behavior. These observations on intra- and international conflicts are true whether the state is Canada, Mexico, Argentina, Spain, Poland, Zimbabwe, Indonesia, Japan, the Soviet Union, or the United States.

To understand conflicts, Harvard law professor Roger Fisher advises that one must be aware that attitudes can obscure the true interests at stake. Defining sovereignty and security as conflicting interests in the Middle East permitted meaningful mediation and negotiation at Camp David. In a letter to the commission toward the close of its work, noted economist Kenneth Boulding reflected upon the basic procedural concepts behind skilled conflict management:

"Conflicts over interests" are situations in which some change makes at least one party better off and the other party worse off, each in their own estimation. If the change is "positive sum," it opens the possibility that both parties may be better off. If the change is "zero sum" or "negative sum," this perception is no longer available.

A "fight" is a situation in which each party to a perceived conflict over interests acts to reduce the welfare of the other. Fights almost always become negative sum and lead to a reduction of the welfare of both parties; the winner may lose less than the loser, but both parties would have been better off if the fight could have been avoided.

A major task of conflict analysis and management is to prevent conflicts from escalating into fights, which make everybody worse off. Institutions of conflict management appear very early in human history: law, diplomacy, arbitration, religious institutions, the family, and athletics. The functioning of these institutions has frequently given way to war, both civil and international, to duels, fistfights, blood feuds, and costly adversary legal battles. Nevertheless, the institutions have always been reestablished after each breakdown or, if they have not, a society has disintegrated and disappeared.

## A Range of Options

The American heritage teaches that one of our most important resources is a vast array of views and problem-solving strategies and skills. Innovative thinking about issues and frequent use of such techniques as negotiation and conciliation have always been characteristic of American democratic traditions and are becoming more and more crucial in international activities. It is the American ability to select from and exercise this range of options that has enabled America, in the words of the Constitution,

> ...to form a more perfect Union, establish Justice, insure domestic Tranquility, provide for the common Defense, promote the general Welfare, and secure the Blessings of Liberty to ourselves and our Posterity.

In fundamental terms, the United States's international policies reflect these purposes, too, and are equally dependent on the continuous presence of a range of options.

With conflict prevalent and debate pronounced over such questions as environmental protection and resource development, urban safety and renovation, and appropriate schooling for youth—which were among the issues addressed before the commission—no one would assert that the United States has devised and honed perfect solutions to its national and community problems. Nor with the delays in achieving enforceable arms limitation agreements or with the Soviet Union's invasion of Afghanistan and direct and indirect activity in Africa, could it be said the United States's international peacemaking policies and actions are invariably successful. At the same time, no one could rightly question the capacity of this nation throughout history to respond to challenges forcefully or through participatory, nonviolent methods.

The commission wants it clearly understood that its findings and recommendations do not contemplate a weakening of American military and diplomatic power. On the contrary, the United States Academy of Peace will, the commission is confident, be viewed as an asset to American military and diplomatic institutions and policies, even beyond their personnel participating in academy programs.

In today's world, it is necessary for the United States to have a well-defined, strong, and flexible military defense capacity. While a profile of this capability is outside the commission's mandate and competence, the commission believes that military capacities ought not to be considered independently from the nonmilitary in considerations of international peace and national security. Military peacemaking options, which themselves form a continuum of intervention strengths, encompass only a part of the nation's total range of options to prevent and respond to harmful international conflict. When the armed component is emphasized and other parts are relatively neglected, questions about the value of the traditional broad range of options tend to arise. If the range of international problem-solving skills is allowed to atrophy, undue pressures and expectations are placed upon military institutions. This damages rather than upgrades defense capabilities.

The commission believes that strategies, tactics, and techniques to meet conflicts of low or intermediate intensity are available for more frequent use. They can reduce tensions before fear, anxiety, and violence interrupt communication, threaten national pride, harden leadership positions, and mobilize military forces; they are critical to the termination of violent conflict. These capacities support and can be part of the careful exercise of military and diplomatic power. Before the commission in Boston, Professor Herbert Kelman testified:

> To establish and maintain peace under the conditions of the contemporary global system requires a variety of new approaches, both within and outside of the framework of traditional diplomacy. Moreover, it requires active attention, not only to the day-to-day issues of national and international politics, but also to the larger social and psychological processes within national and global societies on which the creation of a peaceful and just world order depends in the long run.

Kelman's "variety of new approaches" encompasses the concept of a continuum—a range of options — and is basic to the American experience of conflict resolution.

It is also basic that vacuums be filled. If negotiations are ineffective, or worse if negotiators are short of skill so their efforts are futile, then it is only logical that more unilateral actions will be taken, which ordinarily involve force, or that no response will be available. Also speaking in Boston, Professor Richard Pipes addressed the academy concept with some skepticism while noting American negotiation deficiencies:

> We only have to look on how the British solved the problem in Rhodesia-Zimbabwe. It was a brilliant example of diplomatic skills at the highest level. Here was a situation that to all appearances looked hopeless, and I must say that I expected general carnage to ensue. Yet because of the superb skill of these people, they managed to defuse it and to achieve an all-around peaceful resolution. Now, this is the skill of negotiators. I doubt if we could have done it, not because we lack the good will, but because we lack the skill.

If the United States lacked the mediation and conciliation skills exhibited by the British in Rhodesia-Zimbabwe, but were asked to assume such a responsibility, any failures ultimately would lie with policymakers who had caused an imbalance within the range of peacemaking options. When demands upon one part of the continuum—whether the armed services or the diplomatic corps— exceed realistic capacities, the bias lies not with military or diplomatic planners and decisionmakers, but with those who ill-served them by permitting an unhealthy tilt within the range of options. The commission believes such tendencies contradict the American peace heritage; there is nothing in the British experience that makes them indelibly more proficient than Americans in bringing about peaceful resolutions to difficult international conflicts. In short, the commission believes that maintainence of international peace and national security requires, in addition to military capacity, use of a range of effective options of a problem-solving nature that can leash international violence, manage conflict, and reduce tensions.

## Peace Principles

The resilience of this nation is founded more firmly in peace principles than ordinarily recognized. It is organic to American society that problems can be solved and life improved when there is a wide range of options that permits individual and group creativity. This attitude is deeply embedded in the American national experience. Unlike the European system of education, we are not required in youth to make lifelong career decisions through specialized vocational tracking; Americans from all walks of life enter higher education or training programs and undertake new career directions based on ability, opportunity, and drive without regard to age. American economic principles are reflected today in calls for reduced taxation and regulation and for greater individual and social responsibility, in the family farm and the mom-and-pop store as well as the activities of giant corporations. This tradition offers fluidity and change within processes of stability which Americans share in common.

It is not that the rules of any given time represent agreement by all; rather, rules emerge and change from the many varieties of bartering. The American vision, then, is rarely utopian or even truly ideological; rather, it is a basic belief in the future produced through participation and self-governance. That experience represents a peace principle: conflicts should be resolved with minimal coercion while maintaining public peace and promoting equity and justice. When coercion remains minimal, mutual problem solving becomes a norm. This principle, notably, is neither passive nor a full repudiation of force. It simply sets forth a preferred course which experience shows to be the better way: development and effective use of a full range of options.

A review of constitutional doctrine is quite beyond the scope of this report, but a glimpse can illustrate the operation of that peace principle. It provides evidence of the fundamental nature of that principle to our heritage. Courts review most constitutional challenges to government action using a "rational basis" test. If there is an explicit or even a reconstructed rationale to justify the action as within governmental power, the action is upheld as an expression of representative democracy. When, however, a governmental action limits a "fundamental right," such as religious practice, speech, or freedom from racial discrimination, a different standard applies. Once the government shows under a "strict scrutiny" test that its policy meets an appropriate governmental end, a means test is used. Has the government elected the "least restrictive" or "minimally intrusive" alternative to implement its policy? If the policy purpose is appropriate, but the way it is carried out is overly restrictive or intrusive in light of other less restrictive or intrusive alternatives, the government will be required to use those other means if it still wishes to effectuate its policy.

While recognizing the variety of meanings the word "peace" may evoke, the commission suggests that peace itself may be a fundamental right, calling for us to apply "least restrictive" or "minimally intrusive" principles in devising means for its pursuit. In addition, the commission believes those basic rights we protect and nourish might well be considered integral to an American concept of peace, in the sense that they represent the view of peace as a process that employs both broad participation and access to action and a range of options. The commission notes, however, that a procedural emphasis may have Western roots not understood or accepted by non-Westerners, making comparative perspectives especially important to international peace.

Merging the right to conflict[1] with the rights to create and compete leads to the following rule of conflict resolution: actions taken by parties in a dispute or by a third-party intervenor—an arbitrator, mediator, or conciliator—should follow the view that a more permanent resolution is most likely when the parties in conflict provide each other the greatest degree of freedom and self-interest while reaching an acceptable agreement that resolves the conflict. This is the way to a positive sum result, a win-win outcome. A zero or negative sum result is more likely when a conflict is terminated by force imposed by one party upon the other or by a third party upon both. And, of course, when force is used, intrusion and restriction are greatest and may involve the ultimate measure, physical violence.

This principle is well-known to law enforcement and military planners who devise hierarchies of response mechanisms ranging from the least intrusive presence (perhaps mere visibility) to the use of weapons, which themselves are graded in destructiveness. Writers on conflict resolution represent this diagramatically. Regardless of which technique is invoked, within each there is a similar hierarchy.

Techniques at the lower level of the pyramid would include voluntary limitations in international trade rather than imposed ones, whether the concern is the automotive industry or infant feeding formulas. In human rights concerns where sovereignty matters, United States policy has emphasized least restrictive means, such as persuasion, backed by refuge in this country. Somewhat more intense techniques are illustrated by court diversion programs into community-based institutions. In labor-management disputes, arbitrators may be selected jointly by both parties, often by reviewing lists supplied by the American Arbitration Association with each side challenging a name until common agreement is reached. Peacekeeping techniques, whether in the Middle East or Miami, inject highly visible police or military forces, who represent disputants or are new parties, in an effort to impose some stability and order so that lower level techniques can be used. The presence of these armed forces can cool conflict, but it also risks escalation into violence should complementary lower-level techniques fail.

## PEACEMAKING PROCEDURES:
### VIOLENT CONFLICT PYRAMID

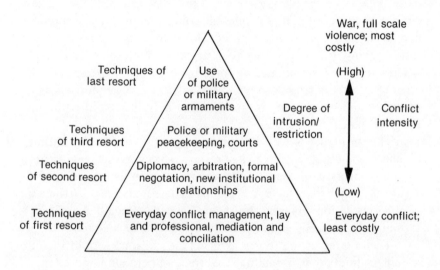

*Adapted from Elise Boulding, "Education for a Disarmed World: In Universities, Military Academies and a Possible National Peace Academy," in American Association for the Advancement of Science, Symposium on Public Opinion, Educational Outreach and Constituency Building for Arms Control, Toronto, January 5, 1981.*

Among the reasons the commission urges greater attention to lower level techniques is that the use of more intrusive or restrictive methods, illustrated at the peak of the violent conflict pyramid, makes conflicts and their management more costly. Options that threaten or employ force are expensive. The commission includes the following expenses within those options:

• Options of intrusion or force risk eruption of conflict into new violence and destruction.

• If the response or intervention option chosen is more forceful than necessary, de-escalation to the appropriate, less intrusive level is difficult.

• More formal, forceful, or restrictived options have greater procedural cost as measured in delay and institutional investment, whether in the form of court backlogs and attorney skirmishing or the logistical, salary, and loss-of-life costs of police or military intervention.

• Force and intrusion often create resentment and inhibit building consensus and reconciliation between the disputing parties.

• Force and restriction may become overriding interests in a conflict, align disputing parties temporarily if the intrusion is by an unwelcome third party, and distract from the real interest.

• A party perceived by others to prefer meeting conflict with force instead of through less intrusive means may lead other parties who anticipate conflict to prepare to meet force with force and to neglect investment in developing less forceful options to meet conflict; maintenance and use of forceful or intrusive options are economically more draining than less restrictive options: the former require substantial hardware and personnel expenditures which are depleted during armed hostilities and may cause balance of payments problems; the latter generally require fewer people, have minimal hardware costs, and may involve stabilizing economic development or humanitarian aid investments which over time may reduce balance of payments problems.

Having noted the cost question, the commission offers some of its thoughts with full acknowledgment that, in its short existence, it was not equipped to undertake original analysis of relative cost matters pertaining to conflict responses at various points along the range of options. To some extent, cost measurements must remain inherently flawed, both because one cannot measure the cost of a conflict that did not escalate into destruction and because one is hard-put to place a dollar figure on the interest that generated a forceful response. When one tries to evaluate what did not happen—to measure a negative—one encounters the fact that certain assumptions may not be shared by all. Perhaps in the end, it becomes a question of values and acceptable risk.

The commission believes that holding true to America's peace heritage requires emphasis on those options which are least restrictive and forceful. The commission believes, further, that those options are virtually without exception less expensive, both in dollar costs and self-confidence; have positive economic benefits through stable trade and cultural relations; and once instituted may permit states and localities dependent on military industries to plan more balanced civil economies through "economic conversion." Dr. Paula Rayman directed the commission's attention to this conversation in Boston and Dr. Richard Williams defined it for the commission in Boulder as "a social, political, and economic process of transferring personnel, resources, and technology from one sector of the economy to another," with planning that alleviates the suffering that attends such economic shifts in communities.

In Washington, testimony reminded the commission of the expense from overreliance on military options to maintain peace, which the commission believes is increased by neglect of the non-military part of the range. Reverend Karl Mattson, Chaplain of Gettysburg College, recalled President Dwight D. Eisenhower's 1953 "cross of iron" speech:

> "Every gun that is made, every warship launched, every rocket fired signifies, in the final sense, a theft from those who hunger and are not fed, those who are cold and not clothed. This world in arms is not spending money alone. It is spending the sweat of its laborers, the genius of its scientists, and the hopes of its children. This is not a way of life at all, in any true sense. Under the cloud of threatening war, it is humanity hanging from a cross of iron."

The commission believes that establishment of the United States Academy of Peace is a direct investment in nonforceful, lower level techniques that can reduce the need for expenditures at higher levels. The more equipped we are to meet conflicts without force, the more we preserve forceful means for the few times they may be truly necessary. A reluctance to make this investment surely will mean more frequent reliance on force, which may disrupt the peaceful norm we desire and exhaust budgetary resources that could be used more profitably elsewhere.

The commission recognizes that internationally our ability to defend our interests with force should remain clear. That potential may, when coupled with other techniques, encourage use of effective and available less restrictive alternatives. When these alternative choices are understood by Americans and others, and their utility and relative cost-effectiveness are further established through experience, then a fundamental part of the American heritage will be affirmed and will move this nation and the world further along the path of international peace.

In this light, the commission has concluded that the United States Academy of Peace will strengthen American security, promote international peace, and reduce the cost of international conflict through research, education and training, and information services on the range of effective responses to international violence and conflict.

## Managing International Conflict

The commission uses three representative stories to set the scene for further discussions directed to the establishment of the United States Academy of Peace. Ambassador Diego Asencio recalls negotiating from captivity in Colombia. Professor Roger Fisher presents a behind-the-scenes picture of the Camp David Middle East mediation. And the Reverend John Adams explains conciliation efforts directed to the release of the American Embassy hostages in Teheran. These first-person accounts make it apparent that clear lines between the three sectors of society-government, private enterprise, and voluntary associations-waver, and that the roles of negotiator, mediator, and conciliator are multifaceted.

*Diego Asencio: Negotiation. Manuel Asencio immigrated to the United States from Spain in 1918. A naturalized American, he returned to his home village of Nijar, married Delores Cortes, and their first child, Diego, was born a United States citizen there. At the age of six months, Diego and his mother sailed to Newark, New Jersey to join Manuel. Diego attended Newark public schools and, at his father's insistence, was tutored in Spanish language and culture. He graduated from the*

*Georgetown University School of Foreign Service, and in 1957, he began a career as a Foreign Service Officer with the Department of State. Ambassador Diego Asencio presently is Assistant Secretary for Consular Affairs. [Since the commission reported, he has become United States Ambassador to Brazil.]*

*His State Department service has included work in Washington on the Alliance for Progress and overseas assignments in Mexico, Panama, Portugal, Brazil, Venezuela, and Colombia, where he was the United States Ambassador from November 1977 through June 1980. When armed guerrillas seized the Dominican Republic's embassy in Bogota and took fifty-seven captives, including twelve ambassadors, one hostage was United States Ambassador Diego Asencio.*[2] *The guerrillas demanded fifty million dollars, release of three hundred and eleven prisoners, and safe exit. Two months later, they took safe passage to Cuba with 1.2 million dollars.*

*The role Ambassador Asencio developed while a hostage in Colombia is one example of highly effective negotiation by government officials involved in international peacemaking. When the hostages helped structure the formalized bargaining setting and used that opportunity to represent their own interests, they became a direct party to the negotiation. Experience gave them a basis to devise and apply innovative negotiating techniques. Ambassador Asencio's account of the negotiations from a hostage's viewpoint illustrates how skilled, culturally attuned, and resourceful individuals can shape fair conclusions out of chaos and violence.*

On February 27, 1979, I went to the National Day Reception at the embassy of the Dominican Republic in Bogota. I had been United States Ambassador to Colombia for two-and-a-half years. A little after noon, two couples dressed in ordinary street clothes walked in with a line of guests and started shooting up the ceiling. Another twelve kids in jogging clothes ran in from the street corner where they had been standing with sports equipment bags. The bags held rifles, shotguns, pistols, and grenades. A shoot-out started between the guerrillas and my security men outside—one was badly wounded—along with police from the National University across the street. For about an hour some two hundred shots were exchanged. Windows were shattered, walls were pockmarked. One guerrilla was killed and a few were wounded, one severely. A guest was badly hurt.

The siege lasted sixty-one days. The first three days I thought I'd be killed. They told me I'd be executed first, since I was the American ambassador.

The group is known as the M-19 Movement. It is a splinter group that originally supported the late '50s candidacy of populist General Gustavo Rojas Pinilla. When he lost—there was some question about the ballot count—they went underground and emerged in the early '70s as a notorious and publicity-conscious outfit. In their first action, they stole Simon Bolivar's sword from a museum to hold "until democracy returned to Colombia." They claim to be nationalists, are militarily well-trained, and support themselves through bank robberies and kidnappings.

When it looked like a siege was in order, they solicited the selection of a central committee from the hostages. The guerrilla commander's view was to use the central committee to control the hostages and as a pressure-point on the Colombian government through our governments. I was elected along with the Mexican and Venezuelan ambassadors and the Papal Nuncio. I later asked that the Brazilian ambassador, a fine international lawyer, be included.

The first, and one of the most important considerations about my role, is what I call "cultural relativity": the ability to bridge different cultures, which presumably a foreign service officer has, if he is a good one. Having been brought up in a culturally diverse neighborhood in New Jersey, I probably had this in ample measure. Also, I had a full command of Spanish, knew Colombian history, politics, and psychology, and had some knowledge of their political platforms and of M-19. With this background, I could serve as a link between the guerrillas and the Colombian government, the United States government, and other governments; could interpret how they were feeling; and could gauge my message accordingly.

The fourth day, the commander called a general meeting to read their position paper setting out demands—amnesty for 311 political prisoners, $50 million ransom, and safe passage out of the country. It was a terrible negotiation document, harsh, with outrageous requests, full of revolutionary cant, insulting the government and the president. It was a prescription for a fight, not a negotiation.

After the meeting, I took the commander aside and suggested the document had deficiencies as a negotiation piece. All it would do is let the right-wing security element in the Colombian government tag M-19 as savages who should be dealt with by force. He asked if I could do better. I said, "Sure, negotiation is part of my business."

With his consent, the Mexican and Brazilian ambassadors and I set out to redraft the document. As experienced negotiators, we know that negotiation documents have to breathe, they need light and flexibility. If "demands" are "non negotiable," there can be no negotiation. We cut out the confrontations and insults, demands they made as if by right, and still kept the negotiation points they wanted, including reference to human rights violations and more responsible government—their talk on dictatorship was pretty crude. It even was fun. We used traditional diplomatic parlance: "The M-19 movement presents its compliments to the negotiators for the government of Colombia and has the honor to make the following points...." They liked it, quite professional stuff.

What we were able to do and they clearly couldn't was to control the document as an instrument. It's a skill that's quite trainable; it's really almost literary, and certainly essential to any negotiation that uses writing. By deft use of language, we were able to rephrase some of the guerrillas' statements without changing the content so they became negotiable interests. When the Colombian government acknowledged the draft, we were in business.

Soon a van with doors off and a table and chairs inside was put in the embassy front yard as the negotiation place. The guerrillas permitted the hostages to talk by phone to their families, and the Colombian government installed a line for us to talk directly to the Foreign Minister. In addition, we had walkie-talkie communication with the military outside. All this time, of course, the building was surrounded by military forces and access to the vicinity was closely controlled. So the stage was set.

From the outset, amnesty for the 311 prisoners was absolutely unacceptable to the Colombian government, legally and politically. Under the Colombian Constitution, the president may only grant amnesty with congressional affirmation. If the president were to grant amnesty unilaterally, he would be subject to impeachment. The government negotiators lectured the guerrillas repeatedly on such legal niceties. "Judicial framework" was elevated to catch phrase, almost a curse word in the guerrillas' frustration.

The hostage central committee quickly became integral to the negotiation process. For most of the process, the Mexican ambassador accompanied the guerrilla negotiator at meetings in the van. After he quit following an argument in which he felt the Colombian representatives insulted him, the Peruvian consul replaced him and subsequently the Bolivian chargé, and by the end we didn't have a hostage at the table. But it wasn't necessary then, as we talked a lot with the guerrillas; we set up an ambassadorial lecture series, had debates, lobbied them before their meetings, and followed every negotiation session with a debriefing. The hostage central committee held daily strategy meetings and kept in close touch with officials on the outside. Still, the situation was so tense we couldn't set up a specific game plan. We had to ad hoc it; if one thing hit a stone wall, we'd try another. Some examples:

• The Brazilian ambassador recalled the use of the Vienna Convention in freeing Ambassador Elbrick. It states that host government care of diplomats supersedes other legal considerations. That change in the "judicial framework" wasn't attractive to the Colombian government.

• We suggested accelerating the court-martials, to which the guerrillas' comrades were subject, or at least the release of a token number of prisoners whose pretrial detention about equalled the probable length of sentence. Again, no go.

• The top echelon of M-19, from number two to about ten, were in prison. We thought number two could be persuaded—our hidden agenda was a little plea-bargaining—to give his blessing to the guerrillas and get them to accept less than their instructions. The Colombian government was dubious: they thought he might just say, "Kill 'em all." Talks went on for two weeks. A Red Cross man came in and taped a message to number two. The Colombian government didn't put the pressure on and a tape came back—"Stay tough."

Then the breakthrough came, obscured in the usual technical prose of an instruction document from the president of Colombia to his negotiators. After a tense meeting in the van, the guerrilla negotiator and Mexican ambassador came back in; both were furious. The negotiator threw a piece of paper—it was the instruction document—on the floor. I picked it up, saw the germ of an idea—bringing in the Organization of American States' Human Rights Commission to observe the court-martial proceedings—and said, "Wait a minute. There's something here."

The hostage central committee began to talk about what this commission might be like. We praised the OAS and its Human Rights Commission to the skies: It would be the greatest thing in the world; think of the institutional impact; think of the benefits to society; you'll go down in history as having done something significant. And the guerrillas began to buy it. It would be a treaty between the Colombian government and the OAS, sanctioned by international law.

At about the same time, Secretary of State Cyrus Vance sent Viron "Pete" Vaky, former assistant secretary for Latin America and former ambassador to Colombia who still knew the Colombian political scene quite well, to meet with the salient members on the scene to get an idea of what the real interests were. This impressed the guerrillas and added momentum to the OAS idea.

In addition, Tom Farer, professor at Rutgers Law School and president of the OAS Human Rights Commission, met with the guerrillas and explained how the commission normally functions and how this agreement would be historically important if the Colombian government let an international organization, the Human Rights Commission, sit in on trials, make observations on fairness, and have a continuing presence in the country to receive allegations of human rights violations. This struck the guerrillas as important and that discussion became pivotal in reaching final settlement of the demand that 311 prisoners be released.

The money side of the demands was handled by a Colombian businessman and a retired Colombian political figure, friends of the hostages. Eventually, about 1.2 million dollars was paid, as by this time the guerrillas were working on the premise that money wasn't really all that necessary to maintain a "pro" status. The final negotiation issue was where everybody would go. The hostage number now was down from fifty-seven to fifteen ambassadors and two others, as people had been released both to show good faith and for medical reasons and the Uruguayan ambassador had escaped, much to the danger of everyone else.

Exit became terribly complex, because the guerrillas wanted to go to the Middle East and take along with them a few of the ambassadors, including me. At this point Fidel Castro came forward—he had offered assistance earlier that was rejected—and said he would accept the guerrillas and the hostages on a humanitarian basis and release the hostages in Havana. The Cuban ambassador came in, and I took him aside and said I wasn't going on any plane unless he assured us that the guerrillas would be disarmed and the plane would be under Cuban military control. I didn't want to end up in the Middle East. He agreed.

So on April 27, the guerrillas and twelve ambassadors flew from Bogota to Havana and I was met there by State Department colleagues. Together we went on to Homestead Air Force Base, where my wife, my daughter, and some other family members were waiting. After a couple of days, the family and I came to Washington.

I think one of the lessons was that those hostages who remained physically and mentally active came out fairly well; those whose defense against the unpleasant situation was to become passive suffered severely; and those with exceptional personal problems, whether physical or psychological, had them aggravated by their captivity. Recognizing this probability, we tried very hard to maintain an acceptable level of morale as part of the whole picture.

There is something called the Stockholm syndrome—fondness for your captors. It really was not applicable in this situation, where we were not sensorily deprived and were fairly well developed as adults. Nevertheless, a number of decisions were taken on the outside based on the thesis that the syndrome was a serious matter. I originally thought it was serious and widely applicable, too. I think, now, that it is an important consideration, but perhaps not all that common. A full-blown study of the Stockholm syndrome is needed. If the United States Academy of Peace did nothing else, that would be a useful contribution to the world. I feel so strongly about it, because I was taking my own emotional temperature and watching my colleagues very carefully; I expected it to manifest itself. I found all sorts of peculiar situations, some of them pathological, but no "syndrome." When I asked one of the Iran hostages about it, he agreed. It may develop sometimes, but for us it was the furthest thing from our minds.

Cultural relativity was a major tool in turning what could have been a disaster into a peaceful end. A cultural relativist, after all, can meet anomalous situations without feeling threatened by cultural differences; whether sheep eyes delicacies or Hispanic closeness, it all is interesting and there to study. This applies to American businessmen who operate internationally no less than to American diplomats or military personnel, even though the functions of business and government are different—one to make profit and the other to act as a channel of communication or means of defense. They all would benefit from training and perspectives that foster cultural relativity, not only with the goal of becoming better negotiators, mediators, and so on, but also to foster greater sensitivity to other cultures and modes of thinking.

To my mind, a good negotiation is one in which everybody wins. If it's a zero-sum game, it's not a real negotiation; it's an imposed outcome. One of the fascinating aspects of this particular experience was that the eventual solution did not contravene Colombian law or affect U.S. policy, yet it was considered an honorable solution by the guerrillas and a realistic and acceptable one by the many governments, hostages, and families concerned.

As a hostage, I was able to use my negotiation skills to bring a sound and safe ending. It worked in a way the guerrillas hadn't foreseen, and it was positive in the sense that they probably could not have carried out this negotiation without our help. The thing would have blown, and I think they realized that. If we hadn't changed the original paper, if we hadn't pointed out the obvious although generally subtle and veiled offer the Colombian government was making, and if we hadn't developed the thought and drafted the agreement, we would have all been in rather deep water.

*Roger Fisher: Mediation. Mediation is a time-tested conflict resolution technique in the private sector. It takes place in a negotiation context and thus requires that disputing parties be ready to negotiate. Upon invitation, a mediator frames a negotiation process or enters an ongoing negotiation. A mediator is not an agent of any of the parties—although in a sense he is an agent of all—and his presence is agreed to. His third party role is more formal than a conciliator's, but he lacks the binding authority of an arbitrator. As a nonpartisan actor, he can cut behind positions, identify interests, and suggest ways for the parties to resolve their conflict. He keeps communication open and can be active in fashioning a fair result. Roger Fisher's description of the United States's mediation strategy at Camp David illustrates a culturally sensitive application of a domestic mediation technique at an international level, and it points to the importance of peacemaking scholar-consultants for international disputes.*

*Roger Fisher is Samuel Williston Professor of Law at Harvard Law School. He is director of the Harvard Negotiation Project, teaches negotiation in such diverse academic settings as Harvard, the Naval War College, the NATO Defense College in Rome, and the State Department's Foreign Service Institute, and advises governments and others involved in international conflict. His writings on negotiation have qualities that are sometimes missing in the works of scholars: both language and organization are direct and simple, without loss of complexity or shading.[3] In two meetings with commissioners in Boston and through other communications, Professor Fisher shared thoughts on international negotiation and mediation and on the peace academy concept.*

Since 1939, when I first came to Harvard College and studied international law, conflict has been my primary professional concern. The goals have been practical. We need to achieve results that work, that permit us to carry on our differences in a less bloody, more efficient fashion. An important part of our job internationally is to carry on conflict better.

I see negotiation broadly: it is a means for people to participate and to accept results that they mutually work out. Participation and consent are fundamental principles of democracy. They are applicable internationally as well as domestically. To make them work, we have to know how conflict should be carried on from any point of view: what a negotiator should do; what a third party, such as a mediator, should do; what a partisan in a crisis should do. Since international conflicts are inevitable, we should be prepared to handle them well.

Before Prime Minister Menachem Begin and President Anwar Sadat came to Camp David, I had the good fortune to sit down with Secretary of State Cyrus Vance to talk about mediation. I shared with him a draft of our International Peace Academy book, *International Mediation: A Working Guide*. It has two principal theses. First, mediation is a skill that can be learned. Mediators are not simply born. We subtitle the book "Ideas for the Practitioner." However much we may know, with more knowledge we can do better. Second, the most effective mediators are active participants in the negotiation process. Certainly mediation facilitates dialogue; but it can be much more than a postal service. If a mediator limits his or her role to asking for people's positions and for concessions, people tend to lock themselves in; movement become more difficult. So, we talked about the process that could be used at Camp David.

We agreed that it would be useful to use a single negotiating text. Various procedures based on a single text were used at the Law of the Sea Conference, by Lord Carrington in mediating a settlement of the Rhodesian-Zimbabwe conflict, and by Henry Kissinger in a portion of his shuttle diplomacy. I have also discussed with Theodore Kheel the use of a single draft text in labor-management disputes. Stimulated in large part by Professor Louis Sohn, we at the Harvard Negotiation Project had developed a particular variation on prior work which we now call the one-text procedure. Although differences between it and other uses of a draft may seem subtle, they are significant. Properly used, it ignores the stated positions of the parties to focus on their underlying interests; it reduces the number of decisions required of each side; it allows the parties to participate in generating a plan before having to decide whether to accept it; and it tends to restructure a conflict so that the parties, rather than confronting each other face to face, are working side by side, facing the shared problem of improving the draft.

The Camp David negotiation in September 1978 was a textbook example of the one-text procedure. The Americans would first listen to the Egyptians and the Israelis. Questions would be designed to illuminate their respective interests, not simply their declared positions. The mediator team would prepare a rough draft, and then ask each side for its criticism: "What would be wrong with something like this? We are not proposing it. In fact, we are not particularly pleased with it ourselves. But what interests of yours would it not take adequately into account?" The mediator team would meet separately, first with one side and then with the other. Neither side would be asked for acceptance or for a concession, but only for criticism. It is hard to make a concession; it is easy to criticize.

Based on the criticisms of Draft 1, a second draft would be prepared and subjected to further criticism. The process would be repeated over and over again. No one would be allowed to reject or accept any paragraph since nothing was yet being proposed. The stance of the mediator would be to see if he could develop a recommendation he would be prepared to make. The whole draft would remain flexible and open until the mediator himself decided to make a recommendation.

The one-text procedure was used by President Carter at Camp David. Not having been there, I cannot do justice to the many elements of timing, stress, personality, and detail involved. However, I had a couple of telephone calls during the meeting and have since discussed it with participants from all three countries. Incidentally, Israeli and Egyptian negotiators at Camp David had been trained at Harvard Law School.

The positions of Egypt and Israel with respect to the Sinai were incompatible. Israel's declared position was that it must retain some of the Sinai. Egypt's declared position was that it must regain every inch. But looking behind their positions, Israel's interest was in security and Egypt's interest was in sovereignty. This difference opened the door for agreement. After a few days, the United States advanced its first draft with one side and then the other. The process of successive nonbinding drafts of a discussion text to which no one was committed continued until the thirteenth day. There had been some twenty three drafts of all or part of the negotiating text which the United States was preparing in light of the criticisms and suggestions of Egypt and Israel. Finally, the United States had decided that this was the best it could do under the circumstances.

To paraphrase the dialogue, President Carter took the draft to Prime Minister Begin and said, "Now is the time." Prime Minister Begin said, "I've made no concessions." President Carter responded, "That's right. But with this draft, you now have a proposal before you. I'm prepared to recommend this. Will you accept it if President Sadat accepts it?'' Only one decision was asked. There were no contingencies. Saying "yes" would not lead to a request for further concessions. Prime Minister Begin said "yes."

President Carter then took the text to President Sadat. "Though you may not like this," he said, "it is the best I can do. Mr. Begin has said 'yes'." President Sadat also was faced then with a decision that was mechanically simple: yes or no. He got a commitment from President Carter to continue as a full participant in the peacemaking process, and then said "yes."

There were, of course, a great many elements which contributed to the success of the Camp David meeting, in particular the enormous dedication and personal effort which those there devoted to the task. One can ask questions about the substance of the Camp David accords, and whether it might have been both possible and wiser to proceed on a basis that included additional Arabs. But those in the business of keeping the world peaceful need every bit of help they can get. Camp David does suggest that technique—method—can help.

Camp David is one of many stories that illustrate the power and importance of methods of coping with differences. We lawyers have spent thousands of years improving the judicial process. Where a judge is involved, we have learned that one question is how to design and maintain a fair process, and that a second question is how a lawyer should argue within that process to obtain a favorable substantive result. But when no judge is involved, as is typically the case internationally, we often fail to distinguish between the task of establishing a fair negotiating process and the questioning of how best to negotiate within that process.

In international affairs, most people most of the time focus their attention on substantive problems. Yet how international affairs are conducted is a problem of procedure, and procedure is likely to determine whether there can be a substantive outcome. Within a family, among neighbors, and within a community, the substantive distribution of assets at any one time is far less important than the way with which differences are dealt. We need to recognize that fact internationally. Within the United States, most of us have learned that making threats and escalating disputes is not the best way to carry on our differences. We have learned that a working relationship is not something that can be bought or sold in exchange for substantive concessions. Again, we need to apply that knowledge to the international situation.

I support the establishment of a peace academy to be concerned with improving the process by which we and others carry on our international affairs. The focus, it seems to me, should be on the international problem. Domestic experience should be studied only to the extent that to do so is expected to yield knowledge relevant to the international problem.

The first task is thus research. The academy itself might gather some knowledge, but I see its task as supporting outside research of a practical nature and perhaps contracting for applied research. A peace academy should be concerned, for example, with designing effective negotiating procedures, standard cease-fire agreements, and checklists for mediators. Its major role would be educational, including both short and longer training programs for mid-career professionals.

The design and continual improvement of such programs is central. Military officers and foreign service personnel should learn the range of ways to influence officers of another government beyond sending formal diplomatic notes or making threats. They should know how to distinguish emotional and perceptual problems from ones involving an objective conflict over interests. They should become expert at looking behind positions for underlying interests, at generating multiple options that could reconcile those interests, and at finding standards for settling a dispute that are independent of the naked will of either side. They should become expert at converting economic and military assets into negotiating power by developing and improving their "BATNA"—the Best Alternative To a Negotiated Agreement. They should understand how to use third parties and how, for example, at a multilateral conference, to behave like one.

Finally, there is a need for public education. Foreign conflict is frequently made worse by domestic political considerations. A public that wants peace may induce its leaders to behave in bellicose ways that make peace more difficult. No one wants a propaganda agency, but certainly it would be as important for a peace academy to have public information materials explaining how international problems are settled as for the Department of Commerce to have public information pamphlets explaining import-export regulations.

Thus, a peace academy, in my view, ought to respond to the needs of people outside of government as well as in government. American businessmen and labor representatives are active throughout the world, and my experience is that they frequently are called upon to exercise peacemaking skill. An academy, then, should be a truly national institution devoted to the international peace interests of us all.

* * *

*Introduction to conciliation.* Voluntary associations are native to American society. Voluntarism in America can be traced to the frontier days, and even back to the Pilgrims, when small communities sought organized ways to express mutual concerns and to execute plans of action. Voluntary associations are an American cement to community. Government as we know it would be impossible without them; whether political parties or simply concerned groups, they are part of the fabric of public life.

In 1975, the Commission on Private Philanthropy and Public Needs, commonly called the Filer Commission, observed:

> On the map of American Society, one of the least charted regions is variously known as the voluntary, the private nonprofit, or simply the third sector. Third, that is, after the often overshadowing worlds of government and business. While [government and business] have been and continue to be micro- scopically examined and analyzed and while their boundaries are for the most part readily identified by experts and laymen alike, the third sector—made up of nongovernmental, nonprofit associations and organizations—remains something of a "terra incognita," barely explored in terms of its inner dynamics and motivations, and its social, economic and political relations to the rest of the world.[4]

For many decades, institutions of higher education have used overseas programs to enrich their academic and cultural offerings. The cumulative result of these exchanges is sounder communication between the United States and other nations and a sharpening of skills in global issues analyses and problem-solving techniques. Based upon research, technical training, seminars, and cross-cultural experiences, more internationally sensitive curricula have developed, although formal education on peace issues still remains diffuse and spotty. Schools of diplomacy offer courses in peace and conflict, but arms control, like many other related topics, continues as a "cottage industry"[5] with scholars scattered and isolated, according to an Arms Control and Disarmament Agency report shared with the commission by Dr. Lawrence D. Weiler of the ACDA.

Religious organizations are the voluntary associations at the forefront of peace activity in the United States. Three short accounts drawn from religious activity help situate the fuller social ministry observations by the Reverend John Adams of the United Methodist Church:

• In St. Louis, Margaret Sonnenday, former international president of the ecumenical Church Women United (founded December 7, 1941), described the organization's activities, including its Causeway program: "Since 1966, church women from 43 countries have walked the Causeway in Africa, Latin America, the Caribbean, East Asia, Cuba, islands of the South Pacific, Australia and the USA" to learn firsthand and develop peace networks among women throughout the world.

• Dr. Roland Warren, who participated in the commission's early planning, spent two years in the Federal Republic of Germany and the German Democratic Republic for the America Friends Service Committee soon after the Berlin Wall went up in 1961. Through almost daily contact with persons on both sides of the wall, he used "Quaker good offices" to clarify, share information while keeping trust, reduce tensions, and suggest opportunities to avert escalation and promote reconciliation.

• Raymond Helmick, a Jesuit priest from the New England Province of the Society of Jesus, described to the commission his decade of activity from London that led him in 1979 to found there with English and Irish Jesuits the Centre of Concern for Human Dignity. Enlightened by his extensive work on areas of conflict and suffering including East Timor, Cyprus, the Middle East, Latin America, and South Africa, the Centre harkens back to 1972 when he was a hod carrier in Belfast along with an American Protestant clergyman. Working in Belfast to develop neighborhood organizations and industries protected from violence led him to conclude that the troubles in Northern Ireland must be addressed through community building, economic development, and more positive roles for the church, both Protestant and Catholic.

Voluntary associations in the United States are broadly engaged in activities that promote international peace. The commission sees them today, as de Toqueville did a century and a half ago, as bedrock institutions in this democracy and as important as government and private enterprise to the peacemaking role of this nation:

> Nothing, in my opinion, is more deserving of our attention than the intellectual and moral associations of America. The political and industrial associations of that country strike us forcibly; but the others elude our observation, or if we discover them, we understand them imperfectly because we have hardly ever seen anything of the kind. It must be acknowledged, however, that they are as necessary to the American people as the former, and perhaps more so. In democratic countries the science of association is the

mother of science; the progress of all the rest depends upon the progress it has made.

Among the laws that rule human societies there is one which seems to be more precise and clear than all others. If men are to remain civilized or to become so, the art of associating together must grow and improve in the same ratio in which the equality of conditions is increased.[6]

\* \* \*

*John Adams: Conciliation. Conciliation is, using de Toqueville's terminology, one "art of associating together" practiced by persons involved in social conflicts. Conciliation is the least structured of the four major conflict resolution techniques. Unlike a negotiator, arbitrator, or mediator, a conciliator frequently works in pre-negotiation situations to establish and maintain communication among disputants and, if appropriate, to move them into more formal bargaining formats. Conciliators may employ fact-finding and observation and help some disputes to be resolved informally. In addition, conciliators play critical roles in helping agreements to be kept and in reconciliation efforts that prevent future conflicts after agreements are reached. The Reverend John Adams's account of the mail exchange for American Embassy personnel held hostage in Iran and their families and of his later activities surrounding the arrest and release of Iranian student demonstrators illustrates conflicts crossing national boundaries and the application of conciliation skills at community, national, and international levels.*

*The Reverend John Adams was one of many members of the clergy engaged in social conflict ministries, and his activities with the United Methodist Church from 1967 to 1980 focused on community and national conflicts throughout the United States.[7] Whether dealing with unpublicized disputes or such well-known conflicts as the urban disorders of 1967 and the Wounded Knee confrontation of 1973, the Reverend Adams's ministry has involved him with numerous government officials and private citizens, principally in the third-party intervenor roles of observer and conciliator.*

In January 1980, John Thomas of the International Indian Treaty Council and I sat in Teheran in the anteroom of the office of Abolhasem Sadegh, Director General of the Foreign Press in the Government of the Islamic Republic of Iran. While we waited after office hours for a scheduled appointment with Mr. Sadegh, we looked at six prominent posters on the walls. In the center of each was a picture postcard from the United States. One was of the White House, another of the United States Capitol, another of the World Trade Center in New York City, and so on. Clustered around these cards from the United States were several photographs, unprofessional ones, obviously taken with someone's personal camera.

They were pictures taken on the Pine Ridge Reservation of the Ogalala Sioux in South Dakota, and they showed the poverty prevalent there. The contrast between the magnificence of the government buildings and commercial centers and the deterioration of the reservation's huts and shanties was striking. More striking, though, was the existence of these posters on the wall of an Iranian government office thousands of miles from the United States.

We learned that Mr. Sadegh had been educated in the United States, become a United States citizen, and for three years been a Vista volunteer on the Pine Ridge Reservation. Later, he renounced his American citizenship, partly because of what he had observed of the treatment of Native Americans, and he returned to Iran.

A discussion of more than two hours developed from an appointment that was to have been twenty minutes, as we shared the concern that brought us to Teheran. John Thomas and I had come to deliver letters and packages to the hostages held at the United States Embassy by Islamic students and to pick up mail from them.

Our presence was a result of John Thomas attending a World Conference of Liberation Movements in Teheran earlier that month at the invitation of the Islamic students. While there, he had spoken about the lack of mail and other contacts between the hostages and their families in the United States. He could do this easily with the students, as a number of them stayed in the same hotel. He was unexpectedly permitted to see one hostage and was given 156 letters from forty-one of the hostages to bring back to their families and friends. Inconvenient and expensive conditions were placed on the delivery of the mail: letters were not to be channeled through the State Department or placed in the U.S. mail. This necessitated personal delivery and hand-carrying of letters.

The International Indian Treaty Council asked the Board of Church and Society of the United Methodist Church to help organize delivery of the letters and to assist in making arrangements for return mail to the hostages. That is how I became involved. I should add here that the State Department knew about our activities and cooperated with the effort. A more formal and fully organized "Hostage Mail Exchange Service" was then established. With its functioning, many hostage families said that "things began to open up for us." Mail flowed between Teheran and the United States more freely through two or three channels. Packages of supplies, photographs, books, and games were permitted into the embassy compound. Tape recordings were taken. Three international telephone calls from hostages to their families were made. Obviously, a line of communication had been offered; the conditions for its operation had been carefully complied with; and an even more open response was given in return.

The mail exchange met a basic human need of the hostages and their families and provided an alternate line of communication with the captors. It also stimulated ongoing communication in an extensive network in Iran and the United States. These communications gave an opportunity to express concern for the condition of the hostages and to urge that the process for gaining their freedom be expedited. The exchanges also gave a forum for the grievances of the Islamic students, which clearly were an important factor in the revolution that was still in progress and in the conflict with the United States that centered around the hostages. Finally, the linkages required in planning and executing the mail exchange undoubtedly helped reduce tensions at critical times and contributed to a climate in which negotiations ultimately could be conducted. The mail exchange was suspended after the aborted April 24-25 rescue mission and was reestablished almost ten weeks later.

On July 27, the Shah died. Three previously planned Iranian demonstrations took place that day on the streets of Washington. These events covered just a few hours and threatened to cancel totally the many constructive earlier initiatives. Demonstrations and counter-demonstrations involved the Iran Freedom Foundation, a group supportive of former Prime Minister Shaphur Bahktiar and the Shah; the Coalition of Iranian Students, which was anti-Shah and pro-democracy, but not necessarily supporters of the Khomeini government; and the Moslem Student Association: Persian Speaking Group that strongly backed the Ayatollah and the form of government being shaped under his authority.

The demonstrations were carefully orchestrated by the police through the issuance of detailed permits in an effort to avoid any direct confrontation between the politically diverse groups. Order deteriorated as the Shah's death, occurring earlier on the exact day, heightened hostility among the factions and increased tension within the police who were assigned to the events. One hundred and ninety-one Iranian students were arrested, principally from the Moslem Student Association. A major new crisis—within the hostage crisis—had erupted.

In the United States, the Moslem Student Association claimed there had been police brutality in Washington and charged that those who were arrested had been beaten in jail, denied use of toilet facilities, and threatened with weapons. A group of Iranian students began a hunger strike on the sidewalk in front of the White House to "condemn the brutality of the barbaric police" and to "demand the immediate unconditional release of those innocent, injured brothers and sisters." They vowed to continue the strike until every single student was released.

Within days, Ayatollah Ruhollah Khomeini charged that the Iranian students were "chained in prison and under torture." Iranian Foreign Minister Sadegh Ghotbzadeh sent a message to United Nations Secretary-General Kurt Waldheim urging him to send a delegation to visit the arrested students. In Teheran, 250,000 Iranians filled the streets around the United States Embassy, protesting the "torture" of the students jailed in Washington.

Late at night on the day of the demonstrations and arrests, I received a telephone call at home from a spokesperson of the Moslem Student Association. He told me that many students had been injured and the association could not locate them to determine their condition or be assured they were receiving adequate medical attention. He asked me to help find them and to give any assistance I could. Although I could not know of the imminent reaction in Iran, I sensed immediately that a serious liability could develop that would delay any resolution of the hostage crisis.

My telephoning to city officials and others began immediately. The next morning, I went to see Robert Klotz, deputy chief of the District of Columbia's Metropolitan Police in charge of the Special Operations Unit, and then contacted Delbert Jackson, director of the District's Department of Corrections. He put me in touch with corrections officials who said it was impossible for them to help me locate particular students, since they had refused to identify themselves at the time of arrest. Lawyers retained by the Moslem Student Association also were denied access to the students, because they could not identify their clients by name. There was an impasse.

I was able to arrange a meeting between Director Jackson and two representatives of the Moslem Student Association and their attorneys. Mr. Jackson stated that the lawyers could go into the D.C. jail as soon as the students gave their names and were placed in individual cells. The student representatives would not cooperate on the matter, since they were protesting what they felt were unwarranted police actions and unjustified arrests. Upon my suggestion, Mr. Jackson granted permission for a small group of us—myself, lawyers, and student interpreters—to enter both cellblocks, where the men and women were being detained separately, to check their conditions.

On July 29, we spent nearly five hours with the confined Iranian students. Already they were showing the effects of their refusal to eat and rejection of medical attention. From the outside, it could be reported as torture. On the inside, it was the result of an active protest.

The student representatives at our meeting after the jail visit demanded release of those jailed and asserted they would talk to no more government officials. They assured us those in the cellblock would go on a dry hunger strike if moved to individual cells. Since neither the lawyers nor the spokespersons for the students wanted any further discussion with the government, I contacted Mr. Jackson and met at his office to go over the situation. He told me that this was one of the worst dilemmas he had faced since assuming his position and that he felt "alone." The federal government was silent.

I left his office and went directly to the Iran Working Group at the State Department. I described to them what I had witnessed in the jail. I alerted them to a crisis that already existed, would probably become more serious, and was basically unknown to them. During a second meeting with Mr. Jackson and the association, initiatives began to be taken within the District government and the next day misdemeanor charges were dropped against the students.

Immediately, however, the Immigration and Naturalization Service notified the District government that it would take custody of the students on detainers in order to investigate the status of their visas. On August 1, with heavy security, the 20 women were transferred to the federal detention center in Manhattan and the 171 men were taken to a new federal correctional facility in Otisville, New York.

The next day, August 2, I was invited to a meeting of the students and their lawyers scheduled for the next morning at a downtown Washington motel. I was glad I attended that particular meeting, for after much heated discussion and fiery criticism of the American government, I heard one of the spokespersons for the Moslem Student Association remark almost casually, "Our committee has agreed that the students who are in prison should now identify themselves." I moved to the edge of my chair and asked, "You are ready for the students to give their names to the authorities?" The reply was that the members of the central committee of the association who were not in prison wanted to make that recommendation to those students who were, but expected many would need to be persuaded that it was the right action after having been on a hunger strike for six days. I then asked, "Do representatives of the United States Government know of this change?"

When they replied, "No, they do not, but you can tell them," I ran to a telephone booth and called the Iran Working Group at the State Department to ask ther assistance in setting up an emergency appointment with David Crosland, the director of the INS. Within an hour after I had returned to my office, Mr. Crosland called. We agreed to meet at 5:30 PM that day in his office. I was to bring the lawyers representing the Moslem Student Association. The spokesperson for the association declined to attend the meeting, but asked me to represent their position.

During the meeting, I asked that the attorneys, along with an interpreter and a spokesperson for the association, be allowed to go, first to Otisville and then to Manhattan, to explain the change and to persuade the students to give their identities. Mr. Crosland responded positively. He said any student who was not "out of status" would be released and not charged with failure to identify himself properly, which is a separate deportable offense under the Immigration and Nationality Act. He asked whether I was willing to go with the delegation. I was. We were on the 9 PM shuttle to New York City.

Early the next morning, a Sunday, we drove up to Otisville and went into the federal correctional facility. We met with the warden, the regional representative of the Federal Bureau of Prisons, INS representatives from the New York City office, and two top INS staff persons from Washington. After a short discussion of security matters, the warden permitted us to have a group meeting with the students by releasing them from their individual cells and locking us all in one room. The students warmly embraced each other and each of us in the delegation. They were weak from the hunger strike, then in its seventh day.

Mohammad Badr, the student spokesperson who travelled with us, asked the group to sit in rows and opened the discussion in Farsi, the language of Iran. He appealed to them to accept the action of the central committee: to give their identities. Among the questions the detained students asked me was whether "this is not a trick to identify the students so that they can be further charged." I replied that I trusted Mr. Crosland, but that I would telephone him at his home to reconfirm clearly the offer he had made.

I immediately called Mr. Crosland from a nearby office. I told him about the situation and that I was being questioned about the offer. He repeated exactly what he stated in his office and added, "This is not an unlimited offer. I must have a prompt reply." I reported back to the group. Within a few moments, they voted to accept the recommendation of the central committee. They then asked for medical attention from an Iranian doctor, who had come up from New York in case he was needed by them.

A representative of the students was dispatched to Manhattan to interpret the offer to the women students being held there. The next morning, their agreement was obtained. By August 5, it became apparent that the overwhelming majority of the students had proper immigration status and could be released. Meanwhile, the reaction from Iran was intensifying and beginning to have deleterious effects upon negotiations over the hostage release. All but one Iranian student was released on August 6, after nine days incarceration. The crisis within the hostage crisis had ended.

On September 12, Ayatollah Khomeini declared that the hostages would be released if the United States government met four conditions. That statement was the first concrete offer made in public by Khomeini to advance the negotiation for the hostages' release. I am convinced that disciplined and professional police performance, coupled with eventual cooperation from the Iranian students and rapid responses by American officials at both local and national levels, helped restore the process of negotiation. It was an example of international peacemaking on the streets of Washington.

There is a discipline for the peaceful solution of conflict. There is theory and there are concepts that can be taught. There are skills to be learned. Many of us did not know this as we were thrust into conflicts. We went into the midst of them out of a respect for all human life and dedication to the peaceful resolution of conflict: the desire to see justice done. We had to learn that commitment is not enough. The desire for peace is not sufficient. Peace is not even based on the saving of human life, as important as that is, for some are dedicated to giving their lives, if necessary, to achieve justice. Peace, we came to see, is not an absence of conflict; it is the presence of justice. That, I hope, will be the promise and legacy of an academy dedicated to peace, that is, to peace with justice.

What the United Methodist Church helped John Thomas to accomplish with the mail exchange and what I, through its offices, was able to do to help resolve the conflicts involved in the arrest and release from prison of Iranian students are examples of the process of conciliation. There are many, many more that others could tell.

The mail exchange partly lowered barriers to the hostages' human right of communication. Conciliation helped the State Department's Iran Working Group and other federal and local officials see and meet the storm developing out of the simple act of refusing to identify oneself. Identity, after all, was the issue that blocked access to the students in the District of Columbia jail and was the sticking point with INS. In Teheran, Washington, Otisville, and Manhattan, John Thomas and then I became trusted messengers and brokers able to suggest ways out of various impasses. Just the doing of that involved so many people that it added to the human face of the situation.

At so many junctures, communication was stifled. Whether from power in Iran or actions and rules in the United States, people took positions that frustrated clarity about their own and other parties' interests. A medium was needed, a way to get the mail through—literally and figuratively. These third party conciliations made it possible, I believe, for the United States and Iran to see their way more clearly in negotiations. With concern over the hostages' health somewhat mitigated and the crisis that began on the streets of Washington defused, the real matter—the release of the hostages—got back on track.

*Concluding Note.* These three first-person accounts represent the societal sectors (government, private enterprise, and voluntary associations) as well as the three prominent types of peacemaking roles which seek agreement among parties to international disputes: negotiation, conciliation, and mediation. The fourth type — arbitration — may be less common in the sometimes chaotic international arena, but it is likely to receive greater use as negotiated agreements are skillfully drawn and directed to future peaceful relationships.

Two facts emerge from the first-person stories: first, the line between international and intranational disputes is blurry and there is much interplay between these levels; and second, opportunities to engage in peacemaking are sometimes unanticipated. This is true for Ambassador Asencio's negotiation success and the Reverend Adams's conciliation assistance as well as for Professor Fisher's mediation advisory role.

\* \* \*

# The Field of Peace Learning

*Defining the Field.* Describing the field of peace learning is no less complicated than defining the field of health. Health focuses on disease and dysfunction and extends beyond to matters of physical and psychological well-being: diet, nutrition, exercise, stress, boredom, and air and water quality. Peace has war and mass destruction as its core concerns and directs additional attention to questions of political and societal structures that reduce harmful conflict and make conflict productive, and to questions of social and interpersonal means to promote affirmative human capacities. While the roots of the health field may be in religion, it now relies heavily on pure and applied science, and science, in our day, carries a sense of certainty. Peace learning has its roots squarely in the humanities, the arts, and religion, and scientific learning, both in methodology and technology, increasingly is applied to questions of peace.

Because both fields involve basic issues of life and death and enlist political and societal decisions, the analogy between health and peace is instructive. There are, however, important differences. In no small measure due to the expenditure of immense sums of money, the health field has developed numerous professional divisions, such as medicine, nursing, and hospital management, and distinct disciplines, such as psychiatry, oncology, and anesthesiology. In this, the health field in the United States has substantial support from the federal government, and the field receives similar attention from other nations' governments, too, particularly in Europe. Many American schools of medicine have benefitted from federal funding, and individuals are assisted through Medicare and Medicaid. Furthermore, the health field has its own federal institution, the National Institutes of Health. In short, the health field is highly organized and has clear popular approval, even if there remain areas of dispute.

A mark of health professionalization is that its practice is viewed by many as outside the scope of lay competence. Peace is not so highly professionalized; neither credentials nor licensing is required for participation. In the commission's view, professionalization of peace-related expertise should be set in the broader context that peace is everyone's business. A too-exclusive professionalization of peacemaking would contradict both our heritage and the extensiveness of American involvement in peace activities.

Not restricting the field to "professionals" does not mean, however, that peace learning shunts aside the development of high professional levels of competence and expertise. The opposite is the case. Peace scholars hold top academic positions, and expertise in practice is increasingly demanded: the Federal Mediation and Conciliation Service, which involves peacemaking in the domestic labor-management arena, requires significant practical experience of most of its mediators, and the State Department now offers a brief course in negotiation at its Foreign Service Institute. It is equally important, the commission believes, that peace learning not be atomized into separated disciplines. The strength of the field of peace learning comes precisely from its multi- and interdisciplinary character. It is the combination of diversity and a fusion of disciplines directed to common goals that defines and invigorates the field. In its research, education, training, and practice, creativity in peace learning advances from the shared insights of anthropology, the arts, economics, geography, the health sciences, history, the humanities, linguistics, philosophy, the physical sciences, political science, psychology, religion, and sociology.

While the commission believes it fortunate that peace is neither fully professionalized nor a single discipline, the commission has established that peace studies is a distinct and definable field of learning for three reasons: it has a literature, courses of study, and professional organizations; it has well-defined assumptions and definitions, and a variety of research methodologies; and it has a strong applied component in the practice of conflict intervention. The commission finds that peace is a legitimate field of learning that encompasses rigorous, interdisciplinary research, education, and training directed toward peacemaking expertise. A brief excursion into the research component of the field will illustrate this judgment.

*Peace Research.* In 1978, the United Nations Educational, Scientific, and Cultural Organization published its third directory of peace research institutions, following earlier editions in 1966 and 1973.[8] The survey identifies 310 peace and conflict research organizations, which include those supporting peace research. Of these, 41 are international and 269 are national research organizations. The United States has 79 of these research groups, more than any other nation. The range is fairly broad, as indicated by inclusion of the following American institutions: the Consortium on Peace Research, Education and Development (COPRED), a group of about one hundred United States and Canadian institutions and organizations headquartered at Kent State University; the Carnegie Endowment for International Peace; the University of Colorado's Institute of Behavioral Science; Duke University's Rule of

Law Research Center; the East-West Center in Hawaii; the Hudson Institute; the Massachusetts Institute of Technology's Center for International Studies; the Conference on Peace Research in History, headquartered at the University of Toledo; the University of Michigan's Correlates of War Project; the United States Arms Control and Disarmament Agency; and Yale University's Department of Political Science, from which the *Journal of Conflict Resolution* is published.

Most institutions are relatively small: two-thirds reported staffs of twenty or less. Budgets, too, are generally modest, leading to specialities even though interests may be more expansive. For example, a prominent Western peace research institution is the Stockholm International Peace Research Institute, which the Swedish government created in 1966 and supports through an annual appropriation of about $1.3 million. Its field of concentration is reflected in its annual publication *World Armaments and Disarmaments Sipri Yearbook.* Because the UNESCO survey relied heavily upon self-definition, the listing of peace and conflict research organizations contains only modest overlap with the 1,755 social science institutions[9] listed in UNESCO's *World Directory of Social Science Institutions* and the many research institutions devoted to scientific and technological issues that concern peace research, such as those which participate in the activities of the Pugwash Conference on Science and World Affairs. In consequence, many organizations whose work touches upon peace questions and many individual peace researchers are not included.

The UNESCO survey shows clearly that peace research is a worldwide activity. It also illustrates how loosely knit and even isolated peace researchers are, which may account to some extent for what the commission views as unfortunate neglect by policymakers of useful knowledge from the field. Still, peace researchers do meet through a number of international organizations. Among them are the International Peace Research Association now headquartered in Tokyo, which has convened biannual conferences since 1964; the International Studies Association, which has sections in North America, the Caribbean, the United Kingdom, and Japan; the Peace Science Society (International); the International Society for Research on Aggression; the International Political Science Association and the International Sociological Association, which each have special research committees on peace and conflict.

Peace researchers gain further linkage through United Nations agencies. These include UNESCO's Division of Human Rights and Peace, which has a budget of $1.2 million, and the United Nations

Institute for Training and Research (UNITAR), which was "set up to enhance the effectiveness of the United Nations in the areas of peace and security and the promotion of socio-economic development"[10] and applies 10 percent of its million dollar budget to peace research; it has a new Center for Disarmament Research in Geneva. Additional linkages may develop through the United Nations University headquartered in Tokyo—which uniquely has no faculty or student body but works to develop collaborative scholarship on world hunger, human and social development, and the use and management of natural resources—and through the University for Peace, recently authorized by a United Nations General Assembly resolution[11] establishing an international center of superior education for postgraduate teaching, research, and dissemination of knowledge, specifically oriented to training for peace. The government of Costa Rica has offered the headquarters site for this new United Nations body. Addressing the commission in New York, Jose Miguel Alfaro, vice president of Costa Rica, shared the peace learning and peacemaking concerns of Costa Rica's President Rodrigo Carazo:

> ... our President said that if we wanted to have a 21st century, it would have to be a peaceful century. And he proposed to change the centuries-old concept "si vis pacem, para bellum"—if you want peace, prepare for war—to a positive outlook on peace as a value in itself, to a concept that could be phrased "si vis pacem, para pacem"—if you want peace, prepare for peace.

Without rigorous research on peace, preparation for peace will continue to be haphazard and difficult. As the commission probed the field of peace learning, it raised sharp questions about the state of peace research, mindful of the danger of false promises and unsubstantiated claims. The commission is satisfied that the research aspect of the field is sufficiently well developed to warrant the establishment of the United States Academy of Peace with research as an important function. Like the disciplines of international relations, group behavior, history, and geography, peace research exhibits substantial debate over methodology. Theory is in the early stages of creative development. Data sets are still inadequate. The proper mix of theoretical investigations and empirical research, the balance between field research and archival and secondary research, and appropriate assumptions and frames of reference are questions of deep concern to peace researchers.

The commission has taken note of a tendency for some outside observers to confuse peace movement activity with peace research, a confusion particularly evident during the anti-war movement of the Vietnam era. Commissioner Elise Boulding commented about activism versus research during a commission meeting in Washington:

> There is perhaps some misperception of the degree to which the "peace movement" has had either input or much interest [in the work of the commission]. Peace researchers are a different category. It may happen that some peace researchers also happen to be advocates of peace in the movement sense, but most researchers are international researchers with a focus on disarmament and non-military solutions to conflict [regardless of]...their personal positions.

On divisions within the field, Dr. J. David Singer, who directs the Correlates of War Project at the University of Michigan, has written:

> ... there can be too much consensus in a field, especially when that field is characterized more by the science of discovery than the science of verification. There are to date few grounds for embracing any particular set of methods within the scientific mode and even fewer for accepting any of the contending theoretical orientations. We just do not know enough yet, and the current diversity is a healthy rather than a dangerous condition. I would even argue that commitment to a common paradigm in any macro-social science discipline today is a sign of atrophy and stagnation, rather than of scholarly advance. Our theoretical and methodological diversity is to me a sign of health, curiosity, and vigor, auguring well for the future of the field.[12]

The commission, too, finds much promise in the different approaches and methods the field is developing as it delves deeper into issues of peace. Ideological conformity in such a field would be counter to our best scholarly traditions and inappropriate to a new national endeavor.

Speaking to the commission in Boulder, Kenneth Boulding reviewed developments that led to the emergence of this profoundly important "new field of human knowledge":

> In its origin, conflict studies owes much to an American historian, Quincy Wright, whose classic work is entitled *A Study of War*,[13]

and to an English meteorologist, Lewis F. Richardson, whose two great works, *Arms and Insecurity* and *Statistics of Deadly Quarrels*,[14] were circulated in manuscript for many years before they were finally published in 1960. The two "founding fathers" in some sense symbolize two sources of the [field], ... one coming out of the study of war, the other coming out of the quest for peace. The first goes into the arms control movement, as reflected, for instance, in the foundation of the Arms Control and Disarmament Agency in the early 1960s. The second goes into the peace research movement, symbolized perhaps in the formation of the International Peace Research Association, under the sponsorship of UNESCO, again in the early 1960s.

What once were different sources have now become identifiable research branches of the field of peace learning: peace as absence of war and peace as social justice. They are complemented by the third branch—peacemaking techniques—which equally reflects the field's concern with policy relevance and application. A brief description of each branch now follows.

*Peace as the Absence of War.* On January 7, 1980, the Council of the American Association for the Advancement of Science adopted the following resolution:

> WHEREAS the present international system contains a positive probability of nuclear war, a situation which the scientific community has made possible. BE IT RESOLVED that the AAAS commends Congress and the President for appointing a Commission on Proposals for the National Academy of Peace and Conflict Resolution and expresses the hope that such an Academy will be established, with the ability to mobilize the scientific community for research and information exchange into the processes by which stable peace and disarmament can be generated and the probability of war reduced.

This resolution is squarely within the peace as absence of war branch of peace research. In a letter to the commission, Randall Forsberg, president and executive director of the Institute for Defense and Disarmament Studies, suggested:

> Two questions have especially important bearing on the relationship between armaments and peace. One is empirical evidence on the correlation between arms races or arms balances and the out-

break of war. The other question involves an analysis of the intended modes of use of specific types of wars. In working for peace there is a decisive distinction to be made, for example, among the following types of war: 1) superpower, unilateral, conventional intervention in smaller countries, such as the USSR in Poland or the U.S. in the Persian Gulf; 2) a conventional war between NATO and the Warsaw Pact; 3) an exchange of nuclear weapons between the United States and the Soviet Union.

In Washington, Lawrence D. Weiler, special assistant for Public and Academic Liaison of the United States Arms Control and Disarmament Agency, testified:

I do not know if the commission will conclude that the arms race — in its broadest political as well as hardware sense — is one of those [critical] areas [requiring increased research and training]. Given the fact that my own professional life has been devoted to this subject, my judgment could possibly be viewed as parochial. I would, therefore, submit for your reflection a statement made years ago by John Foster Dulles: ''... [The] destructive power inherent in matter must be controlled by the idealism of the spirit and the wisdom of the mind. They alone stand between us and a lifeless planet. There are plenty of problems in the world, many of them interconnected. But there is no problem which compares with this central, universal problem of saving the human race from extinction....'' I have personally become increasingly concerned by the gap between the magnitude and significance of the problem of the arms race and the resources that we as a society devote to understanding and dealing with it.... We have not as a society matched our resources to what we proclaim to see as one of mankind's greatest dangers.

Congruent with Dr. Weiler's testimony, the commission believes that the academy should and will devote significant resources to questions of war and the arms race, nuclear and other, in collaboration with the Arms Control and Disarmament Agency and other government and non-government institutions that focus on those issues.

A number of scholars investigate these questions and others that pertain to global and national conditions leading to war or permitting the conduct of large as well as contained wars, and to ways international and other major conflicts can be waged without war. The commission cites the work of two such scholars to illustrate the peace as absence of war research branch of the field. They are Dr. J. David Singer and Dr. Gene

Sharp. Their work represents this branch's uses of historical and political science modes of analysis, including comparative and qualitative case studies and systems theory. Singer's work is heavily quantitative and employs computer technology. Sharp prefers non-quantitative description influenced by classical political theory. Sharp is an apostle of nonviolent action as a political tool and of a nonmilitary civilian defense. Singer works to develop predictive schema useful to policymakers in preventing war. Each recognizes the inevitability of international conflict and believes that scholarship can be policy-relevant and can reduce the possibility of mass destruction while advancing security interests and national goals.

Singer's work is informed by the view that

> ... the better our knowledge about the processes by which groups move from incompatible interests to conflict to mass violence, the more readily we can distinguish between those factors which are beyond our control and those which we had best try to modify. If, near the brink, it is too late to change certain structural, cultural, or material properties of the system, but still possible to change others, the knowledge which permits us to make that distinction is of no mean consequence.[15]

Singer makes every effort to state clearly his assumptions and values and encourages others to make use of the extensive and painstakingly developed data bank of the Correlates of War Project. He recognizes the interdependency of peace and justice, but argues that

> ... war, and the recurrent preparation for war, may well be a greater obstacle to the achievement of justice than the opposite. That is, we may be able to reduce the incidence of war while injustice remains, but are quite unlikely to reduce the incidence of injustice while war remains an accepted condition of the human community. As long as war is a regular mode of human problem-solving—and today its legitimacy remains virtually unchallenged—people and resources will continue to be mobilized for war. The material and psychological consequences of such continuing mobilization can hardly be conducive to the growth of civilized discourse, generous cooperation, human liberties, or economic development.[16]

Like other peace researchers, Singer is concerned that his type of work on issues of peace and war be presented in ways that facilitate appropriate attention from policymakers. Too often, he suggests, peace researchers succumb to impenetrable prose, and quantitative work on peace is manipulated to fit a policymaker's preconceptions or is ignored because it is less familiar than military or industrial studies. He suggests:

> Although our progress in the generation of knowledge has been painfully slow, that pace seems breathtaking in contrast to the rate at which political elites and the attentive public have taken an interest in the findings, concepts, and methods of recent research on conflict and war. [17]

Singer and his colleague Michael Wallace suggest that policymakers should be encouraged by the quality of empirical research on peace as the absence of war:

> ... the early warning indicators strategy is already showing considerable promise; in less than two years, the research community in North America has generated a significant number of indicators that are not only useful "omens" for the policymaker but also demonstrably systematic and reliable....And, judging from the growing conceptual and methodological sophistication displayed in these essays [in *To Augur Well*], we have only begun to tap the possibilities inherent in this approach. The day will never arrive when "calculation will replace argumentation" in the foreign policy process, but perhaps it is not too much to hope that the "mix" may in due course be modified.[18]

Sharp's work is historical rather than mathematical. It represents important philosophical traditions and is one historian-political scientist's effort to address issues of war, conflict, and peace with practicality and a new set of research concepts. Sharp's major and seminal contribution is *The Politics of Nonviolent Action*. His premise is that:

> Basically, there appear to be two views of the nature of power. One can see people as dependent upon the good will, the decisions and the support of their government or of any other hierarchical system to which they belong. Or, conversely, one can see that government or system as dependent upon the people's good will, decisions and support....Nonviolent action is based on the second of these views: that governments depend upon people, that power is pluralistic, and that political power is fragile because it depends on many groups for reinforcement of its power sources. The first view — that people depend on governments, that political power is monolithic,

that it can really come from a few men, and that it is durable and self-perpetuating — appears to underlie most political violence.[19]

Sharp describes nonviolent action as a powerful technique that is neither passive nor submissive, does not depend solely upon psychological persuasion, does not require that its users be "good" people or that its goals be "good," and is not limited to intranational conflicts within a democratic system.[20] After he establishes theoretical premises in Part I, "Power and Struggle," he presents a thesaurus of 196 nonviolent action methods in Part II, "The Methods of Nonviolent Action," and then a tactical handbook in Part III, "The Dynamics of Nonviolent Action." The thrust of his work is to describe, with massive historical evidence, how and why "to apply nonviolent action in place of violence in the crucial conflicts of today and tomorrow." [21]

Sharp's most recent book, *Social Power and Political Freedom,*[22] continues the themes set in *The Politics of Nonviolent Action,* but is considerably shorter and written in a more popular style than the earlier work. In his "Introduction" to *Social Power and Political Freedom,* United States Senator Mark O. Hatfield of Oregon comments on Sharp's rational pragmatism by quoting General Omar N. Bradley's November 11, 1948, Armistice Day Address concerning what Hatfield terms the limits to "what the mind of man can do alone":

"With the monstrous weapons man already has, humanity is in danger of being trapped in this world by its moral adolescence. Our knowledge of science has clearly outstripped our capacity to control it. We have too many men of science, too few men of god. We have grasped the mystery of the atom and rejected the Sermon on the Mount. Man is stumbling blindly through spiritual darkness while toying with the precarious secrets of life and death....The world has achieved brilliance without wisdom, power without conscience. Ours is a world of nuclear giants and ethical infants. We know more about war than we know about peace; more about killing, than we know about living."

Hatfield urges that "Dr. Sharp's intuitive grasp and understanding of the practical vehicles for just such an application of divine principles make this work monumental in its time," even though "the case he presents...is not made on moral or theological truths; rather it rests on history. Therefore, Sharp's case has relevance to all, no matter what their theological or moral persuasion." [23]

Sharp's work is not heavily theological, but in Boston he spoke to the commission on conflicts that come from humanity's universal reverence for life and the need for dignified relationships:

> I think that the attention [of an academy] should be primarily, though not exclusively, focused on what I call acute conflicts. These are the conflicts in which the issues at stake are perceived by one or both parties [to be] of extreme importance [and] on which compromise is normally not possible. Now, this means there are many other types of conflict in which compromise and those means of conflict resolution such as arbitration, conciliation, negotiation, and so forth, are useful, and they should receive attention also. But the most serious ones are those in which people believe they cannot compromise because of moral principle, because of the societal and political consequences, and therefore, the people are prepared to fight. And normally that means they are willing to fight by violent means.

*Peace as Social Justice.* As is clear from the statements of Singer and Sharp in the preceding section, peace as absence of war does not shut out the concerns of peace as social justice. Singer simply suggests a priority relationship between the two, and Sharp may agree that, when reduced to fundamentals, social justice is the basis for conflicts over which there is no "compromise because of moral principle."

The World Order Models Project represents one aspect of the movement in research toward peace as social justice. Saul Mendlovitz writes that the World Order Models Project

> ... was initially conceived in response to pedagogical needs related to the study of the problem of the elimination of war as a human social institution....It soon became clear that the subject matter would have to be expanded to include the related problems of economic well-being and social justice, if we were to generate a world interest in this inquiry.... Many persons ... argued that it was impossible to deal adequately with war prevention without taking into account poverty and social injustice; that as an empirical matter, these matters were so inextricably interwoven, they should be seen as part of the definition of the problem of war prevention. More importantly, however, it became increasingly clear that while peace, in the sense of the elimination of international violence, might have a very high priority with individuals in the industrialized sector of the globe, economic well-being and social justice received a much higher rating in the Third World.[24]

These attitudinal differences that reflect value weightings in various cultures were illustrated to the commission by Dr. Donald McNemar. After speaking about structural and institutional violence which arguably allows a black South African half the life-span of a white, he stated:

> People view various values quite differently. If you talked with Africans and said, "Let's talk about what kind of future world we want," we'll discover various values. The Americans [would say], "Peace is terribly important and the environment is becoming even more so." The Africans [would say], "You've got your priorities wrong. Until southern Africa is resolved, we can't talk about peace as being a prime value. We may have to use war in order to resolve that issue."

A major European proponent of research into peace as social justice is Johan Galtung, first holder of the Chair in Peace Research at the University of Oslo. Tightly linking peace and violence, Galtung suggests that "in a conflict, [when] there are incompatible goals...in the system of interaction, it [is] clear that an asymmetric relationship must always be one of conflict, i.e., involving structural and possibly also personal violence."[25] Galtung illustrates his view of violence through an "heuristic device [of two questions] ... to show how untenable the classical conception [is] in terms of direct violence between states":

> (i) Violence is deprival of life, like in a battle; it is intended and is a quick process. But what if it is not intended, and/or takes place slowly like in a slum? Is that not violence? It might even be argued that it is usually more violent, for if the victim dies 32 years old in a battle he is usually in good health the moment before, whereas a slow death is usually preceded by a process of increasing near-death. (ii) Imagine a country engaged in no external war at all. Is that country in a stage of peace if internal wars are raging, or if the other type of violence discussed above is rampant?[26]

Having agreed, then, to probe beyond the immediate questions of peace as absence of war, peace as social justice research seeks to identify at least decently arguable if not yet scientifically causal explanations of fundamental social discord and human misery and to suggest ways to overcome them. Like the other two branches of the field—peace as absence of war and peacemaking techniques—peace as social justice researchers work as problem-solvers. Marek Thee, editor of the *Bulletin of Peace Proposals,* describes substantive issues in peace research as shifting along a continuum from a narrow to a wide matrix of concerns involving a great variety of types of studies. On his continuum, peace as absence of war would limit itself to the top two categories, while peace as social justice would explore all the categories.

### THEE'S PEACE RESEARCH CONTINUUM*

| | Focus: ⟶ | Subject: ⟶ | Goal: |
|---|---|---|---|
| **1** | The nation-state in the international system | International relations General international system studies | Realization of United Nations ideals |
| **2** | Manifest physical violence | War/peace Armaments/dis-armament studies | Abolition of war |
| **3** | Structural socio-economic violence | Underdevelopment/ development studies | Satisfaction of basic human needs Social justice Equality of nations |
| **4** | Repressive political violence | Human rights studies | Human autonomy and self realization |
| **5** | Alternative futures | World order Workable utopia studies | Progressive transfor-mation of the human society |

*Marek Thee, "Scope and Priorities in Peace Research," paper prepared for Consultations in Pease Research, United Nations University, Tokyo, December 6, 1980.*

Peace as social justice is prescriptive as well as descriptive in approaching "future worlds." It requires straight statements of operative values. Dr. Elise Boulding writes:

> One thing that the development of futurism, the first cousin of peace research, has done for twentieth century science is to deal a deathblow to the old discussions about value-free science. In envisioning alternative futures, the first thing futurists have to do is to clarify their values and priorities, and to lay out their working assumptions about the nature of the human conditions and the potentials of the social order.[27]

The five values adopted by the World Order Models Project— peace, ecological stability, economic well-being, social justice, and participation — represent this type of value and priority clarification.[28] Social justice, which may be the clearest principle next to peace, includes "life, health, freedom, basic material comforts, and equal social status."[29] Its Biblical roots are found in the Hebraic concept of "Shalom." Because of its clarity and its ties with long-standing concerns of social activists in the United States, the commission believes that social justice best identifies this branch of peace research.

The commission sees research on peace as social justice as highly important to development of the field of peace learning. Without it, both peace as absence of war and peacemaking techniques may lose the value base they need and the constant challenge to their own assumptions. Despite its importance, it has less immediate importance to policymakers than the other two branches. The difficulty for the commission, specifically in regard to the United States Academy of Peace funding original research from the peace as social justice branch, is that the work in that part of the field tends "to adopt the more traditional analytic interpretive style of research, rather than the more methodologically sophisticated behavioral science approach."[30] This is due less to research style preferences than to the scope of questions involved, the high cost of complex and rigorous empirical analyses, and the difficulty in obtaining sufficiently precise data on these issues globally.

Peace as social justice may not be the most useful priority research area for the academy at this time, but from the pedagogical side, it should be an integral part of the academy's education and training programs and information services. This will keep the public and policymakers abreast of what is being done in the area in this country and elsewhere and will be important to practitioners and researchers who are more active in the other two branches of the field of peace learning— peace as absence of war and peacemaking techniques.

*Peacemaking Techniques.* The third major branch of the field of peace learning is peacemaking techniques. The commission expects the academy to focus substantial attention on research about peacemaking techniques, through the study of peace, conflict, and social processes and such analyses as strategic formulations in bargaining and gaming. Knowledge from peace as absence of war and peace as social justice research remain vital to peacemaking techniques. Dr. Daniel Levinson pointed to this in testimony before the commission in Los Angeles:

My message is that a successful effort to do something fundamental about conflict, in all its forms and in all its locations, must look at its sources and causal factors as well as techniques of resolution. A better understanding than we now have of the causes of conflict would not only provide a rationale for methods of conflict resolution, it might also suggest effective methods to prevent conflicts from developing in the first place. Prevention is always better than cure.

To a large extent, research in peacemaking techniques and the training that can develop from it draw from the behavioral sciences. They are directed to application both by individuals and by groups. A question that resounded throughout the commission's public seminars, for example, was "Can conflict resolution techniques be taught?" There was almost universal consensus that the skills of the four basic peacemaking techniques—negotiation, conciliation, mediation, and arbitration — are teachable. These techniques form a continuum; what one learns about one technique is useful to another. Negotiators represent a party's positions and interests. Conciliators work at both preliminary and subsequent stages to a formal negotiation. Like conciliators, mediators and arbitrators are third parties who help disputants reach accords, with the difference being that an arbitrator can impose an outcome and a mediator can only suggest one.

Speaking about training and education in peacemaking, Eldrin Bell, Atlanta's deputy director of police, responded to the question, "Can peacemaking be taught?":

The answer seems implicit. Surely the Reverend Martin Luther King, Jr. and Mahatma Gandhi taught the theories of nonviolence they advocated as much as they espoused them. The question of peaceful resolution to conflict can even be answered with the local efforts of our domestic violence teams. Out of 2,300 referrals, we have had only four homicides. Even the number of repeat referrals has been lower than we had originally anticipated.

Echoing the view of Theodore Kheel, who assured the commission in New York that negotiation and mediation can be taught, Richard D. Fincher of the American Arbitration Association stated to the commission in Boston: "The theory and skills required in effective conflict resolution can clearly be taught. Since 1968, the AAA has conducted training for hundreds of aspiring neutrals and has developed a curriculum that provides the optimal blend of theory and case simulation.'' In Washington, Dr. Wayne Horvitz of the Federal Mediation and Conciliation Service testified: ''There is a body of mediators which says, 'Mediators are born and not made.' I happen to think that that is a lot of malarkey.''

Addressing the diplomatic side of peacemaking, Professor Richard Pipes suggested to the commission in Boston:

> We're not really training diplomats at Fletcher or Georgetown; we're training people in international relations....The art of negotiating in international relations is a great skill acquired partly through teaching, partly through experience, and partly through teaching accumulated experience. There are certain things you can be taught. For example, if you're going to sit down with the Russians, we know that certain things have to be prepared. With Russians, you have to be extremely specific. You have to work out a [detailed] agenda. You have to keep very good records. You have to spell out in greatest detail every term you're going to use. Nothing must be left to a simple sort of general understanding. This is just one of the many rules that have been established in dealing with the Russians that can be taught, and I believe properly trained diplomats can achieve a tremendous amount in defusing international tension.

And Ambassador Diego Asencio urged building upon our capacities as cultural relativists:

> When you find yourself in a situation that is anomalous because of cultural differences, you don't feel threatened, [but] rather interested.... A person who is conditioned to reacting that way is able, even if he gets sent in improperly and inadequately trained, to pick up these perceptions as he goes along and to study the society in those terms....There is no question in my mind that these are teachable traits and, approached properly, the whole idea, particularly in the international context, is bridging these gaps.

Research in peacemaking techniques is intimately tied to training as well as to education, and that results in rather different media and scholarly attention than is common to peace as absence of war and peace as social justice research. Some work is synthesized into book-length studies, such as Kriesberg's *The Sociology of Social Conflicts*, Deutsch's *The Resolution of Conflict*, Curle's *Making Peace*, Burton's *Conflict and Communication* and *Deviance, Terrorism and War*, and

Wehr's *Conflict Regulation*[31]. Other work of great value appears as handbooks or monographs: Fisher's *International Mediation,* the International Peace Academy's *Peacekeeper's Handbook,* Laue's "Intervening in Community Conflicts," Rip and Lincoln's "Impartial Intervention into Community Disputes," and the Ford Foundation's "New Approaches to Conflict Resolution."[32] And there are a number of useful collections of essays and studies, including Bermant, Kelman, and Warwick's *The Ethics of Social Intervention,* Wilkenfeld's *Conflict Behavior and Linkage Politics,* and Smith's *Conflict Resolution: Contributions of the Behavioral Sciences.*[33]

The range of questions addressed by research in peacemaking techniques is large and is joined by a common interest in applicability. It includes techniques for reaching arms limitation agreements, border settlements, interstate environmental accords, and decisions on locating contested community facilities. Success to date in application has been rather mixed. Lawrence D. Weiler suggested that the literature is extensive, but too confined within academic walls: "Thus, if there is a need with respect to this field, it is not research on the techniques as such, but it is to make them more relevant and to expose practitioners to them in some form of post-graduate study."

The commission suggests that research is substantial, but has not exhausted the questions and dilemmas of peacemaking techniques. It is true, however, that translation into readily usable form has been inadequate. Because of its complementary program and delivery system structure, the United States Academy of Peace should be able to remedy this deficiency in the field substantially and in a relatively short period of time.

Issues may be defined situationally, as Dr. Philip Jacob did for the commission in Hawaii, with the focus kept on performance. Dr. Jacob suggested four basic areas requiring research on techniques. First is communication, encompassing perceptional and behavioral aspects of direct and third parties to conflicts, mass media, public opinion, and technological instruments. Second is peacekeeping, both in methodology and in establishing a reservoir of effectively trained people. Third is negotiation, mediation, conciliation, and arbitration, including the internal processes of such teams and their relationships with their own governments or organizations. And fourth is social change strategies which extend beyond the immediate crisis and include forecasting. Dr. Jacob said it is here that "traditional diplomacy is extremely weak. Very little time is left to address the fundamental problems of peacemaking, and it is crisis after crisis."

Although research on peacemaking techniques is extensive, it may be the research area of least systematic attention, perhaps because it requires a blend of practitioner experience, scholarly dissection, and educational and training interests. Yet it is also the one that harbors the most immediate payoff. One can foresee, for example, peacemaking technique courses enriching the curriculum of the Naval War College. At the commission's Boston public seminar, Rear Admiral Edward F. Welch, Jr., president of the college, reported that the faculty uses a multidisciplinary curriculum in the school's three basic courses of study—strategy and policy, management, and naval operations—to meet its commitment "to furthering the essential continuance of peace and the resolution of conflict by peaceful means."

Research on peacemaking techniques is pragmatic and looks at all the actors in conflict roles. Richard Pipes told the commission that the United States has even relied on Soviet translators, and thus a Soviet record, "in all major negotiations conducted with the Soviet Union over the past ten years." Unlike us, he said,

> The Russians have an academy of international relations where they have an incredibly tough program. It lasts six years ... [and] negotiations are part of it. It's a school for diplomats in which negotiation is one of the things they teach and, by all accounts, they produce superb negotiators.... Now, we have a great and long record of experience in negotiating with the Soviet Union. I brought with me a volume which has been put out very recently by the Committee on Foreign Affairs called "Soviet Diplomacy and Negotiating Behavior." This is a superb volume ... [by] Joseph Whelan working for the Congressional Research Service, with just incredible evidence of our experience negotiating with the Soviet Union since 1918 virtually to the present. [It] shows there are certain patterns which we run into, there are certain mistakes we commit, there are certain patterns of Soviet behavior which we ought to know.
>
> ... I believe we need far more attention to be paid to the teaching of negotiating techniques. This is a very ancient art and developed first in the Italian city-states in the 14th century; it has a long tradition behind it—how states deal with each other even though they are very hostile to each other. We ought to teach people: in particular, what kinds of experience we have in negotiating with countries which have set different outlooks on life and different interests, such as the Communist block.

The commission wholly agrees that our diplomats must be highly skilled in negtiations so they can effectively represent the nation's goals in pursuing peace even in the most difficult of circumstances. But we need not and ought not to limit our training or the research on which it must be based to diplomatic officials and situations alone. Full involvement of the citizenry in civic matters is a fundamental American process. While the Soviet Union develops an elite cadre of negotiators, the United States develops negotiating skills throughout its people—as befits a democracy. Today's banker may become tomorrow's diplomat and a haberdasher may become president. To be true to our heritage and our interests, peacemaking research and its broad scale application should receive significant attention by the United States Academy of Peace.

## Conclusion

The Commission on Proposals for the National Academy of Peace and Conflict Resolution presents its final report with confidence. The commission looks forward to the establishment of the United States Academy of Peace as a living symbol and practical instrument for the nation's dedication to international peace.

This report responds fully to the questions mandated to the commission by the Congress and the president. The commission found that the knowledge and skills developed by the field of peace learning remain fragmented and underused. The commission also established that the field has scientifically testable theories and hypotheses, is devoted to pragmatism and application, is international in scope, and has critical importance to the nation's goal of promoting peace among the nations and peoples of the world.

The commission was heartened by the extent of international peace activities of persons from government, private enterprise, and voluntary associations. The commission has proposed an academy design that is efficient and responsive to the peace interests of the federal government, private and public institutions of higher education, and persons from many walks of life. The academy will be accessible. Although the academy will not have policy or intervention authority itself, it will situate the field of peace learning squarely in education and policy determinations and will extend the field's knowledge and skills to persons from all three sectors of the nation.

As a visible, focused, national investment, the academy will be organically American, based in the nation's rich but unsung peace heritage. "To read de Toqueville and look at us today," commission vice chairman James Laue noted, "one is astonished and really delighted at how we have built on what we have been and transmitted that sense of association and problem-solving across the generations, even though many of our ancestors came here long after he left our shores." As a contribution to the nation and the world, the academy will be a permanent beacon for those principles of peace that make America a cherished ideal.

No problems of our age surpass those of international peace, conflicts, and war. Throughout the nation, the commission heard deep concern, worry, and even outrage over the violence and threats of violence, particularly nuclear, that are part of our daily lives. The commission also found a people proud of its peace heritage and determined to bring its full measure to bear upon these crucial issues of life and death, freedom and justice. When opportunity is clear and the need pressing for fusion between the worlds of learning and public affairs, this nation responds: the Morrill Act created the land grant college system to transform and unify an expanding nation; the military service academies educate and train a needed sophisticated, professional officer corps; and the National Academy of Sciences informs the federal government on controversial scientific questions. The United States Academy of Peace comes from this tradition: a new institution to meet critical needs of the nation as a whole.

Earlier in this report, the commission discussed extension of national conflict resolution methods to international disputes. It made clear that the academy's focus is international peace, but that the broad role of Americans internationally as well as the blurring of national and international lines make it imperative that the academy address the question of transferability. The commission reserved to these concluding pages a final thought on the relationship between international and national conflict resolution experience. It is this: primary attention to questions of international peace may bring important dividends to the United States as a society with its own conflicts. Many people who have been involved in international peace activities report new insights in their understanding of conflicts at all levels of society. Moreover, comparison with other societies and cultures—through such activities as international business, Peace Corps service, and refugee resettlement—offers fresh perspectives, refined sensitivities, and creative new approaches to problems we face within the nation.

Finally, the commission believes that we as a nation have an obligation, a sacred duty, to do what we can to gain control over elements of our destiny. We must, as we have in the past, provide standards and leadership to reduce the causes of war, to prevent violence and destruction, to secure freedom and justice, and to promote peace among nations. Americans never have been a passive people, content to sit back while events plunge on. The need for this nation's stewardship of peace never has been clearer.

In his preface to this report, commission chairman Spark Matsunaga states: "If peace is a risk, never won for sure but held for the day, then we must know its ways and means surely today and tomorrow." To today's youth and to generations yet to be born, the United States Academy of Peace represents a promise that the nation will take that risk. The wise person approaches international peace with no less trepidation than war, and the commission is clear that the academy is not the only institution for the pursuit of peace. As a nation, we are active on many fronts; the academy will strengthen those peace efforts. The commission is deeply certain that the academy is an opportunity not to be passed by. At this critical time in the nation's history, the commission urges the Congress, the president, and the people of the United States to consider carefully and favorably the immediate establishment of the United States Academy of Peace.

# Notes

## PART ONE

## The Just-War Tradition

This essay in many respects draws substantially on the efforts of others. In the sections, ''The Medieval Perspective'' and ''The Post-Medieval Reaction,'' I have relied on two outstanding studies: Frederick H. Russell, *The Just War in the Middle Ages* (Cambridge: Cambridge University Press, 1975) and ''Five Classic Just-War Theories: A Study in the Thought of Thomas Aquinas, Vitoria, Suarez, Gentili, and Grotius,'' written by LeRoy B. Walters, Jr. (unpublished Ph.D. dissertation, Yale University, 1971). Walters's study is long overdue for publication. I have also profited from the discussions of just-war categories in the writings of my colleague, James F. Childress, *Moral Responsibility in Conflicts: Essays on Nonviolence, War, Conscience* (Baton Rouge and London: Louisiana State University Press, 1982). In addition, I have relied to some extent on the historical reflections of James T. Johnson in *Just War Tradition and the Restraint of War: A Moral and Historical Inquiry* (Princeton, Princeton University Press, 1961); the more policy-oriented analysis of William V. O'Brien, *The Conduct of Just and Limited War* (New York: Praeger Publishers, 1983); Michael Walzer, *Just and Unjust Wars* (New York: Basic Books, Inc., 1977); Ralph B. Potter, *War and Moral Discourse* (Richmond, VA: John Knox Press, 1969); and Roland H. Bainton, *Christian Attitudes toward War and Peace* (Nashville: Abingdon Press, 1960).

1. Commission on Proposals for the National Academy of Peace and Conflict Resolution, *To Establish The United States Academy of Peace* (Washington, D.C.: Government Printing Office, 1981), p. 34.

2. Aristotle, *Nicomachean Ethics* (New York: Bobbs-Merrill, Inc., 1962), p. 90.

3. Cicero, *Laws (De Republica, de Legibus)*, trans. Clinton Walker Keyes (Cambridge, Mass.: Harvard University Press, 1927) pp. I, X, 28-29.

4. Frederick H. Russell, The Just War in the Middle Ages (Cambridge: Cambridge University Press, 1975), pp. 5-6.

5. These questions are my own revision and elaboration of four principal questions suggested by LeRoy Walters in his fine unpublished paper, ''The Simple Structure of the Just-War Theory.''

6. Augustine, *City of God*, trans. Marcus Dods (New York: Modern Library, 1950), pp. XIX, 7.

7. Russell, *Just War*, p.21. For a conflicting view, see Roland H. Bainton, *Christian Attitudes toward War and Peace* (Nashville: Abingdon Press, 1960), p. 99.

8. Ibid,. p. 97.

9. Russell, *Just War*, pp. 19-20 (italics added).

10. Bainton, *Christian Attitudes*, pp. 118-121.

11. Cited in Walters, "Five Classic Just-War Theories: Thomas Aquinas, Vitoria, Suarez, Gentili, and Grotius" (Ph.D. diss,. Yale University, 1971), p. 43.

12. Ibid., pp. 43-44.

13. Brian Tierney, *The Crisis of Church and State, 1050-1300* (Englewood Cliffs, N.J.: Prentice-Hall, Inc., 1964), p. 118.

14. Russell, *Just War,* p. 194.

15. Bainton, *Christian Attitudes*, p. 112.

16. Ibid., p. 113.

17. Ibid., p. 112.

18. Ibid., pp. 112-13.

19. Russell, *Just War*, p. 210.

20. Walters, "Five Classic Just-War Theories," p. 84.

21. Ibid., p. 115.

22. Eric D'Arcy, *Conscience and Its Right to Freedom* (London: Sheed & Ward, 1979), pp. 153-54.

23. A.P. D'Entreves, ed., *Aquinas: Selected Political Writings* (Oxford: Blackwell, 1959), p. 179.

24. Cited in D'Arcy, *Conscience and Its Right to Freedom,* p. 159.

25. Cited in Walters, "Five Classic Just-War Theories," p. 150.

26. Ibid.

27. Ibid., p. 187.

28. Ibid., p. 161.

29. See James T. Johnson, *Just War Tradition and the Restraint of War: A Moral and Historical Inquiry* (Princeton: Princeton University Press, 1981), p. 131ff.

30. Ibid., p. 149ff.

31. Walters, "Five Classic Just-War Theories," p. 223.

32. Hugo Grotius, *Prolegomena to the Law of War and Peace*, trans. Francis W. Kelsey (New York: Liberal Arts Press, 1957), p. 21.

33. Ibid., p. 18; cf. Grotius, *The Rights of War and Peace (De Jure Belli; ac Pacis)*,trans. Francis W. Kelsey (Oxford: Clarendon Press, 1925), Bk. III, ch. 1., "What is Lawful in War."

34. Ibid.; p. 10. cf. *Rights of War and Peace*, I,10.

35. Ibid., II, XXVI, 3.

36. Ibid., II, XXVI, 4.

37. Ibid.

38. Ibid.

39. Grotius, *Rights of War and Peace*, II, XX, 40

40. Walters, "Five Classic Just-War Theories," p. 352.

41. Ibid., p. 316; cf. Grotius, *Rights of War and Peace*, II, 24,7.

42. Walters, "Five Classic Just-War Theories," pp. 393-394.

43. Ibid., p. 364-365; cf. p. 384.

44. Ibid., p. 370.

45. Ibid., p. 325; cf. Grotius, *Rights of War and Peace* II, XXI, 12-13.

46. See Michael Walzer, *Just and Unjust Wars* (New York: Basic Books, 1977), p. 58 ff.

47. Frederick O. Bonkovsky, *International Norms and National Policy* (Grand Rapids, Mich.: Eerdmans, 1980), p. 85.

48. Myres B. McDougal and Florentino P. Feliciano, *Law and Minimum World Public Order* (New Haven: Yale University Press, 1967), p. 132.

49. See Walzer, *Just and Unjust Wars*, pp. 61-63.

50. This tradition has more recently led to an important discussion of the possibility of instituting "*selective* conscientious objection," whereby individuals might give conscientious reasons for non-participation in selected wars. See the interesting discussion in Childress's essay, "Policies Toward Conscientious Objectors to Military Service," in James F. Childress, ed.

*Moral Responsibility in Conflicts: Essays on Nonviolence, War and Conscience* (Baton Rouge and London: Lousiana State University Press, 1982), chap. 6.

51. William V. O'Brien, *The Conduct of Just and Limited War* (New York: Praeger Publishers, 1983), pp. 91-126.

52. Walzer, *Just and Unjust Wars*, pp. 97-101.

53. See Ralph B. Potter, *War and Moral Discourse* (Richmond, Va.: John Knox Press, 1969), pp. 43-46.

54. Paul Ramsey, *War and Christian Conscience* (Durham, N.C.: Duke University Press, 1961), esp. chaps. 8 and 11.

55. Leon Wieseltier, "Nuclear War, Nuclear Peace," *New Republic*, Jan. 10 and 17, 1983, p. 24.

56. Michael Novak, *Moral Clarity in the Nuclear Age* (Nashville, Tenn.: Thomas Nelson, 1983), pp. 62-63.

57. Jim Castelli, ed., *The Bishops and the Bomb* (Garden City, N.Y.: Doubleday, 1983), pp. 235-244 (paragraphs 162-199, "Pastoral Letter on War and Peace ").

58. Walzer, *Just and Unjust Wars*, p. 269.

## Peacekeeping as a Military Mission

1. See David R. Segal, Jesse J. Harris, Joseph M. Rothberg, and David H. Marlow, "Paratroopers as Peacekeepers," *Armed Forces and Society* 10 (1984), pp. 487-506.

2. Quincy Wright, *A Study of War*, 2d ed. (Chicago: University of Chicago Press, 1965), pp. 33-41.

3. Stanislav Andreski, *Military Organization and Society*, 2d. ed. (Berkeley: University of California Press, 1968), p.7.

4. Maury D. Feld, *The Structure of Violence* (Beverly Hills: Sage Publications, 1977), p. 13.

5. Morris Janowitz, *Military Conflict* (Beverly Hills: Sage Publications, 1975), pp. 70-88. See also Jacques Van Doorn, "The Decline of the Mass Army in the West," *Armed Forces and Society* 2 (1975), pp. 147-157.

6. Jacques Van Doorn, *The Soldier and Social Change* (Beverly Hills: Sage Publications, 1975), pp. 51-64.

7. Harold D. Lasswell, "The Garrison State," *American Journal of Sociology* 46 (1941), pp. 45-68; and Harold D. Lasswell, "Sino-Japanese Crisis: The Garrison State Versus the Civilian State," *China Quarterly* 11 (1937), pp. 643-49.

8. Harold D. Lasswell, "The Garrison State Hypothesis Today," in Samuel P. Huntington, ed., *Changing Patterns of Military Politics* (New York: Free Press, 1962), pp. 51-70.

9. For example, C. Wright Mills, *The Power Elite* (New York: Oxford University Press, 1956) and Seymour Melman, *Pentagon Capitalism* (New York: McGraw-Hill, 1970).

10. See R.E. Canjar, "Politics, Peace, and Production: A Structural-Materialist View of War" (forthcoming).

11. See D.K. Palit, *War in the Deterrent Age* (New York: A.S. Barnes, 1966).

12. Morris Janowitz, *The Professional Soldier* (New York: Free Press, 1960), p. 418 (emphasis added).

13. Ibid., p. 420.

14. Ibid., p. 419.

15. Ibid., pp. 424-25.

16. Morris Janowitz, "Toward a Redefinition of Military Strategy in International Relations," *World Politics* 26 (1974), pp. 499-500.

17. Morris Janowitz, "Stabilizing Military Systems," *Military Review* 55 (1975), p. 6.

18. Morris Janowitz, "Beyond Deterrence: Alternative Conceptual Dimensions," in Ellen P. Stern, ed., *The Limits of Military Intervention* (Beverly Hills: Sage Publications, 1977), pp. 384-385.

19. Morris Janowitz, "Civic Consciousness and Military Performance," in Morris Janowitz and Stephen D. Wesbrook, eds., *The Political Education of Soldiers* (Beverly Hills: Sage Publications, 1983), pp. 76-77.

20. The UN peacekeeping missions of this period were: Greece (1947); Palestine (1949); Indonesia (1949); Kashmir (1949); Egypt (1956); Lebanon (1958); Congo (1960); West New Guinea (1962); Yemen (1962); Cyprus (1964); India and Pakistan (1965); Suez Canal (1967).

21. Larry L. Fabian, *Soldiers Without Enemies* (Washington: The Brookings Institution, 1971).

22. Charles C. Moskos, "UN Peacekeepers: The Constabulary Ethic and Military Professionalism," *Armed Forces and Society* 1 (1975), pp. 388-401. See also David R. Segal and Barbara Foley Meeker, "Peacekeeping and Warfighting: Attitude Organization and Change among Combat Soldiers on Constabulary Duty" (Paper presented at the 79th annual meeting of the American Sociological Association, San Antonio, Texas, August 27-31, 1984).

23. Charles C. Moskos, *Peace Soldiers: The Sociology of a Unified United Nations Military Force* (Chicago: University of Chicago Press, 1976), p. 7.

24. Francis Paul Walters, *A History of the League of Nations* (London: Oxford University Press, 1952), p. 142.

25. Ibid., p. 592.

26. See Ibid., p. 593, and Moskos, *Peace Soldiers,* p. 19.

27. Moskos, *Peace Soldiers*, p. 16.

28. Ernest A. Gross, *The United Nations: Structure for Peace* (New York: Harper and Brothers, 1962), p. 58.

29. John G. Stoessinger, *The United Nations and the Superpowers—United States-Soviet Interactions at the United Nations* (New York: Random House, 1965), p. 62.

30. Ibid.

31. Arthur Lee Burns and Nina Heathcote, *Peacekeeping by UN Forces—from Suez to the Congo* (New York: Praeger, 1963), p. 7.

32. Ibid., p. 20.

33. Stoessinger, *The United Nations and the Superpowers*, p. 71.

34. Moskos, *Peace Soldiers*, p. 19.

35. Stoessinger, *The United Nations and the Superpowers*, p. 78.

36. Burns and Heathcote, *Peacekeeping by UN Forces*, p. 27.

37. Ibid., p. 32.

38. King Gordon, *The United Nations in the Congo* (Washington: Carnegie Endowment for International Peace, 1962), p. 104.

39. Linda B. Miller, *World Order and Local Disorder—The United Nations and Internal Conflicts* (Princeton: Princeton University Press, 1967), p. 74.

40. Ibid., p. 86.

41. Ibid., pp. 88-89.

42. Burns and Heathcote, *Peacekeeping by UN Forces*, p. 59.

43. Ibid., p. 67, Gordon, *The United Nations in the Congo*, p. 104.

44. Burns and Heathcote, *Peacekeeping by UN Forces*, p. 161.

45. Moskos, *Peace Soldiers*, p. 31.

46. Ibid., p. 48.

47. Miller, *World Order and Local Disorder*, p. 127.

48. Alistair Taylor, "Peacekeeping: the International Context," in Alistair Taylor et al., *Peacekeeping* (Canada: Canadian Institute of International Affairs, 1968), p. 174.

49. James A. Stegenga, *The United Nations Force in Cyprus* (Columbus: Ohio State University Press, 1968), p. 95.

50. Moskos, *Peace Soldiers*, pp. 56-57.

51. Ibid., p. 84.

52. Ibid., p. 134.

53. Segal, Harris, Rothberg, and Marlowe, "Paratroopers as Peacekeepers."

54. See Moskos, "UN Peacekeepers," and Janowitz, "Beyond Deterrence."

55. For example, Indar J. Rikhye, Michael Harbottle, and Bjorn Egge, *The Thin Blue Line* (New Haven: Yale University Press, 1974), p. 115.

56. Jesse J. Harris and David R. Segal, "Observations from the Sinai: The Boredom Factor," *Armed Forces and Society* 11 (February, 1985) pp. 235-248.

57. William W. Haddad, "Lebanon in Despair," *Current History* 84 (January, 1983), p. 15.

58. Norman F. Howard,"Lebanon's Clouded Future," *Current History* 76 (January, 1979)̈, p. 15.

59. Augustus Richard Norton, "Observations on U.N. Peacekeeping" (Presentation to the International Meeting of the Inter-University Seminar on Armed Forces and Society, Chicago, Illinois, October 24, 1983).

60. Haddad, "Lebanon in Despair," p.18.

61. See Janowitz and Wesbrook, *The Political Education of Soldiers*.

62. *Report of the DoD Commission on Beirut International Airport Terrorist Act, October 23, 1983* (20 December 1983; Washington: U.S. Government Printing Office, 1984).

63. Miller, *World Order and Local Disorder*, p. 151.

# Reflections on Social Justice and Migration

1. Elie Wiesel in "Conference on Ethical Issues and Moral Principles in U.S. Refugee Policy," (Washington, D.C.: Office of the U.S. Coordinator for Refugee Affairs, March 1983), p.4; reproduced in edited version as, Elie Wiesel, "We Have Witnessed...A New Category of Stranger—The Refugee," in *Refugee Reports* 4, special issue, December 16, 1983 (New York: American Council for Nationalities Service, 1983).

2. For a good discussion of the difficulties in tabulating accurate statistics on refugee populations, see the editor's note in U.S. Committee for Refugees, *World Refugee Survey 1983* (New York: American Council for Nationalities Services, 1983), pp. 60-61.

3. One of the finest resources on this subject is George H. Sabine, *A History of Political Theory*, 4th ed. (New York: Holt, Rinehart & Winston, 1973).

4. ECOSOC Official Records, Fourteenth Session, 632nd meeting, July 7, 1952.

5. Peter Odegard, *Religion and Politics* (Dobbs Ferry: Oceana Publications, 1960), p. 23.

6. Statement of Edward Derwinski, counselor of the Department of State, before the Senate Judiciary Committee, September 26, 1983. U.S. Department of State, Bureau of Public Affairs, Washington, D.C. "Current Policy U.S. Department of State," no. 517, September 26, 1983.

7. Henry Shue, *Basic Rights: Subsistence, Affluence and U.S. Foreign Policy* (Princeton: Princeton University Press, 1980), p. 20. The ideas expressed here on the role and definition of basic rights are drawn from Shue's work.

8. Richard Sterling, *Macropolitics: International Relations in a Global Society* (New York: Alfred A. Knopf, 1974), p. 564.

9. Animesh Ghoshal, "Political vs. Economic Refugees," in U.S. Select Commission on Immigration and Refugee Policy, *U.S. Immigration Policy and the National Interest: Appendix C* (Washington, D.C.: U.S. Government Printing Office, 1981), pp. 210-225.

10. Articles 3, 4, 5, and 9. Reprinted in "Human Rights. A compilation of international instruments of the United Nations" (New York: United Nations, 1967). (Hereafter cited as "UN compilation.")

11. "UN compilation," Articles 7, 8, 10, 18, 19, 20.

12. Ibid., Article 21.

13. Ibid., Articles 22 through 26.

14. See Ronald S. Scheinman, "The Office of the United Nations High Commissioner for Refugees and the Contemporary International System" (Ph. D. diss., University of California, Santa Barbara, 1974). Chapter 1, "The Politics of Humanitarianism."

15. These were the arrangements of July 5, 1922; May 31, 1924; May 12, 1926; June 30, 1928; July 30, 1935, the agreement of October 15, 1946; the conventions of October 28, 1933 and February 10, 1938; and the protocol of September 14, 1939.

16. Art. 1 (A) (2), Convention Relating to the Status of Refugees. Done at Geneva on July 28, 1951; entry into force April 22, 1954; text, United Nations Treaty Series no. 2545, vol. 189, p. 137.

17. Atle Grahl-Madsen, "Identifying the World's Refugees" in *The Annals of the American Academy of Political and Social Science,* no. 467, May 1983, pp. 11-23.

18. Ibid. at 19: *Gesetz über Massnahmen fur im Rahmen humanitärer Hilfsaktionen aufgenommene Flüchtlinge,* July 22, 1980.

19. Grahl-Madsen, "Identifying the World's Refugees," p. 14.

20. Stephen Young, "Who is a Refugee? A Theory of Persecution," in *In Defense of the Alien: Volume V—Refugees and Territorial Asylum,* proceedings of the 1982 Annual Legal Conference on Refugees and Territorial Asylum, ed. Lydio F. Tomasi (Staten Island, N.Y: Center for Migration Studies, 1983), p. 45.

21. Ibid.

22. Earl C. Huyck and Leon F. Bouvier, "The Demography of Refugees," in *The Annals,* no. 467, May 1983,, p. 41.

23. Grahl-Madsen, "Identifying the World's Refugees," p. 16.

24. Gilbert Loescher and John Scanlan, "Human Rights, U.S. Foreign Policy and Haitian Refugees," *Journal of Interamerican Studies and World Affairs,* vol. 26, no. 3, August 1984, p. 316.

25. Ibid.

26. Ibid.

27. Matts Lundahl, *Peasants and Poverty: A Study of Haiti* (London: Croom-Helm, 1979), p. 636. Cited in ibid.

28. It is not necessary in this discussion to examine as well the evidence of torture, imprisonment, harassment, and the denial of such basic civil rights as free speech and assembly contained in litigation brought by Haitian asylum claimants against the U.S. government. See for example, *Haitian Refugee Center* v. *Civiletti,* 503 F. Supp. 442 (S.D. Fla. 1980).

29. U.S. State Department, *Country Reports on Human Rights Practices for 1979* (Washington, D.C.: 1980), p. 344. Cited in Loescher and Scanlan, "...Haitian Refugees," p. 317. Two years later the Department of State reported that it "*appears* that the government is *attempting* to curtail fiscal and administrative practices of previous years...which undercut Haiti's development efforts...." *Country Reports on Human Rights Practices for 1982,* p. 463. (emphasis added).

30. Roslyn D. Roberts, "Impediments to Economic and Social Change in Haiti" (Washington, D.C.: Library of Congress, Congressional Research Service, June 19, 1978.) Quoted in Loescher and Scanlan, "...Haitian Refugees."p. 317.

31. Revenues were quoted at $269 million; expenditures at $195 million. Noted in Young, "Who Is a Refugee?" p. 43.

32. World Bank, Latin America and the Caribbean Regional Office. *Memorandum of the Haitian Economy,* report no. 3444-HA, May 31, 1981, p. IV. Cited in Loescher and Scanlan, "... Haitian Refugees," p. 317.

33. Lundahl, *Peasants and Poverty*, p. 641.

34. I am indebted to Professor Aristide Zolberg of the New School for Social Research for this insight.

35. "Refugees," no. 23 (November 1983), p. 1. Published by the Public Information Section, Office of the UN High Commissioner for Refugees, Geneva, Switzerland.

36. The UNHCR *Handbook on Procedures and Criteria for Determining Refugee Status* takes the position that an applicant could normally qualify by being a member of a group against which general, or even random, persecutory action is directed. In a case involving this principle which reached the U.S. Supreme Court in 1983, the government took the position that the "particular [applicant] alien had to prove he 'would be singled out for persecution upon his return' to his country of origin, and the evidence he would furnish had to specifically [relate] to the respondent." See "Brief for the Committee on Migration and Refugee Affairs of the American Council of Voluntary Agencies for Foreign Service and the Washington Lawyers Committee for Civil Rights Under Law as Amici Curiae in Support of Respondent," pp. 7, 8, 9, filed August 29, 1983 *INC v. Steric,* 467 U.S. __, 104 S. Ct. 2489 (No. 82-973, June 5, 1984).

37. "Conference on Ethical Issues." One of the most compelling presentations was by Michael Teitelbaum, a former staff director of the U.S. Select Committee on Population. Here is what he said, in part:

> Whom shall we admit? And based on what criteria? Should we save, for example, the young?...What about the old, the skilled, perhaps?...The most desperate, but how do we define that? The most deserving, but again who are they? Should there be equality? We are all in favor of equality. Equality by what? By country? By region? By social class? By race? And what do we mean by "equality"? Do we mean equal numbers? Do we mean equal percentages of potential population? What about the provision in the 1980 Refugee Act that specially singled out those of special humanitarian concern to the United States? ... And finally, what about asylees? Do we have a justification, a good justification, for granting them permanent residence when they have, in effect, jumped the queue of worthy seekers? (p. 21).

Even though Teitelbaum favors a narrow (Convention) definition, these choices still must be made. His most concrete policy advice was that it is ethically dangerous to use refugee admissions as "hostile acts aimed at foreign adversaries," p. 22. International law also tells us this. (For example, Article II(2) of the OAU Convention states that "the grant of asylum...is a peaceful and humanitarian act and shall not be regarded as an unfriendly act by any Member State.") Still, it would appear much harder for nationals of "friendly" countries to obtain refugee status or asylum.

38. Categories based on Chapter 2 of Forecasting International, "Political, Economic and Social Stability in 21 Nations Including Long-Term Impacts of Major Internal Political Shifts in the European Community" (Arlington, Va.: 1980). Marvin J. Cetron, program manager, Anne Kusener Nelson, principal investigator.

39. USAID director M. Peter McPherson, quoted in *The Washington Post*, January 7, 1984, p. A-6.

40. See for example, "Report on Latin America: The Great Dilemma for American Business" in *International Strategic Issues* (Washington, D.C.: Sage Associates, 1982.) Sage provides a private forecasting service to business, and in the 1982 spring-summer forecast, it advised its clientele "to exercise extreme caution in their investment and marketing strategies in Latin America. The central theme of those strategies must be to protect and limit the exposure of capital investments, even while aggressively pursuing sales and product developments in the area." Ibid., p. 2.

41. See for example, Charles William Maynes, "If the Poor Countries Go Under, We'll Sink With Them" *The Washington Post*, September 18, 1983, p. C-20. "In Chile, the International Monetary Fund is demanding a 50 percent cut in government spending, even though Chile's unemployment rate has risen from 4 percent to 26 percent in the last two years. In Argentina, following IMF guidelines, the government is attempting to cut its budget deficit by an astonishing *two-thirds*, even though the unemployment rate has tripled in the last two years. It is no coincidence that there have been massive street demonstrations in those two Countries in the past few weeks. . . . 'Cuts in public spending' is a euphemism for saying that health, education and welfare budgets are being slashed. . . . the IMF-imposed austerity measures that lead to improved balance-of-payments results today will lead to higher rates of infant mortality, illiteracy, and malnutrition tomorrow." (emphasis in original.)

42. Per capita GNP alone is not a useful measure of economic growth. Where the gap between the wealthiest and the poorest in society attains multiples of thirty or forty or more, and the wealthiest class is a narrowly based elite that allows no, or only very limited, access to others via an educational system or other generally accessible system of ascription, a formula for political violence is present. It was analysis based in part on study of the mathematical gap between the wealthiest and poorest that enabled Marvin Cetron to project the overthrow of the

Shah of Iran before any western intelligence service, and to project the creation of what became the Solidarity movement in Poland. See Cetron, ''21-Nation Study.''

43. ''Population Handbook: International Edition.'' (Washington D.C.: Population Reference Bureau, 1980) p. 59, and chart, p. 60. See also Final Report and Recommendations of the Select Commission on Immigration and Refugee Policy with Supplemental Views by Commissioners, *U.S. Immigration Policy and the National Interest* (Washington D.C.: U.S. Government Printing Office, 1981), p. 19.

44. ''World's Population Grows by 82 Million,'' *The Washington Post*, August 31, 1983, p. 4.

45. Leon F. Bouvier, ''The Other Population Problem: Impact of International Migration,'' *Interaction* 3, No. 1, Spring 1983, p. 11.

46. Maynes, ''If the Poor Countries Go Under''. p. C-1.

47. Maxwell Taylor, ''The Forgotten Factor in Central America,'' *The Washington Post*, August 30, 1983, p. A-19.

48. Harry E. Cross and Leon F. Bouvier, ''Conflict in Central America: The Population Factor,'' (unpubl. paper, The Futures Group, Washington D.C., August 1983), Table 3.

49. Maynes, ''If the Poor Countries Go Under,'' p. C-2.

50. Testimony of Loy Bilderback, California State University, Fresno, before the National Bipartisan Commission on Central America. September 7, 1983, p. 1.

51. Cross and Bouvier, ''Conflict in Central America,'' p. 1.

52. Maynes, ''If the Poor Countries Go Under,'' p. C-2.

53. Bilderback testimony, p. 1.

54. Taylor, ''The Forgotten Factor.''

55. Cross and Bouvier, ''Conflict in Central America,'' pp.2-4 (emphasis added).

56. Bilderback testimony, p. 1 and chart, p. 11.

57. Jacques Vernant, *Les Réfugiés dans l'Après-guerre* (Monaco: Editions du Rocher, 1953), pp. 43, 45.

58. On the roles played by controlling and non-controlling actors in the design of the UNHCR statute, see Scheinman "The Office of the United Nations High Commissioner for Refugees," chapters 2 and 3.

59. Vernant, *Les Réfugiés,* pp. 43, 45.

60. General Assembly Resolution 1166 (XII), 723d Plenary Session, November 26, 1957.

61. Letter dated May 13, 1983, of Dr. Jiri Toman, honorary secretary, Fridtjof Nansen Centre Preparatory Committee, to participants and prospective members of the centre.

62. Scheinman, "The Office of the United Nations High Commissioner for Refugees," p. 67.

63. USCR, *World Refugee Survey 1983*, Table 5, p. 62: to Guinea Bissau (1975, 45,000); to Angola (1975, 300,000); to Mozambique (1975, 84,000); to Zaire from Angola (1978, 150,000); to Burma from Bangladesh(1978, 200,000); to Nicaragua (1979, 100,000); to Angola from Zaire (1979, 50,000); to Equatorial Guinea (1979, 30,000); to Uganda (1979, 30,000); to Cambodia from Thailand, Vietnam, Laos (1979-82, 420,000); to Laos from Thailand (1979-82, 11,000); to Zimbabwe (1980, 250,000); to Chad (1981-82, 150,000); to Ethiopia from Sudan (1981-82, 61,000).

64. Ibid, Table 1, p. 61.

65. "Country Reports on Human Rights Practices for 1981" (Washington D.C.: U.S. Department of State, 1982), pp.79-84.

66. Richard Feen, "Our Brothers's Keeper? Theories of Obligation in U.S. Refugee Policy," in USCR, *World Refugee Survey 1983,* p. 47.

67. Scheinman, "The Office of the United Nations High Commissioner for Refugees," p. 224.

68. David Ford, the Deputy U.S. Coordinator for Refugee Affairs, presented an idea along these lines in a speech at Northampton College, Massachusetts, on November 17, 1983.

69. See Ronald S. Scheinman, "Refugees: Goodbye to the Good Old Days," in *The Annals,* no. 467, May 1983, pp. 84 et seq.;and Ronald S. Scheinman and Norman L. Zucker, "Refugee Policy," *The New York Times,* May 24, 1981, p. 19e.

70. See Howard Adelman, "Palestinian Refugees: Defining the Humanitarian Problem," Table 5, p. 25, in USCR, *World Refugee Survey 1983*, and pp. 20-27, for a clear treatment of defining and counting Palestinian refugees.

71. The situation with respect to legal protection of Palestinians is extraordinarily complex. Both the UNHCR Statute (Art. 7c) and the 1951 Convention (Art. ID) stipulate that persons who continue to receive "protection or assistance" from other organs or agencies of the

United Nations are not within UNHCR's competence. UNRWA, which *is* a United Nations agency, does *not* have a protection function. The result is that Palestinians are left without protection. The political reality behind this apparent aberration is that the Palestinian leadership has not wanted the UN to exercise a protection function because it would imply a durable solution outside the territory Palestinians claim. However, in practice, some measure of protection is provided. UNHCR considers itself responsible for Palestinians outside the geographic area of UNRWA operations, and it may request a host government to issue a travel document. UNHCR also may offer modest aid. But governments outside the Middle East frequently contend that Palestinians already have a place of firm resettlement. In those situations, the UNHCR role focuses on preventing or delaying deportation, particularly if to an area such as Lebanon, ridden with sectarian and political violence. Within the area of UNRWA operations, UNRWA performs one fundamental protection service: requests to host governments to issue travel documents to Palestinians who need them. But the full meaning of protection encompasses such areas as real and intellectual property, civil status, employment, and public education. These are matters UNRWA is not equipped to pursue. The texts of the UNHCR Statute and 1951 Convention can be found in "Collection of International Instruments Concerning Refugees," 2d ed. (Geneva: Office of the United Nations High Commissioner for Refugees, 1979). The UNRWA Statute is found in UN Document A/RES/302 of December 8, 1949.

72. Roger P. Winter, "1982—The Year in Review," in USCR, *World Refugee Survey 1983*, p. 3-4. On the Ugandan incident, see Roger P. Winter, "Refugees in Uganda and Rwanda: The Banyarwanda Tragedy," ibid., pp. 28-31.

73. The Thai Government denies these events occurred as reported and states that it has no such "pushoff" policy. It states that it has a policy of discouraging seaworthy boats from landing in Thailand, and it says the government helps boat-people who wish voluntarily to continue their voyage. A variety of observers, including officials of the U.S. State Department and the UNHCR, report differently, based on interviews with refugees and other fact-finding efforts. Not only are "pushoffs" done, they say, but those actions represent a policy of the Thai government which is implemented by the Thai navy and marine police and independent persons whose boats are under contract. These boats rammed and sank the refugee boat, causing the loss of life. See American Council for Nationalities Service, *Refugee Reports* 5, February 10,1984, pp. 5-6, February 24, 1984, p. 3, and March 23, 1984, pp. 4-5; *Bangkok World* in English, January 30, 1984, pp. 1-2; *Bangkok Post* in English, February 9, 1984, p. 5; see generally U.S. Committee for Refugees, *Vietnamese Boat People:Pirates' Vulnerable Prey* (New York: American Council for Nationalities Service, February 1984).

74. Aristide Zolberg, "The Formation of New States as a Refugee-generating Process," in *The Annals of the American Academy of Political and Social Science,* no. 467, May 1983, pp. 31 and 32.

75. "[A]sylum seekers are only a tiny fraction of the total number of today's legal and illegal immigrants. The numbers alone, therefore, are not conclusive justification of such a restrictive behavior." Gilbert Jaeger, "The Definition of Refugee: Restrictive versus Expanding Trends," in USCR, *World Refugee Survey 1983*, p. 9.

76. In some cases, these resettlements were carried out in the context of labor-recruitment programs drawn from a combination of national and international initiatives. Known by such names as "Westward Ho," "Balt Cygnet," "Black Diamond," and "Grand National,"

they met with mixed success. Host governments occasionally sought to exact a price, in terms of commitment to particular sectors of the economy such as mining, in exchange for resettlement opportunity. See Scheinman, "The Office of the United Nations High Commissioner for Refugees," pp. 43-47.

77. Feen, "Our Brother's Keeper."

78. Jaeger, "Definition of a Refugee," p. 9.

79. Feen, "Our Brother's Keeper."

80. See Note 76.

81. Article 1(2). OAU Convention of September 10, 1969 Governing the Specific Aspects of Refugee Problems in Africa. In "Collection of International Instruments Concerning Refugees," p. 194.

82. See Jaeger, "Definition of Refugee,"; and Scheinman, "Refugees: Goodbye to the Good Old Days," p. 88.

83. Atle Grahl-Madsen, "Identifying the World's Refugees," in *The Annals*, no. 467, May 1983, p. 22.

## PART THREE

## Excerpts from the Report: "To Establish the U.S. Academy of Peace"

1. Paul Wehr, *Conflict Regulation* (Boulder, Colo.: Westview Press, 1979), pp. 4-5.

2. Ambassador Asencio and his wife later published a book on his experiences: Diego Asencio and Nancy Asencio, *Our Man is Inside* (Boston: The Atlantic Monthly Press, 1983).

3. Roger Fisher's books include: with William Ury, *Getting to Yes: Negotiating Agreement Without Giving In* (Boston: Houghton Mifflin, 1981); *International Mediation: A Working Guide* (New York: International Peace Academy, April 1978 Draft Edition); *International Crises and the Role of Law* (New York: Oxford University Press, 1978); and *International Conflict for Beginners* (New York: Harper and Row, 1969).

4. Commission on Private Philanthropy and Public Needs, *Giving in America: Toward a Stronger Voluntary Sector* (Washington, D.C., 1975), p. 31.

5. United States Arms Control and Disarmament Agency, "Report to Congress on Arms Control Education and Academy Study Centers" (January 1979), pp. iii and 14.

6. Alexis de Toqueville, *Democracy in America* (first pub. 1835; New York: Vintage, 1945), Vol. II, p. 118.

7. The Rev. John Adams wrote about his social ministry in John P. Adams, *At the Heart of the Whirlwind* (New York: Harper and Row, 1976), and Adams, "Ministries in the Midst of Social Conflict," *Engage/Social Action Forum,* No. 43 (Washington D.C.: United Methodist Church, August 1978), pp. 17-24, and "Practical Matters of Peace," *E/SA Forum,* No. 70 (April 1981). The Rev. John Adams moved from Washington to a church in Fort Wayne, Indiana. He died in December 1983.

8. UNESCO, *Peace Research: Trend Report and World Directory* (Paris: UNESCO Reports and Papers in the Social Sciences, No. 43, 1978/1979).

9. Ibid., p. 21 ("Data from *World Directory of Social Science Institutions,"* UNESCO, 1977).

10. Ibid., p. 58.

11. Res. No. 355 of the 2d Commission of the United Nations, 25th Ordinary Session of the General Assembly, adopted December 5, 1980.

12. J. David Singer, "Introduction" to J. David Singer and associates, *Explaining War: Selected Papers From The Correlates of War Project* (Beverly Hills, Calif.: Sage, 1979), pp. 18-19.

13. Quincy Wright, *A Study of War,* 2d ed.(Chicago: University of Chicago Press, 1965, orig. pub., 1942).

14. Lewis F. Richardson, *Arms and Insecurity: A Mathematical Study of The Causes and Origins of War* (Pittsburgh: Boxwood Press, 1960) and *Statistics of Deadly Quarrels* (Pittsburgh: Boxwood Press, 1960).

15. Singer, "The Peace Researcher and Foreign Policy Prediction," *Peace Science Society (International)* Papers, XXI, 1973, p. 12.

16. Singer, "Preface" to Juergen Dedring, *Recent Advances in Peace and Conflict Resolution: A Critical Survey* (UNITAR: Beverly Hills, Calif.: Sage, 1976), p. 8.

17. Singer, "Introduction" to *Explaining War,* p. 17.

18. J. David Singer and Michael D. Wallace, "Introduction" to *To Augur Well: Early Warning Indicators in World Politics,* (ed. J. David Singer and Michael D. Wallace (Beverly Hills, Calif.: Sage, 1979), p. 14. See also, Singer, "Accounting for International War: The State of the Discipline," *American Review of Sociology* 6, (1980), pp. 349-67.

19. Gene Sharp, *The Politics of Nonviolent Action:* Part I — *Power and Struggle,* Part II — *The Methods of Nonviolent Action,* Part III — *The Dynamics of Nonviolent Action* (Boston: Porter Sargent, 1973), p. 8.

20. Ibid., pp. 70-71.

21. Ibid., p. 810.

22. Gene Sharp, *Social Power and Political Freedom* (Boston: Porter Sargent, 1980).

23. Mark Hatfield, "Introduction" to Sharp, *Social Power,* ibid., p. ix.

24. Saul Mendlovitz, "General Introduction" to Richard A. Falk, *A Study of Future Worlds* (New York: Free Press, 1975), pp. xix-xx.

25. Dedring, *Recent Advances,* p. 43.

26. Johan Galtung, "Towards a Definition of Peace Research," United Nations University Project, Geneva (presented at the UNESCO Meeting in Co-ordination and Development of Research, Information, and Documentation on Peace, Paris, August 28, 1978), p. 4.

27. Elise Boulding, "Foreword" to Dedring, *Recent Advances,* p. 2.

28. Dedring, *Recent Advances,* p. 55.

29. Ibid., p. 56.

30. Mendlovitz, "General Introduction," p. xxii.

31. Louis Kriesberg, *The Sociology of Social Conflicts* (Englewood Cliffs, N.J.: Prentice-Hall, 1973); Morton Deutsch, *The Resolution of Conflict: Constructive and Destructive Processes* (New Haven, Conn.: Yale University Press, 1973); Adam Curle, *Making Peace* (New York, London: Barnes and Noble, Tavistock, 1971); John Burton, *Conflict and Communication: The Use of Controlled Communication in International Relations* (New York: Oxford University Press, 1969) and *Deviance, Terrorism and War* (London: Martin Robertson, 1979); and Paul Wehr, *Conflict Regulation.*

32. Roger Fisher, *International Mediation: A Working Guide — Ideas for the Practitioner* (New York: International Peace Academy, April 1978 draft edition); *Peacekeeper's Handbook* (New York: International Peace Academy, 1978); James H. Laue, ed.,"Intervening in Community Conflicts," *The Journal of Intergroup Relations* (special issue), 9 (Summer 1981); Rip and Lincoln, "Impartial Intervention in Community Conflict," (New York: American Arbitration Association, 1975); and "New Approaches to Conflict Regulation" (New York: Ford Foundation, 1978).

33. Gordon Berment, Herbert C. Kelman, and Donald P. Warwick, eds., *The Ethics of Social Intervention* (New York: John Wiley, 1978); Jonathan Wilkenfeld, ed., *Conflict Behavior and Linkage Politics* (New York: David Mckay, 1973); Clagett G. Smith, ed., *Conflict Resolution: Contributions of the Behavioral Sciences* (Notre Dame, Ind.: University of Notre Dame Press, 1971).

# Appendix

On October 19, 1984, President Ronald Reagan signed Public Law 98-525, the Defense Authorization Act. Title XVII of that Act established the national institute of peace.

## United States Institute of Peace Act

*Short Title*

Sec. 1701. This may be cited as the "United States Institute of Peace Act."

**Declaration of Findings and Purposes**

Sec. 1702. (a) The Congress finds and declares that—

(1) a living institution embodying the heritage, ideals, and concerns, of the American people for peace would be a significant response to the deep public need for the Nation to develop fully a range of effective options, in addition to armed capacity, that can leash international violence and manage international conflict;

(2) people throughout the world are fearful of nuclear war, are divided by war and threats of war, are experiencing social and cultural hostilities from rapid international change and real and perceived conflicts over interests, and are diverted from peace by the lack of problem-solving skills for dealing with such conflicts;

(3) many potentially destructive conflicts among nations and peoples have been resolved constructively and with cost efficiency at the international, national, and community levels through proper use of such techniques as negotiation, conciliation, mediation, and arbitration;

(4) there is a national need to examine the disciplines in the social, behavioral, and physical sciences and the arts and humanities with regard to the history, nature, elements, and future of peace processes, and to bring together and develop new and tested techniques to promote peaceful economic, political, social, and cultural relations in the world;

(5) existing institutions providing programs in international affairs, diplomacy, conflict resolution, and peace studies are essential to further development of techniques to promote peaceful resolution of international conflict, and the peacemaking activities of people in such institutions, government, private enterprise, and voluntary associations can be strengthened by a national institution devoted to international peace research, education and training, and information services;

(6) there is a need for Federal leadership to expand and support the existing inter-

national peace and conflict resolution efforts of the Nation and to develop new comprehensive peace education and training programs, basic and applied research projects, and programs providing peace information;

(7) the Commission on Proposals for the National Academy of Peace and Conflict Resolution, created by the Education Amendments of 1978, recommended establishing an academy as a highly desirable investment to further the Nation's interest in promoting international peace;

(8) an institute strengthening and symbolizing the fruitful relation between the world of learning and the world of public affairs, would be the most efficient and immediate means for the Nation to enlarge its capacity to promote the peaceful resolution of international conflicts; and

(9) the establishment of such an institute is an appropriate investment by the people of this Nation to advance the history, science, art, and practice of international peace and the resolution of conflicts among nations without the use of violence.

(b) It is the purpose of this title to establish an independent, nonprofit, national institute to serve the people and the Government through the widest possible range of education and training, basic and applied research opportunities, and peace information services on the means to promote international peace and the resolution of conflicts among the nations and peoples of the world without recourse to violence.

## DEFINITIONS

SEC. 1703. As used in this title, the term—

(1) "Institute" means the United States Institute of Peace established by this title; and

(2) "Board" means the Board of Directors of the Institute.

### Establishment of the Institute

SEC. 1704. (a) There is hereby established the United States Institute of Peace.

(b) The Institute is an independent nonprofit corporation and an organization described in section 170(c)(2)(B) of the Internal Revenue Code of 1954. The Institute does not have the power to issue any shares of stock or to declare or pay any dividends.

(c) As determined by the Board, the Institute may establish, under the laws of the District of Columbia, a legal entity which is capable of receiving, holding, and investing public funds for purposes in furtherance of the Institute under this title. The Institute may designate such legal entity as the "Endowment of the United States Institute for Peace".

(d) The Institute is liable for the acts of its directors, officers, employees, and agents when acting within the scope of their authority.

(e)(1) The Institute has the sole and exclusive right to use and to allow or refuse others the use of the terms "United States Institute of Peace", "Jennings Randolph Program for International Peace", and "Endowment of the United States Institute for Peace" and the use of any official United States Institute of Peace emblem, badge, seal, and other mark of recognition or any colorable simulation thereof. No powers or privileges hereby granted shall interfere or conflict with established or vested rights secured as of September 1, 1981.

(2) Notwithstanding any other provisions of this title, the Institute may use "United States" or "U.S." or any other reference to the United States Government or Nation in its title or in its corporate seal, emblem, badge, or other mark of recognition or colorable simulation thereof in any fiscal year only if there is an authorization of appropriations for the Institute for such fiscal year provided by law.

## POWERS AND DUTIES

SEC. 1705. (a) The Institute may exercise the powers conferred upon a nonprofit corporation by the District of Columbia Nonprofit Corporation Act consistent with this title, except for section 5(o) of the District of Columbia Nonprofit Corporation Act (D.C. Code, sec. 29-1005(o).

(b) The Institute, acting through the Board, may—

(1) establish a Jennings Randolph Program for International Peace and appoint, for periods of up to two years, scholars and leaders in peace from the United States and abroad to pursue scholarly inquiry and

other appropriate forms of communication on international peace and conflict resolution and, as appropriate, provide stipends, grants, fellowships, and other support to the leaders and scholars;

(2) enter into formal and informal relationships with other institutions, public and private, for purposes not inconsistent with this title;

(3) conduct research and make studies, particularly of an interdisciplinary or of a multidisciplinary nature, into the causes of war and other international conflicts and the elements of peace among the nations and peoples of the world, including peace theories, methods, techniques, programs, and systems, and into the experiences of the United States and other nations in resolving conflicts with justice and dignity and without violence as they pertain to the advancement of international peace and conflict resolution, placing particular emphasis on realistic approaches to past successes and failures in the quest for peace and arms control and utilizing to the maximum extent possible United States Government documents and classified materials from the Department of State, the Department of Defense, the Arms Control and Disarmament Agency, and the intelligence community;

(4) develop programs to make international peace and conflict resolution research, education, and training more available and useful to persons in government, private enterprise, and voluntary associations, including the creation of handbooks and other practical materials;

(5) provide, promote, and support peace education and research programs at graduate and postgraduate levels;

(6) conduct training, symposia, and continuing education programs for practitioners, policymakers, policy implementers, and citizens and noncitizens directed to developing their skills in international peace and conflict resolution;

(7) develop, for publication or other public communication, and disseminate, the carefully selected products of the Institute;

(8) establish a clearinghouse and other means for disseminating information, including classified information that is properly safeguarded, from the field of peace learning to the public and to government personnel with appropriate security clearances;

(9) recommend to the Congress the establishment of a United States Medal of Peace to be awarded under such procedures as the Congress may determine, except that no person associated with the Institute may receive the United States Medal of Peace; and

(10) secure directly, upon request of the president of the Institute to the head of any Federal department or agency and in accordance with section 552 of title 5, United States Code (relating to freedom of information), information necessary to enable the Institute to carry out the purposes of this title if such release of the information would not unduly interfere with the proper functioning of a department or agency, including classified information if the Institute staff and members of the Board who have access to such classified information obtain appropriate security clearances from the Department of Defense and the Department of State.

(c) The Institute may undertake extension and outreach activities under this title by making grants and entering into contracts with institutions of postsecondary, community, secondary, and elementary education (including combinations of such institutions), with public and private educational, training, or research institutions (including the American Federation of Labor—the Congress of Industrial Organizations) and libraries, and with public departments and agencies (including State and territorial departments of education and of commerce). No grant may be made to an institution unless it is a nonprofit or official public institution, and at least one-fourth of the Institute's annual appropriations shall be paid to such nonprofit and official public institutions. A grant or contract may be made to—

(1) initiate, strengthen, and support basic and applied research on international peace and conflict resolution;

(2) promote and advance the study of international peace and conflict resolution by educational, training, and research institutions, departments, and agencies;

(3) educate the Nation about and educate and train individuals in peace and conflict

resolution theories, methods, techniques, programs, and systems;

(4) assist the Institute in its publication, clearinghouse, and other information services programs;

(5) assist the Institute in the study of conflict resolution between free trade unions and Communist-dominated organizations in the context of the global struggle for the protection of human rights; and

(6) promote the other purposes of this title.

(d) The Institute may respond to the request of a department or agency of the United States Government to investigate, examine, study, and report on any issue within the Institute's competence, including the study of past negotiating histories and the use of classified materials.

(e) The Institute may enter into contracts for the proper operation of the Institute.

(f) The Institute may fix the duties of its officers, employees, and agents, and establish such advisory committees, councils, or other bodies, as the efficient administration of the business and purposes of the Institute may require.

(g)(1) Except as provided in paragraphs (2) and (3), the Institute may obtain grants and contracts, including contracts for classified research for the Department of State, the Department of Defense, the Arms Control and Disarmament Agency, and the intelligence community, and receive gifts and contributions from government at all levels.

(2) The Institute may not accept any gift, contribution, or grant from, or enter into any contract with, a foreign government, any agency or instrumentality of such government, any international organization, or any foreign national, except that the Institute may accept the payment of tuition by foreign nationals for instruction provided by the Institute. For purposes of this paragraph, the term—

(A) "foreign national" means—

(i) a natural person who is a citizen of a foreign country or who owes permanent allegiance to a foreign country; and

(ii) a corporation or other legal entity in which natural persons who are nationals of a foreign country own, directly or indirectly, more than 50 percent of the outstanding capital stock or other beneficial interest in such legal entity; and

(B) "person" means a natural person, partnership, association, other unincorporated body, or corporation.

(3) Notwithstanding any other provision of this title, the Institute and the legal entity described in section 1704(c) may not obtain any grant or contract or receive any gift or contribution from any private agency, organization, corporation or other legal entity, institution, or individual.

(h) The Institute may charge and collect subscription fees and develop, for publication or other public communications, and disseminate, periodicals and other materials.

(i) The Institute may charge and collect fees and other participation costs from persons and institutions participating in the Institute's direct activities authorized in subsection (b).

(j) The Institute may sue and be sued, complain, and defend in any court of competent jurisdiction.

(k) The Institute may adopt, alter, use, and display a corporate seal, emblem, badge, and other mark of recognition and colorable simulations thereof.

(l) The Institute may do any and all lawful acts and things necessary or desirable to carry out the objectives and purposes of this title.

(m) The Institute shall not itself undertake to influence the passage or defeat of any legislation by the Congress of the United States or by any State or local legislative bodies, or by the United Nations, except that personnel of the Institute may testify or make other appropriate communication when formally requested to do so by a legislative body, a committee, or a member thereof.

(n) The Institute may obtain administrative support services from the Administrator of General Services on a reimbursable basis.

## BOARD OF DIRECTORS

SEC. 1706. (a) The powers of the Institute shall be vested in a Board of Directors unless otherwise specified in this title.

The Board shall consist of fifteen voting members as follows:

(1) The Secretary of State (or if the Secretary so designates, another officer of the Department of State who was appointed with the advice and consent of the Senate).

(2) The Secretary of Defense (of if the Secretary so designates, another officer of the Department of Defense who was appointed with the advice and consent of the Senate).

(3) The Director of the Arms Control and Disarmament Agency (or if the Director so designates, another officer of that Agency who was appointed with the advice and consent of the Senate).

(4) The president of the National Defense University (or if the president so designates, the vice president of the National Defense University).

(5) Eleven individuals appointed by the President, by and with the advice and consent of the Senate.

(c) Not more than eight voting members of the Board, (including members described in paragraphs (1) through (4) of subsection (b)) may be members of the same political party.

(d)(1) Each individual appointed to the Board under subsection (b)(5) shall have appropriate practical or academic experience in peace and conflict resolution efforts of the United States.

(2) Officers and employees of the United States Government may not be appointed to the Board under subsection (b)(5).

(e)(1) Members of the Board appointed under subsection (b)(5) shall be appointed to four year terms, except that—

(A) the term of six of the members initially appointed shall be two years, as designated by the President at the time of their nominations;

(B) a member may continue to serve until his or her successor is appointed; and

(C) a member appointed to replace a member whose term has not expired shall be appointed to serve the remainder of that term.

(2) The terms of the members of the Board initially appointed under subsection (b)(5) shall begin of January 20, 1985, and subsequent terms shall begin upon the expiration of the preceding term, regardless of when a member is appointed to fill that term.

(3) The President may not nominate an individual for appointment to the Board under subsection (b)(5) prior to January 20, 1985, but shall submit the names of eleven nominees for initial Board membership

under subsection (b)(5) not later than ninety days after that date. If the Senate rejects such a nomination or if such a nomination is withdrawn, the President shall submit the name of a new nominee within fifteen days.

(4) An individual appointed as a member of the Board under subsection (b)(5) may not be appointed to more than two terms on the Board.

(f) A member of the Board appointed under subsection (b)(5) may be removed by the President—

(1) in consultation with the Board, for conviction of a felony, malfeasance in office, persistent neglect of duties, or inability to discharge duties;

(2) upon the recommendation of eight voting members of the Board; or

(3) upon the recommendation of a majority of the members of the Committee on Foreign Affairs and the Committee on Education and Labor of the House of Representatives and a majority of the members of the Committee on Foreign Relations and the Committee on Labor and Human Resources of the Senate.

A recommendation made in accordance with paragraph (2) may be made only pursuant to action taken at a meeting of the Board, which may be closed pursuant to the procedures of subsection (h)(3). Only members who are present may vote. A record of the vote shall be maintained. The President shall be informed immediately by the Board of the recommendation.

(g) No member of the Board may participate in any decision, action, or recommendation with respect to any matter which directly and financially benefits the member or pertains specifically to any public body or any private or nonprofit firm or organization with which the member is then formerly associated or has been formally associated within a period of two years, except that this subsection shall not be construed to prohibit an ex officio member of the Board from participation in actions of the Board which pertain specifically to the public body of which that member is an officer.

(h) Meetings of the Board shall be conducted as follows:

(1) The President shall stipulate by name the nominee who shall be the first Chairman of the Board. The first Chairman shall

serve for a term of three years. Thereafter, the Board shall elect a Chairman every three years from among the directors appointed by the President under subsection (b)(5) and may elect a Vice Chairman if so provided by the Institute's bylaws.

(2) The Board shall meet at least semiannually, at any time pursuant to the call of the Chairman or as requested in writing to the Chairman by at least five members of the Board. A majority of the members of the Board shall constitute a quorum for any Board meeting.

(3) All meetings of the Board shall be open to public observation and shall be preceded by reasonable public notice. Notice in the Federal Register shall be deemed to be reasonable public notice for purposes of the preceding sentence. In exceptional circumstances, the Board may close those portions of a meeting, upon a majority vote of its members present and with the vote taken in public session, which are likely to disclose information likely to affect adversely any ongoing peace proceeding or activity or to disclose information or matters exempted from public disclosure pursuant to subsection (c) of section 552b of title 5, United States Code.

(i) A director appointed by the President under subsection (b)(5) shall be entitled to receive the daily equivalent of the annual rate of basic pay in effect for grade GS-18 of the General Schedule under section 5332 of title 5, United States Code, for each day during which the director is engaged in the performance of duties as a member of the Board.

(j) While away from his home or regular place of business in the performance of duties for the Institute, a director shall be allowed travel expenses, including a per diem in lieu of subsistence, not to exceed the expenses allowed persons employed intermittently in Government service under section 5703(b) of title 5, United States Code.

## OFFICERS AND EMPLOYEES

Sec. 1707. (a) The Board shall appoint the president of the Institute and such other officers as the Board determines to be necessary. The president of the Institute shall be a nonvoting ex officio member of the Board. All officers shall serve at the pleasure of the Board. The president shall be appointed for

an explicit term of years. Notwithstanding any other provision of law limiting the payment of compensation, the president and other officers appointed by the Board shall be compensated at rates determined by the Board, but no greater than that payable for level I of the Executive Schedule under chapter 53 of title 5, United States Code.

(b) Subject to the provisions of section 1705(g)(3), the Board shall authorize the president and any other officials or employees it designates to receive and disburse public moneys, obtain and make grants, enter into contracts, establish and collect fees, and undertake all other activities necessary for the efficient and proper functioning of the Institute.

(c) The president, subject to Institute's bylaws and general policies established by the Board, may appoint, fix the compensation of, and remove such employees of the Institute as the president determines necessary to carry out the purposes of the Institute. In determining employee rates of compensation, the president shall be governed by the provisions of title 5, United States Code, relating to classification and General Schedule pay rates.

(d)(1) The president may request the assignment of any Federal officer or employee to the Institute by an appropriate department, agency, or congressional official or Member of Congress and may enter into an agreement for such assignment, if the affected officer or employee agrees to such assignment and such assignment causes no prejudice to the salary, benefits, status, or advancement within the department, agency, or congressional staff of such officer or employee.

(2) The Secretary of State, the Secretary of Defense, the Director of the Arms Control and Disarmament Agency, and the Director of Central Intelligence each may assign officers and employees of his respective department or agency, on a rotating basis to be determined by the Board, to the Institute if the affected officer or employee agrees to such assignment and such assignment causes no prejudice to the salary, benefits, status, or advancement within the respective department or agency of such officer or employee.

(e) No officer or full-time employee of the Institute may receive any salary or other compensation for services from any source other than the Institute during the officer's or employee's period of employment by the Institute, except as authorized by the Board.

(f)(1) Officers and employees of the Institute shall not be considered officers and employees of the Federal Government except for purposes of the provisions of title 28, United States Code, which relate to Federal tort claims liability, and the provisions of title 5, United States Code, which relate to compensation and benefits, including the following provisions: chapter 51 (relating to classification); subchapters I and III of chapter 53 (relating to pay rates); subchapter I of chapter 81 (relating to compensation for work injuries); chapter 83 (relating to civil service retirement); chapter 87 (relating to life insurance); and chapter 89 (relating to health insurance). The Institute shall make contributions at the same rates applicable to agencies of the Federal Government under the provisions of title 5 referred to in this section.

(2) No Federal funds shall be used to pay for private fringe benefit programs. The Institute shall not make long-term commitments to employees that are inconsistent with rules and regulations applicable to Federal employees.

(g) No part of the financial resources, income, or assets of the Institute or of any legal entity created by the Institute shall inure to any agent, employee, officer, or director or be distributable to any such person during the life of the corporation or upon dissolution or final liquidation. Nothing in this section may be construed to prevent the payment of reasonable compensation for services or expenses to the directors, officers, employees, and agents of the Institute in amounts approved in accordance with the provisions of this title.

(h) The Institute shall not make loans to its directors, officers, employees, or agents, or to any legal entity created by the Institute. A director, officer, employee, or agent who votes for or assents to the making of a loan or who participates in the making of a loan shall be jointly and severally liable to the Institute for the amount of the loan until repayment thereof.

## PROCEDURES AND RECORDS

SEC. 1708. (a) The Institute shall monitor and evaluate and provide for independent evaluation if necessary of programs supported in whole or in part under this title to ensure that the provisions of this title and the bylaws, rules, regulations, and guidelines promulgated pursuant to this title are adhered to.

(b) The Institute shall prescribe procedures to ensure that grants, contracts, and financial support under this title are not suspended unless the grantee, contractor, or person or entity receiving financial support has been given reasonable notice and opportunity to show cause why the action should not be taken.

(c) In selecting persons to participate in Institute activities, the Institute may consider a person's practical experience or equivalency in peace study and activity as well as other formal requirements.

(d) The Institute shall keep correct and complete books and records of account, including separate and distinct accounts of receipts and disbursements of Federal funds. The Institute's annual financial report shall identify the use of such funding and shall present a clear description of the full financial situation of the Institute.

(e) The Institute shall keep minutes of the proceedings of its Board and of any committees having authority under the Board.

(f) The Institute shall keep a record of the names and addresses of its Board members; copies of this title, of any other Acts relating to the Institute, and of all Institute bylaws, rules, regulations, and guidelines; required minutes of proceeding; a record of all applications and proposals and issued or received contracts and grants; and financial records of the Institute. All items required by this subsection may be inspected by any Board member or the member's agent or attorney for any proper purpose at any reasonable time.

(g) The accounts of the Institute shall be audited annually in accordance with generally accepted auditing standards by independent certified public accountants or independent licensed public accountants, certified or licensed by a regulatory authority of a State or other political subdivision of the United States on or before December 31, 1970. The audit shall be conducted at the place or places where the accounts of the Institute are normally kept. All books, accounts, financial records, files, and other papers, things, and property belonging to or in use by the Institute and necessary to facilitate the audit shall be made available to the person or persons conducting the audit, and full facilities for verifying transactions with the balances or securities held by depositories, fiscal agents, and custodians shall be afforded to such person or persons.

(h) The Institute shall provide a report of the audit to the President and to each House of Congress no later than six months following the close of the fiscal year for which the audit is made. The report shall set forth the scope of the audit and include such statements, together with the independent auditor's opinion of those statements, as are necessary to present fairly the Institute's assets and liabilities, surplus or deficit, with reasonable detail, including a statement of the Institute's income and expenses during the year, including a schedule of all contracts and grants requiring payments in excess of $5,000 and any payments of compensation, salaries, or fees at a rate in excess of $5,000 per year. The report shall be produced in sufficient copies for the public.

(i) The Institute and its directors, officers, employees, and agents shall be subject to the provisions of section 552 of title 5, United States Code (relating to freedom of information).

## INDEPENDENCE AND LIMITATIONS

SEC. 1709. (a) Nothing in this title may be construed as limiting the authority of the Office of Management and Budget to review and submit comments on the Institute's budget request at the time it is transmitted to the Congress.

(b) No political test or political qualification may be used in selecting, appointing, promoting, or taking any other personnel action with respect to any officer, employee, agent, or recipient of Institute funds or services or in selecting or monitoring any grantee, contractor, person, or entity receiving financial assistance under this title.

## FUNDING

SEC. 1710. (a) For the purpose of carrying out this title (except for paragraph (9) of section 1705(b)), there are authorized to be appropriated $6,000,000 for the fiscal year 1985 and $10,000,000 for the fiscal year 1986. Monies appropriated for the fiscal year 1985

shall remain available to the Institute through the fiscal year 1986.

(b) The Board of Directors may transfer to the legal entity authorized to be established under section 1704(c) any funds not obligated or expended from appropriations to the Institute for a fiscal year, and such funds shall remain available for obligation or expenditure for the purposes of such legal entity without regard to fiscal year limitations. Any use by such entity of appropriated funds shall be reported to each House of the Congress and to the President of the United States.

(c) Any authority provided by this title to enter into contracts shall be effective for a fiscal year only to such extent or in such amounts as are provided in appropriation Acts.

## DISSOLUTION OR LIQUIDATION

SEC. 1711. Upon dissolution or final liquidation of the Institute or of any legal entity created pursuant to this title, all income and assets of the Institute or other legal entity shall revert to the United States Treasury.

## REPORTING REQUIREMENT AND REQUIREMENT TO HOLD HEARINGS

SEC. 1712. Beginning two years after the date of enactment of this title, and at intervals of two years thereafter, the Chairman of the Board shall prepare and transmit to the Congress and the President a report detailing the progress the Institute has made in carrying out the purposes of this title during the preceding two-year period. The President shall prepare and transmit to the Congress within a reasonable time after the receipt of such report the written comments and recommendations of the appropriate agencies of the United States with respect to the contents of such report and their recommendations with respect to any legislation which may be required concerning the Institute. After receipt of such report by the Congress, the Committee on Foreign Affairs and the Committee on Education and Labor of the House of Representatives and the Committee on Foreign Relations and the Committee on Labor and Human Resources of the Senate shall hold hearings to review the findings and recommendations of such report and the written comments received from the President.

# Index

Best Alternative to a Negotiated Agreement(BATNA), 188
Bierman, Rep. Fred, 159
Bilderback, Loy, 89
Bill of Rights, 158
Bishop, Prime Minister Maurice, 65
*Bloody Tenet of Persecution*, 7
bombing, 64, 128
border settlements, 215
boredom, among peacekeepers, 44, 59, 61, 66
Boulding, Dr. Elise, 161, 203, 211
Boulding, Dr. Kenneth, and conflict management, 3, 136
Dr. Kenneth, and conflict management v. conflict resolution, 139
Dr. Kenneth, and procedural conflicts of conflict management, 168-69
Dr. Kenneth, and new field of human knowledge, 145, 203
boundary, and refugees, 83f
Bouvier, Leon, 77-78, 90
Bradley, General Omar, 140-41, 208
Brazil, 49, 53, 56; U.S. Ambassador to, see Ascencio, Ambassador Diego
Brind, Major General, 49
British, 48, 51, 52
British Empire, 129, 137
*Bulletin of Peace Proposals*, 210-11
Bureau of Peace and Friendship, 159
Burger, Chief Justice Warren E., 149
Burke, Edmund, 73
Burnett, Henry, 161
Burns, Major General E. L. M., 52
Burton, Professor John, 150; *Conflict and Communication* by, 214; *Deviance, Terrorism and War* by, 214
Butler, Nicholas Murray, 71

Calvin, John, 20
Cambodia, xi, 72
Camp David, xi, 4, 149, 168, 184-87
Canada, 52, 53, 55, 168
Canadian Institute of International Peace, 151
Carazo, President Rodrigo, 202
Caribbean, 84
Caribbean Peacekeeping Force(CPF), 65, 67
Carnegie Endowment for International Peace, 200
Carrington, Lord, 185
Carter, President Jimmy, 60, 161, 186
Castro, Fidel, 182
Catholic bishops, 1, 34
Catholics, persecution of, 72
Causeway program, 190
cease-fire, 51, 58, 188
Center for Disarmament Research, 202
Center for International Affairs, 147

Center for International Peace, 133
Center for International Studies, at MIT, 201
Center for Study of Democratic Institutions, 3
Central America, population dynamics of, 89-91
Centre of Concern for Human Dignity, 190
Chad, 72, 87
Charny, Dr. Israel, 138-39
Chile, 230f41
China, 71, 129
Christian Family Movement, on peace academy, 160
Christians, 8-9, 72
church and state, 11, 16
Church Women United, 190
Cicero, 1, 8-11, 97
citizens, involved in peacemaking, 130, 133, 217; and state, 69-71
citizenship, for Palestinians, 101; and refugees, 97-98
civil disobedience, 17-18, 22
civil rights, and political refugees, 73
Civil War, U.S., 158
civilians in war, 25, 28, 41, 58; see also noncombatants
clergy, exempt from combat, 12, 15
Coalition of Iranian Students, 193
coercion, 7-8, 172
collective guilt and punishment, Grotius on, 22
Colombia, 4, 48-49, 178
American hostages in, xi
constitution of, 180
court-martial trials in, 181-82
and UNEF force, 53
combat readiness, in elite combat unit, 44
combatant, versus noncombatant, 39
Commerce, U.S. Department of, 114
Commission on Private Philanthropy and Public Needs, 189
Commission on Proposals for National Academy of Peace, 1-4, 8, 113, 157, 161-219
communist conspiracy, in Grenada, 67-68
community dispute resolution centers, 149
conciliation, 143, 146, 189-98, 213
Conference on Peace Research in History, 201
conflict, circle of, 146
dealing with it constructively, 138-40
as minor and arbitrary cause of war, 128
and violence, 138, 143
conflict management, 3, 123-25, 168
as academic field, 145-46
antagonism toward, 125-28
in armed services, 132
and domestic tensions, 148-50

hope of, 153-54
and national peace institute, 129
procedural concepts of, 168-69
types of, 143
versus peace research, 123
conflict resolution, xi; and freedom, 173
and National Peace Institute, 114
teaching of, 213
and U.S. military, 38-39
versus conflict management, 139
conflicts, definition of, 167-68; and fights,
168-69; over interests, 168
Confucius, 166
Congo, peacekeeping in, 45, 53, 67
conscientious objection, 1, 17-18, 22, 29;
selective, 222f50
Consortium on Peace Research, Education
& Development(COPRED), 122, 144,
200
constabulary, concept of, 42-47; as role of
combat troops, 66
Constitution, U.S., 112, 158, 169
Convention on the Prevention and Punishment of the Crime of Genocide, 28
COPRED, see Consortium on Peace
Research, Education and Develop-
ment(COPRED)
Correlates of War Project, 201, 203, 206
corruption, 77, 84, 105
Costa Rica, 56, 89, 133, 202
counterforce, 33
court diversion programs, 173
Covenant of the League of Nations, 27
Crosland, David, 196-97
Cross, Harry, 90
"cross of iron" speech, 176
crusaders, 14-15
Cuba, guerrillas went to, 178
Cubans, 65, 72
cultural relativity, 179, 183, 214
Curle, Making Peace by, 214
Cyprus crisis, 56-58

Darwin, Charles, 158
de Toqueville, 190-91, 218
de Vitoria, Francisco, 20
Declaration of Independence, 157-58
declaration of war, in Vietnam, 31
defending against enemies, 16
Defense Authorization Act, ix, 111
defense of allies, 23
defense spending, ix
defensive wars, in early modern times, 23
Dellenback, Rep. John, 161
Democratic party, 148
Denmark, 52, 53
Department of Agriculture Graduate School,
113

Department of Peace, ix, 159-60; see also
National Peace Institute
deterrence, 36, 134-35; as peacekeeping
strategy, 41-42, 68
and nuclear weapons, 34, 35
Deuteronomy, holy wars in, 9
Deutsch, Resolution of Conflict by, 214
Djibouti, 101
diplomats, conflict management users, 124;
and arms control courses, 189
Dirksen, Senator Everett, 160
disarmament, and just-war theory, 1; of
frontiers, 128
discrimination, Augustine on, 12; and noncombatant immunity, 24-25;
with nuclear weapons, 32
displaced persons, 106, see also forced
migrants
divorce mediation, 149
domestic violence teams, 213
Dominican Republic, 55-56; Colombian embassy of, 178-84
invasion of, 65
peacekeeping in, 67
double effect, principle of, 25
Dresden, 127, 128
Dulles, John Foster, 205
Dunfey, John, 161

East-West Center, 201
Eastern Europe, refugees from, 95, 96
ecological stability, value of World Order
Model Project, 212
economic equality, 73
economic refugee, 77-79
economic security, 73
economic survival, and forced migrants, 69
economic well-being, value of World Order
Model Project, 212
economics, and peace learning, 200
education, 169; role of federal government
in, 112-13
education and training, function of National
Institute of Peace, ix
Egypt, 51, 59
Egyptians, at Camp David, 185-87
Einstein, Albert, 137, 138
Eisenhower, President Dwight, 159, 176
El Salvador, 81, 87, 89
Elbrick, Ambassador, 181
election process, as peacekeeping method,
1; in United States, 148
Elementary and Secondary Education bill,
161
enemies, randomness of, 128
environmental accords, 215
environmental protection, 169
Equatorial Guinea, 82, 97
equity and justice, 172

peace information services, 166
peace issues, academic work on, 143-44
peace learning, compared to health field,
199
definition of, 198-99
field of, 198-200
knowledge and skills in, 217
multidisciplinary, 200
peace management, disciplines for, 2
peace movement, not peace research, 203
"Peace on Earth," 140
peace principles, 171-77
peace research, 122, 200-09, 211
Peace Research Section, of International
Studies Association, 122
Peace Science Society, 201
peace studies, and National Peace Institute,
114
peace through strength, 68
peace-related expertise, professionalization
of, 199-200
peaceful intention, 24
Peacekeeper's Handbook, 215
peacekeeping, xi
affirmative approaches toward, 135
as American military mission, 38
and boredom, see boredom
force for, 1-2, 57, 62-63
as military mission, 38, 65-68
and military professionalism, 61
and police or military force, 173-74
and political system, 67
superpower involvement in, 46-47
value of, 68
peacemaking, affirmative approaches to, 134
as instrument of power, 119
methods of, 1; see also elections, mediation, negotiation
by military, 170
science of, 142-48
techniques of, 204, 212-13
Pearson, Lester, 52
Pell, Senator Claiborne, 161
persecution, 70-71, 74, 82-83, 98
Peru, 50
Phalange in Lebanon, 63-64
philosophy, and peace learning, 200
physical security, 73
Pinilla, General Gustavo Rojas, 179
Pipes, Professor Richard, 147, 171, 214,
216
Plato, 71
PLO, see Palestine Liberation Organization
poisons, 25
Pol Pot, 82
Poland, 28, 49, 128, 168
police, 80, 197
police brutality, 194
political rights, and political refugees, 73

political science, part of peace studies, 144,
200
political violence, from unemployment, 89
politicians, conflict management users, 124
Politics of Nonviolent Action, 207-08
pope, role of, 22-23
Pope John Paul II, 34
Pope Urban II, 14
population growth, 85-91
population movements, and refugee events,
81
positivist position, 26-27, 29
preemptive attack, 42
preventive war, 42
prisoners, enslavement according to
Aquinas, 19; treatment of, 25-26
prisoners of war, 28
problem-solving strategies, 146, 169
property, and legitimated threat system, 125
Protestants, persecution of, 72
Protocol Relating to the Status of Refugees,
75
Proudhon, property is theft, 125
psychology, and peace learning, 144, 200
public education, 188
Pugwash Conference on Science and World
Affairs, 201
punishment of wrongdoing, in early modern
times, 23
Purple Heart, 36, 38

Ramsey, Paul, 33-34
Randolph, Sen. Jennings, 2-3
and Commission on Proposals for
National Academy of Peace, 160, 165
introduced peace academy bill, 161, 163
writing by, 111-21
Rayman, Dr. Paula, 176
Reagan, President Ronald, 64, 165
Reagan administration, military targeting
strategy, 33
reasonable hope of success, justified war
conditions of, 24
refugee, definition of, 72, 74-76, 82, 91
definition by Grahl-Madsen, 78, 106-07
as economic migrant, 75
solution to problems, 95
Elie Wiesel as, 69
Refugee Act of 1980, 75, 83f
refugee assistance, nongovernmental, 92
refugee movements, and democratization,
81-82; not transitory, 70-71
refugee resettlement, 94, 106, 218
refugee status, and diplomacy, 81
refugees, xi; causes of, 71-72
and civil rights of, 76
communications and, 87
deportation of, 75
economic development for, 105-06

health care of, 76
legal protection for, 92f
number of, 96, 97, 103
pre-planning for, 106
and resettlement as positive goal, 103-04
restrictions on admission of, 81-82
safety of, 76
and undocumented aliens, 103
see also forced migrants
religious organizations, and peace movement, 189-90, 200
religious persecutions, 11-12, 13, 21, 71, 72
religious wars, 137
repatriation, of refugees, 95-96
reprisals, Augustine on, 12
Republican party, 148
restraint, in Thomas Aquinas, 16
retaliatory strikes, and just-war theory, 1
retaliation, law of, 136
revenge, Augustine on, 11
revolution, in early modern thought, 23
Rhodesia-Zimbabwe, 171, 185
Richardson, Lewis F., 122, 204
Rip and Lincoln, "Impartial Intervention in Community Disputes," 215
Roman law, 73
Roosevelt, President Franklin, 159
Royal Canadian Air Force, 52
Rule of Law Research Center, Duke University, 200
Rush, Dr. Benjamin, ix, 158
Rush-Banneker idea, 159, 160
Russia, and academy of international relations, 214, 216
forced migrants in, 72
and League of Nations intervention in Lithuania, 49
Rwanda, 72, 102

Saar, 49-50
Saar International Force, 45
Sadat, President Anwar, 60, 185-87
Sadegh, Abolhasem, 191
safe havens, 99-100, 106
Salvadorans, 106
Saunders, Harold H., 119, 151
Scanlan, John, 78
Scheinman, Ronald S., 69
schools of diplomacy, and arms control courses, 189
Schuman, Dr. Frederick, 159
scientific learning, and peace learning, 199
Segal, David R., 38
Selassie, Haile, 159
self realization, and forced migration, 71-80
Shah, death of, 193
Shalom, ix, 212
Sharp, Dr. Gene, 205-09

Short, Dr. Joseph, 7-8
Shue, Henry, 72, 77
simultaneous justice, 24
Sinai, 66-68, 185
Singer, Dr. J. David, 145, 203, 205-07, 209
slavery, 74, 158
Smith, Conflict Resolution: Contributions of Behavioral Sciences, 215
Smith, Langdon, 136
social change strategy, includes forecasting, 215
social contract, and refugees, 83
social justice, 69
failure of and migration, 71
history of, 70
and international laws, 73-74
value of World Order Model Project, 212
Social Power & Political Freedom, 208
social responsibility, of government, 79
social science, and peace management, 2
social unrest, from investment policies, 86
Society of Friends, 149
sociology, and peace learning, 144, 200
Sohn, Professor Louis, 185
soldiers, in peacekeeping role, 66
political education of, 66
Sonnenday, Margaret, 190
South Africa, lifespan in, 210
South Korea, 50-51
South Yemen, 62
sovereignty, and security, 168
Soviet Diplomacy & Negotiating Behavior, 216
Soviet Union, in Afghanistan, 42, 86, 169
in Africa, 169
boycott of United Nations by, 50
and China, 128
and destruction of scientific genetics, 125
international & intranational conflicts in, 168
in Poland, 205
and repatriation efforts, 95, 96
and trained negotiators, 147
and United States, 46
Spain, 20, 102-03, 168
Spanish Inquisition, 124
Spanish Republicans, as forced migrants, 72
Sri Lanka, forced migration from, 87
St. Augustine, see Augustine
St. Bartholomew Day Massacre, 72
St. Paul, 8; Letter to the Romans by, 9
stable peace, 128-29, 136
Stalin, Josef, 45
state, legitimacy of, 9
State, U.S. Department of, 141, 147, 192; and conflicts with national peace institute, 130
Iran Working Group of, 195, 196, 198

negotiation taught in, 200
peace division in, 160
refugee aid meeting by, 84
site of ACDA, 117
state sovereignty, and human rights abuses, 94
*Statistics of Deadly Quarrels*, 204
Sterling, Richard, 73
Stockholm International Peace Research Institute, 201
Stockholm syndrome, 183
Stoics, 8, 11
*Study of War*, 203
Suarez, Francisco, 20, 22
success, as basis for resorting to force, 24
Sudanese, 55, 72
Suez, 67
Suez Canal, 51
Sumner, William Graham, 134
Swallow, Captain Chan, 132
Sweden, 53, 55, 76
Syria, 59-60, 101

taxes, as threat system, 125
Taylor, Maxwell, 89, 90-91
technology transfer, and migration, 86
Templars, monastic military order, 15
Tennyson, Alfred Lord, 3, 158-59
tension criterion, 146
terrorism, 66, 86
Thailand, 99, 102
Thee, Marek, 210
Third World, 81
Thomas Aquinas, 1, 16-19, 191, 197
    anticipates early modern thought, 22
    just-war thinking of, 30
Thurmond, Sen. Strom, 165
*To Establish the US Academy of Peace*, 157
tontons macoutes, 80
torture, right to be protected from, 74
Toynbee, Arnold, 137
Trudeau, Prime Minister Pierre, 151
Truman, President Harry, 159

U.S. Commission on National Academy of Peace and Conflict Resolution, 157
U.S. Department; see under other part of name: Agriculture, Commerce, Health and Human Services, Justice, Labor, State
U.S. House Armed Services Investigations Subcommittee, 64
U.S. Joint Chiefs of Staff, 64
U.S. Senate Labor Committee, 114, 115, 117
Uganda, Rwandan refugees rejected from, 102
underlying interests, 188
unemployment, 89, 104

Uniformed Services University of the Health Sciences, 113
unilateral disarmament, 35, 119
United Methodist Church, 191, 192, 197
United Nations, charter of, 27
    forces in Congo, 53-55
    international armed force in, 45
    message from Iran, 194
    and migration forces, 2
    military peacekeeping of, 45-47, 51, 62-63, 67
    protected persons of, 106
    purpose of, 141
    and Truman, 159
    U.S. mission to, 162
    and Vietnam conflict, 31
United Nations Convention Relating to the Status of Refugees, 74-75
United Nations Disengagement Observer Force, 60
United Nations Economic and Social Council, 71
United Nations Educational, Scientific & Cultural Organization(UNESCO), 200, 201
United Nations Emergency Force(UNEF), 52-53, 59
United Nations Force in Cyprus (UNFICYP), 47-48, 58, 63, 66
United Nations Fund for Durable Solutions, 94, 100
United Nations High Commissioner for Refugees(UNHCR), 71, 75-76, 82, 91, 92, 93, 94, 98-100, 105
United Nations Institute for Training and Research(UNITAR), 201-02
United Nations Interim Force in Lebanon, 62-63
United Nations Korean Reconstruction Agency(UNKRA), 91, 92, 94
United Nations Relief and Rehabilitation Administration(UNRRA), 91, 92, 94, 96
United Nations Truce Supervision Organization(UNTSO), 59
United Nations University, 202
United States Academy of Peace, see National Institute of Peace
United States Air Force, 44, 113, 148
United States Armed Services, and conflict management in, 132
United States Army War College, 65, 148
United States Marines, 63-64, 66-67
United States, attitude toward refugees in, 104
    and Genocide Treaty, 28
    in Grenada, 42, 51, 64-65, 86
    and Haitian refugees, 102
    immigration reform in, 75
    and international relations by specialists, x